THE
UNITED STATES

······· OF ·······

OPI IDS

THE
UNITED STATES
OF
OPI🇺🇸IDS

A PRESCRIPTION FOR
LIBERATING A NATION IN PAIN

HARRY NELSON

FOREWORD BY LISA MARIE PRESLEY

ForbesBooks

Published by ForbesBooks, Charleston, South Carolina.
Member of Advantage Media Group.

ForbesBooks is a registered trademark, and the ForbesBooks colophon is a trademark of Forbes Media, LLC.

Printed in the United States of America.

10 9 8 7 6 5 4 3 2 1

ISBN: 978-1-946633-32-3
LCCN: 2019930201

Cover design by George Stevens.
Layout design by Carly Blake.

Advantage Media Group is proud to be a part of the Tree Neutral® program. Tree Neutral offsets the number of trees consumed in the production and printing of this book by taking proactive steps such as planting trees in direct proportion to the number of trees used to print books. To learn more about Tree Neutral, please visit **www.treeneutral.com**.

Since 1917, the Forbes mission has remained constant. Global Champions of Entrepreneurial Capitalism. ForbesBooks exists to further that aim by bringing the Stories, Passion, and Knowledge of top thought leaders to the forefront. ForbesBooks brings you The Best in Business. To be considered for publication, please visit **www.forbesbooks.com**.

Dedicated to my children, Ami, Noa, Aiden, and Leila.
May you realize your capacity to take on challenges not only
in the lives of the people close to you but in the world around
us, and bring healing in the process.

TABLE OF CONTENTS

"*The best way out is always through.*"
ROBERT FROST

"*Do not despair of our present difficulties but believe always in the promise and greatness of America, because nothing is inevitable here. Americans never quit. We never surrender. We never hide from history. We make history.*"
JOHN S. MCCAIN

OPIOID OVERDOSE DEATHS: VISUALIZING A NATION IN PAIN*

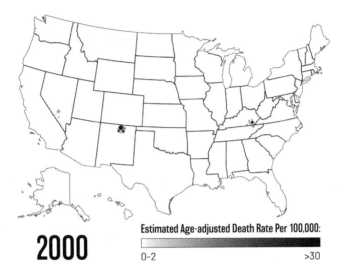

Estimated Age-adjusted Death Rate Per 100,000:

2000

0-2   >30

In 2000, 11,000 people died from opioid overdoses in the US, attributed to overprescribing of and abuse of OxyContin.

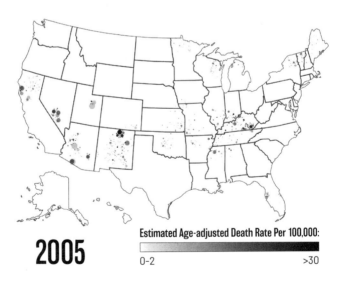

Estimated Age-adjusted Death Rate Per 100,000:

2005

0-2   >30

In 2005, 15,000 people died from opioid overdoses in the US as "hot zones" emerged across the country.

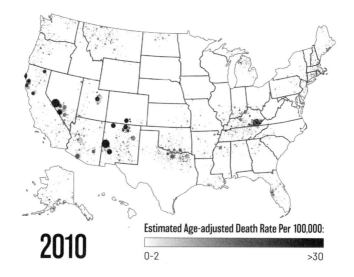

2010

Estimated Age-adjusted Death Rate Per 100,000:

0-2   >30

In 2010, 20,000 people died from opioid overdoses in the US as heroin filled the void after a crackdown on overprescribing.

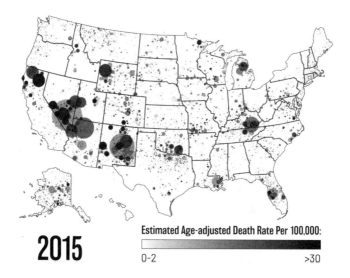

2015

Estimated Age-adjusted Death Rate Per 100,000:

0-2   >30

In 2015, 33,000 people died from opioid overdoses in the US as illegal sources of fentanyl drove an accelerating death toll.

---

* The data depicted in these images is based on the Centers for Disease Control and Prevention's (CDC) National Center for Health Statistics (NCHS) publications "Drug Poisoning Death Rates by County" for the respective years. Current and more detailed information, including CDC's Data Visualization Gallery, is available at https://www.cdc.gov/nchs/data-visualization/drug-poisoning-mortality/index.htm.

FOREWORD

WHEN HARRY FIRST APPROACHED ME about contributing to *The United States of Opioids: A Prescription for Liberating a Nation in Pain,* I was ambivalent. I had never openly spoken in public about my own addiction to opioids and painkillers. I wasn't sure that I was ready to share on such a personal topic.

Then, in August 2018, I decided that it was time. I was on *The Today Show* to promote my latest album, *Where No One Stands Alone,* a tribute to my father. Jenna Bush Hager asked me a direct question in the interview about addiction. The timing was no accident. I decided to share. It wasn't easy to talk about such a painful topic, but it was too important not to speak out.

"I'm not perfect," I said. "My father wasn't perfect, no one's perfect. It's what you do with it after you learn and then you try to help others with it."

The realization that led me to share my experience publicly on this topic and to contribute this foreword was this desire to help other people. As I write this, I think of my four children, who gave me the purpose to heal, and the countless parents who have lost children to opioids and other drugs. Across America and the world, people are dying in mind-boggling numbers because of opioid and other drug overdoses. Many more people are suffering silently, addicted to opioids and other substances. I am writing this in the hope that I can play a small part in focusing attention on this terrible crisis.

I experienced firsthand how hard it is to cut through all of the bad information out there to get help. We all need to educate ourselves and the people around us on the dangers of opioids and other drugs, and understand what we can do to keep ourselves and the people we love safe. In writing *The United States of Opioids*, Harry has provided not just a must-read account of the story of the opioid crisis, but essential tools that all of us can use to prevent more harm and intervene in the lives of everyone around us who needs help.

Whether you are a person struggling with opioids yourself, or a parent worried about your children or friends and family, the first challenge is getting access to good information. The opioid crisis is not happening to other people. It is not only a problem for doctors and addiction treatment professionals. Harry has taken lessons learned working inside our health system and distilled them into practical tools to drive positive change.

A separate challenge is the issue of shame. We live in a culture of shame that keeps us afraid of being honest about what we are dealing with. We are embarrassed to be vulnerable. We are so afraid of being stigmatized, of being judged, that we do not talk about what's really going on. We allow shame to prevent us from reaching out for help.

This is a unique challenge for people living with fame. I have seen it up close with too many people I have loved. I have experienced it myself. It is hard to understand what exactly is going wrong. How much of this crisis is about people in pain? Drug companies? Doctors now knowing what they are doing? I have seen too many times the tragic consequences of drugs taking people from us too soon. What I know is that, at one and the same time, the danger is avoidable, and yet none of us is immune from it. Acknowledging that we are all at risk is a not a measure of weakness, but of honesty.

You may read this and wonder how, after losing people close to me, I also fell prey to opioids. I was recovering after the birth of my daughters, Vivienne and Finley, when a doctor prescribed me opioids for pain. What makes opioids so dangerous is their addictiveness. It only took a short-term prescription of opioids in the hospital for me to feel the need to keep taking them.

It was a difficult path to overcome this dependence, and to put my life back together. Even in recent years, I have seen too many people I loved struggle with addiction and die tragically from this epidemic.

It is time for us to say goodbye to shame about addiction. We have to stop blaming and judging ourselves and the people around us.

We need to do what we can, to use our resources and creativity to overcome this problem. That starts with sharing our stories. It is time that we do so and that we dedicate ourselves to doing what we can to prevent more people from dying, and to support the people around us who are living with addiction.

Where do we go from here? Harry has written a powerful book that is a starting point. *The United States of Opioids* is a call to action with tangible steps that we can all take. Harry delivers insights into the challenges facing our health system—doctors, hospitals, and addiction treatment providers—and also offers steps that we can all take as parents and with everyone else in our lives. This message is essential and timely. I hope that you will join in the work of taking on the opioid crisis.

I am grateful to be alive today, and to have four beautiful children who have given me a sense of purpose that has carried me through dark times. If you are reading this, I hope you are able to join me in feeling that same sense of gratitude and purpose in your life. If you are not, I hope you will use *The United States of Opioids* to find the strength and the help that you need, and to get to a place of strength and support.

LISA MARIE PRESLEY

INTRODUCTION

THIS IS PERSONAL.

In 2009, the drug overdose story of the year was Michael Jackson. He had taken a lethal mix of opioids, benzodiazepines (highly addictive anti-anxiety medications and sedatives that are a frequent complicating factor in many overdoses), and the anesthetic propofol, injected to force sleep. The doctor in charge when Jackson died, Conrad Murray, was arrested and charged criminally. As a healthcare lawyer who has worked with many doctors involved in opioid issues, I found myself taking calls from several other doctors who had also treated Jackson and were worried they'd be investigated next. The first doctor to reach me was beside himself. He told me he'd prescribed painkillers to Jackson under false names to protect his famous patient's privacy.

These calls fit a pattern: doctors were second-guessing whether they had given the celebrity too much leeway and applied relaxed standards in prescribing. Critical documentation to justify the prescription was missing. My job was to help the doctor understand what questions to expect from the medical board, and to strategize about how to take accountability and respond when the medical board and the Drug Enforcement Administration (DEA) investigated.

I tried to reassure this doctor that it wouldn't be the end of the world; no matter what mistakes he had made, there was still a chance to express remorse, demonstrate self-awareness, and establish that he took compliance seriously. I told the doctor that I'd been down this path many times, and that he needed to take a deep breath and not panic. After nearly an hour on the phone, he seemed calmer and made an appointment to come into the office the next afternoon.

He didn't show up for our appointment. I had a feeling something was wrong. Sure enough, I got the news a few days later: he had been found dead after having taken a lethal dose of opioids, ending his own life.

Even now, nearly a decade later, I think about this doctor frequently. It wasn't even a story that made the newspaper. This doctor was just one more faceless victim of the massive crisis we all now face.

Closer to home, I have watched three good friends, whose kids are just a few years older than mine, struggle with addiction and recovery, relapses and setbacks, and the continual challenge to stay clean. The most painful stories, of course, are of kids—and adults— who aren't coming back. I think of Mark, a twenty-year-old whose parents got him into treatment. He took off a few weeks later, leaving the treatment program to use again. After spending days looking for him, his parents finally found him living on the street, and persuaded him to try again to get clean. He seemed ready. The last thing he decided to do before resuming treatment was to use up the last of his stash. It would turn out to be the last thing he ever did: he overdosed and died en route to the hospital.

There is no single pattern to the lives ended or disrupted by this crisis. The risks cut across socioeconomics, age, race, ethnicity, and geography. The victims of this crisis are as likely as not to have been raised in loving, stable homes. Sometimes, their stories begin with something medical—a surgery or a condition involving pain leading to medication. Sometimes, they expand the circle of addiction by sharing these highly addictive medications with friends and relatives. Sometimes, their stories are as simple as someone feeling lonely and isolated and self-medicating away the anxiety.

These stories have come together not only in an incomprehensible and steadily climbing overdose death toll—the face of the crisis—but also in countless numbers of people struggling without solutions for their pain and without options to treat addiction effectively. I write this book in the hope that, together, with a deeper understanding of the underlying challenge and the options ahead of us, we can stem the tide, save lives, and improve care for people struggling with pain and for people living with addiction.

Before we can solve the opioid crisis, we all need to understand it—not just policy wonks, doctors, and law enforcement, but also educators, employers, parents, and peers. We need to come to terms with the people and problems whose care we have ignored. We need to come to terms with the gaps in our treatment of addiction, which are a legacy of treating addiction as an issue separate and distinct from the rest of healthcare. Ultimately, we need to address and fix the culture of shame that prevents so many people from getting the help they need.

I also hope this book will help guide the many people suffering personally and watching uncertain what to do as loved ones, children, and friends struggle. I believe we all have a role to play in addressing this challenge.

THIS IS VERY, VERY FRUSTRATING.

I've learned a lot about the history of opioids, pain medicine, and addiction treatment over my twenty-five years as a healthcare lawyer.

With lawsuits continuing to pile up against drug manufacturers and the story still unfolding, I didn't set out to write the definitive opioid crisis history, but rather to try to do something about a problem that I fear is going to get much worse.

I've had a front-row seat as the opioid crisis has unfolded because my clients—mostly healthcare providers and life sciences companies—have brought me their hardest problems to solve. Drug treatment programs reeling from patient overdoses or being stonewalled by insurance companies ask for guidance on how to turn their operations around. Telehealth ventures and developers of new drugs and devices bring their cutting-edge technologies, seeking guidance on how to persuade state and federal regulators to bless their new approaches.

While I have learned so much from this vantage point, the specific legal problems I and other lawyers in my firm solve are mostly confidential. Clients who hire us to address big challenges don't necessarily want us to publicize our successes, since most people didn't know there were even problems that needed to be solved. Similarly, clients working on new technologies don't want competitors to learn what they're working on.

While working in secret is part of the responsibility of being a lawyer, the growth of the opioid crisis over the past two decades led me to the perspective that I had to find a way to do something to share critical information. More and more of my clients were affected, directly or indirectly, by opioids. I worked closely with doctors who fell prey to the addictive power of opioids themselves. I worked with pharmacies and other providers who were clueless about their responsibilities with regard to opioids. As an expert on healthcare regulatory issues, I was going crazy watching complicated legal problems get in the way of tackling this crisis. It was this frustration, as well as my keen professional and personal interest in the subject, that first inspired me to delve into the fascinating and deeply disturbing history behind this crisis. I write this book with a handful of personal stories (shared with permission) and many insights gleaned from seeing the distinct moving pieces in this unfolding story.

THIS IS FOR YOU—BECAUSE WE ARE ALL AFFECTED.

In this book, I will guide you through the opioid crisis, offering a detailed narrative followed by "takeaways" summing up key points. Ultimately, I take a final hard look at the big picture and end up, in spite of everything, with a clear-eyed message of hope—a prescription for liberating a nation in pain.

Chapter One begins with understanding how the crisis has unfolded over the past two decades in three "waves" of death by opioid in the United States, as total overdose deaths reach unfathomable numbers. It is important to understand how the current crisis combines legal and illegal sources of opioids, as well as how the response to the crisis on the ground has emerged slowly to address the crisis.

If, like many Americans, you're uncertain what exactly an opioid is and how many varieties of opioids there are, **Chapter Two** has the answers you need. You'll also find out why opioids are so addictive, and how they kill people.

The history of opioid use and abuse in the United States is convoluted and full of intrigue, reflecting the growing pains of the nation from its founding to present day, with a national crackdown in the early 1900s holding many lessons for today. **Chapter Three** explores this history of regulatory efforts that set the stage for the current crisis.

Large pharmaceutical companies have pushed hard to sell the opioids they manufacture, with a singular role played by Big Pharma villain Artie Sackler and his company, Purdue Pharma. Was the price they paid when found guilty of FDA violations fair? **Chapter Four** looks at this sorry history.

Doctors have been singled out for blame in overprescribing opioids, accused of fueling the crisis. **Chapter Five** assesses the various points of health system failure, as we have gone from designating pain as a "fifth vital sign" to making doctors and hospitals reluctant to treat patients in pain.

Though it's easy to point fingers at Big Pharma and overprescribing doctors, there are other underlying causes fueling the drive to consume opioids, and I explore them in **Chapter Six**. Behavioral health issues run wide and deep in the United States, as does consumerism, a demand for instant gratification, and the allure and dangers of social media. Is the opioid crisis attributable to a breakdown in social and spiritual connections and a loss of hope?

With one in ten American adults addicted to opioids and other drugs, how is it that so little attention is paid to the lack of access to effective addiction treatment? **Chapter Seven** looks at the history of addiction treatment and the work ahead as treatment and recovery have begun to be integrated into US healthcare and as insurance has factored into the picture. We also explore the unique challenge of predatory practices by those seeking to profit on the availability of funding for addiction treatment.

It's nearly impossible to avoid the subject of cannabis deregulation and psychedelics within the context of a book about drug use and abuse. Acknowledging the inevitable, I tackle the multipronged question of how they fit into the opioid picture in **Chapter Eight**.

What work is already underway to respond to the opioid crisis? Is it helping? In **Chapter Nine** I've organized these priorities into seven "pillars" of government and healthcare policy that, applied together, will reduce the death toll and other harm caused by the opioid crisis.

How can we truly liberate a nation in pain? As much as systemic reforms can reduce the harm caused by our descent into the United States of Opioids, I believe that our real hope for a solution will come in the form of more personal outreach in our families, workplaces, and communities as we take on, through social and spiritual connection, the underlying suffering that has driven the crisis. **Chapter Ten** offers information everyone needs to understand in order to take part personally in the work ahead. It also offers some concluding thoughts about how we can all contribute to finding a solution to the opioid crisis.

Since the first step in solving any problem—besides recognizing that the problem actually exists—is developing an understanding of the facts and complexities, I have included various resources at the end of this book with specific information that may be of interest to particular groups of readers, including a **glossary** of terms, a **resource guide** to find additional information and places to seek help, and **graphics and data** to visualize and quantify some of the key challenges.

CHAPTER 1

INITIAL RESPONSES TO A STAGGERING OPIOID CRISIS

"Here's why we're so concerned. To be blunt, what you might buy and use, thinking it's a good time, could cost you your life."

**T.J. JORDAN, ASSISTANT DIRECTOR,
TENNESSEE BUREAU OF INVESTIGATIONS**[1]

THE OPIOID CRISIS—the impact of legally prescribed and illegally obtained opioid-based painkillers—is a uniquely American health disaster that has exploded over the past two decades.* Put simply, the opioid crisis is American healthcare's self-inflicted wound.

Before we get to the story of how or why the opioid crisis unfolded, it's worth considering how opioid and other drug overdoses have been part of our consciousness for much longer than the past two decades.

OPIOID OVERDOSE AS AN AMERICAN STORY

While we commonly use 1999 as the start date of the opioid crisis based on the notable statistical uptick that began that year, most people can tick off celebrity overdoses that called attention to the problem long before then. Certain big ones stand out. My parents, in their seventies, remember Marilyn Monroe overdosing in Los Angeles at the age of thirty-six in 1962. For many baby boomers in their sixties, that moment was Elvis's death at age forty-two in 1977, originally attributed by a medical examiner to a heart attack, but linked to opioids and other drugs. The celebrity overdose that marked my entry

---

* Throughout this book, I refer to the "opioid crisis." Some people use the term "opioid epidemic." Others use the terms interchangeably. According to Google's dictionary function, which uses the *Pocket Oxford English Dictionary*, an epidemic is "a widespread occurrence of an infectious disease in a community at a particular time" or "a sudden, widespread occurrence of a particular undesirable phenomenon." Opioids, overdoses, and addiction are not infectious and, far from being a sudden development, they have been a slow-moving, mass casualty event—which is why, two decades in, there is still so little understanding of what is happening and how to stop it. It's tempting to call opioids a "pandemic"—a "disease prevalent over a whole country or the world." I stuck with the "opioid crisis" for its breadth. Google and Oxford define crisis as a "time of intense difficulty, trouble, or danger," with synonyms of "emergency, disaster, catastrophe, and calamity." The second definition adds another critical layer of meaning: "A time when a difficult or important decision must be made," as in a "crisis point of history," with synonyms including "critical point, turning point, crossroads, watershed, moment of truth." We are living in just such a time.

into this morbid topic came in 1982, when I was fourteen.

I remember watching the news alert that thirty-three-year-old John Belushi had overdosed on heroin and cocaine. And there have been many other tragic high-profile opioid deaths more recently: Heath Ledger, Chris Farley, Michael Jackson, Amy Winehouse, Prince, Tom Petty, Whitney Houston, and so many more.

So it's not as if 1999, the year by which we mark the onset of the opioid crisis statistically, was a "clean" beginning. It is more accurate to think of that year as the time when the problem began to get much, much worse. The biggest unknown is how much worse things will get, and when, if ever, they will get better.

BREAKING THROUGH WORST-CASE PROJECTIONS— TOWARD A MILLION DEAD

As it unfolded in slow motion from the late 1990s, the opioid crisis worsened for well over a decade before its magnitude began to register with the national psyche. Even then, each year brought new evidence that the problem was much worse than we had previously thought.

How many people have died as a result of opioids since 1999? The Centers for Disease Control (CDC), reports that between 1999 and 2016, roughly 630,000 people died of drug overdoses.[2] According to the CDC, roughly 350,000 of these deaths were opioid-related.[3] More recently, CDC reported 72,000 drug deaths in 2017, of which roughly 49,000 were opioid-related, a jump from 42,000 opioid-related deaths in the previous year, 2016.[4] This bring the total from 1999 through 2017 to over 700,000 deaths.

While the estimate used to be that slightly more than half of these deaths were opioid-related, the CDC now puts the estimate at closer to two-thirds of all drug deaths.[5]

Moreover, according to a recent study by the University of Pittsburgh,[6] errors in reporting causes of death since 1999 have likely resulted in undercounting of opioid deaths by seventy thousand.[7] This undercounting occurs because the mechanism of death in an opioid overdose is essentially the same as in a heart attack or stroke: oxygenated blood flow is cut off, by suppressed breathing with opioids and by an obstruction in a heart attack or stroke. The pathway may be different, but the end result—brain tissue death—looks the same, leading to the reporting undercounting.

Adding in these undercounted deaths, the total drug-related deaths may already be closing on eight hundred thousand total drug deaths and close to half a million opioid deaths from 1999 to 2018. If the year-over-year rate of increases in the numbers remain consistent, the data puts us roughly seven years out from the number of one million Americans dead of opioid-related deaths over the quarter century from 2000 to 2025.[*]

This is a mind-numbing, staggering loss of life and potential. Consider the collective pain and trauma of the families, friends, and loved ones of this epidemic's victims. If you haven't lost someone to opioid addiction yourself, you almost certainly know others who have.

How did we get to this horrific point? Although we often talk about opioids as a singular crisis, a closer look reveals three distinct waves of opioid deaths. (See Graphics and Data for a visual of the three waves.) The first wave lasted roughly a decade, beginning in the late 1990s, as increasing volumes of physician-prescribed opioid painkillers led to steady rise in the death rate. The death rate climbed from 1 death per 100,000 people in 1999 to 4 per 100,000 in 2010. In 2012 alone, American doctors wrote 259 million opioid prescrip-

---

[*] As a comparison for the death toll, the total number of soldiers who gave their lives in all American conflicts is roughly 1.264 million, roughly half in the Civil War and half in all other wars combined.

tions for pain, enough to provide every single person in the country over the age of eighteen with his or her own thirty-day supply of painkillers.[8] American doctors were prescribing and pharmacies were dispensing enough opioids each year to keep our adult population on a schedule of one pill every four hours for an entire month!

As the government sprang into action, cracking down on physicians who were overprescribing opioids, the supply of these drugs became much scarcer, while demand remained as high as ever. People increasingly turned to the black market, sparking the second wave of deaths. In this second wave of the crisis beginning in 2010, the popularity of a crudely processed form of heroin known as "black tar" began to surge, beginning a continuing climb of roughly 20 percent year over year. Roughly 80 percent of new black tar heroin users were people who became addicted to prescription painkillers, were turned away by their doctors, and turned instead to heroin.[9]

Susan is a good example.* In her early twenties, she began to experience severe and persistent pain in different parts of her body. She visited doctor after doctor, including physical medicine doctors, pain specialists, and neurologists, in search of a solution. No one could offer a convincing diagnosis or tell her what to do about it. Several doctors who Susan saw prescribed different opioid medications to see what would work, enabling her to function, and she tried a few options. The pills didn't change the repetitive cycle of pain, but they did allow her to sleep through the night.

The problem came when Susan's doctor retired. All of a sudden, she needed a new doctor willing to prescribe opioids. The problem was that several doctors she was referred to seemed suspicious of her motives; she had unwittingly acquired the profile of a drug-seeking

---

* First names have been changed and last names omitted to protect the privacy of many of the people who shared their stories with me.

patient and could not find anyone willing to prescribe. The fact that she had gotten scripts from multiple doctors looking for answers to her pain had set off alarm bells with both new doctors and pharmacies. After a particularly excruciating stretch without medication, a "friend" suggested heroin as a last resort. At first Susan resisted, thinking the solution could not possibly be a street drug. Soon enough, though, she was using, and then addicted to, heroin. Over the past five years, Susan has cycled between heroin and Suboxone. She has tried to switch completely off of heroin but finds the weaker relief of Suboxone insufficient when the worst pains return. So far, Susan has been one of the lucky ones. Between the late 2000s and 2017, the death toll from heroin shot up eightfold, from roughly two thousand to almost sixteen thousand Americans—a number that is still rising.[10]

Sheila Scott was one of the thousands of parents to lose a child, her twenty-three-year-old son Luke, beloved for his work as a production assistant on the television show, *Goliath*. Luke overdosed in 2016. I sat down with Sheila to talk about Luke and the book she wrote, *lukelove. My boy, My grief, My journal: Losing a child to opioids*. Sheila brought to my attention the organization GRASP (Grief Recovery After Substance Passing), with chapters across North America full of grieving parents and others who have lost loved ones to heroin and other opioids.

To reframe the heartbreak and grief, consider that with half a million people in America having died opioid-related deaths in past twenty years, we already have millions of grieving parents, siblings, and other loved ones across America whose children, brothers, and sisters are dead. How many more will die before we find a way out of this crisis?

Heroin is almost benign in comparison to the fentanyl that began to show up around 2013. While heroin was the first drug to fill the void for people unable to get prescription opioids, drug traffickers found a cheaper and more potent product to sell in fentanyl.

Fentanyl marks the third wave of deaths in the opioid crisis. As a synthetic, manmade creation, fentanyl is roughly thirty-five-times more powerful than heroin. While heroin has continued to play a role, fentanyl has become a much deadlier killer. In just three short years, from 2013 to 2016, the death rate soared from 1 death per 100,000, to 6 per 100,000 people—an increase of almost *90 percent* year-over-year.

It's hard to express the enormity of the fentanyl problem. Cheap and easy to manufacture, as well as odorless, fentanyl entered the US market largely from Mexico, where it is made by cartels, and from China, where it is made in clandestine labs and sold online, without any resistance. Without any infrastructure deployed to detect and intercept it, fentanyl became a favorite of drug traffickers, who began counterfeiting or cutting more expensive illegal drugs with fentanyl to increase their profit margins. Drug dealers would sell counterfeits to people trying to buy Percocet or OxyContin on the black market, giving them fentanyl. Drug dealers would sell fentanyl-laced versions of cocaine and heroin to people on the street, raising the risk of overdose deaths exponentially. Fentanyl's potency, in turn, led to vastly more deaths.[*]

If fentanyl isn't deadly enough, carfentanil—a medication designed to anesthetize elephants and other large land mammals—is now showing up at crime scenes and autopsies. Sold under the brand name Wildnil (hinting at its wildlife-intended uses), carfentanil is one hundred times more powerful than fentanyl (and a thousand times more powerful than morphine).[11] Some traffickers distribute carfen-

---

[*] In a curious irony and acknowledgment of its potency, in 2018, Nebraska became the first state to execute a prisoner on death row with fentanyl.

tanil as loose grains, like salt, except much deadlier and absorbable through the skin.

PERSONAL EXPERIENCES

For me, the opioid crisis came into focus gradually over the course of responding both professionally and personally to one unfolding tragedy after another: overdose deaths; suicides; people cycling through wilderness therapy, therapeutic boarding schools, treatment programs, and sober living homes; and people living in unrelieved pain.

In thinking about how to help others understand this crisis, I could not stop thinking about Kate O'Neill's obituary for her thirty-year-old sister, Madelyn Ellen Linsenmeir, who died of an overdose in October 2018. In writing this book, I interviewed parents and siblings who lost loved ones to opioids, but O'Neill managed to capture something essential in her writing about her sister:[12]

> *Madelyn was a born performer and had a singing voice so beautiful it would stop people on the street. Whether she was onstage in a musical or around the kitchen table with her family, when she shared her voice, she shared her light. . . .*

> *When she was 16, she moved with her parents from Vermont to Florida to attend a performing arts high school. Soon after she tried OxyContin for the first time at a high school party, and so began a relationship with opiates that would dominate the rest of her life. . . .*

> *To some, Maddie was just a junkie—when they saw her addiction, they stopped seeing her. And what a loss for them. Because Maddie was hilarious, and warm, and fearless, and resilient. . . . In a system that seems to have hardened itself*

against addicts and is failing them every day, she befriended and delighted cops, social workers, public defenders and doctors, who advocated for and believed in her 'til the end. She was adored as a daughter, sister, niece, cousin, friend and mother, and being loved by Madelyn was a constantly astonishing gift.

During the past two years especially, her disease brought her to places of incredible darkness, and this darkness compounded on itself, as each unspeakable thing that happened to her and each horrible thing she did in the name of her disease exponentially increased her pain and shame. For twelve days this summer, she was home, and for most of that time she was sober. For those twelve wonderful days, full of swimming and Disney movies and family dinners, we believed as we always did that she would overcome her disease and make the life for herself we knew she deserved. We believed this until the moment she took her last breath. But her addiction stalked her and stole her once again. Though we would have paid any ransom to have her back, any price in the world, this disease would not let her go until she was gone....

Madelyn's story is like far too many others' stories whose addictions simply would not relent, despite interventions from family and repeated efforts to get sober. For someone who struggles with addiction, the lines between sobriety, drug use, and overdose—between life and death—are razor thin. The personal losses to parents, siblings, grandparents, children, friends, and communities from this crisis are staggering.

In writing this book, I heard so many heartbreaking personal stories of love and loss and shame and lives cut short. It's important to hear these stories, and it's critical to understand where the personal story meets the systemic call to action. Understanding how the US healthcare system, emergency responses, addiction treatment resources, pharmaceutical marketing, and regulations have responded to and shaped this crisis is essential to plotting the way through and beyond the opioid crisis.

FIRST RESPONSES

The national responses to the growing death toll began to spike in the late 1990s. The opioid crisis has generated many responses, but few solutions. As the casualties mounted and began to garner attention, a number of mechanisms and approaches slowly took shape to control the damage. These "first responses" not only tell the story of how the opioid crisis unfolded but continue to play a central role in how the opioid crisis is being addressed.

One "front line" group called upon to respond to the opioid crisis was hospital emergency room personnel. By 2009, roughly 1.2 million hospital ER visits had been reported for opioid (and other drug) overdoses, with OxyContin as the single leading culprit.[13] The other front-line responders—paramedics, emergency medical technicians (EMTs), police officers, firefighters, and other rescuers—were called to the scene after a 911 call for emergency assistance. To encourage more 911 calls, California and other states passed laws providing that any drug offenses like intoxication or possession of opioids or other illegal drugs discovered through a 911 call would not be prosecuted. The idea was to ensure that the people would not be afraid to call first responders when an overdose occurred.

The biggest problem with opioids is that, in pursuit of pain management or the pleasurable feeling of euphoria (sometimes both), patients accidentally kill themselves. The reason for these deaths is that opioids suppress the respiratory system. The telltale signs of opioid overdose is an unconscious or sleepy person who is difficult to wake, with slow, shallow, weak breathing, and pupils that are much smaller than ordinary.

The biggest problem with opioids is that, in pursuit of pain management or the pleasurable feeling of euphoria (sometimes both), patients accidentally kill themselves.

The slowdown in breathing deprives the brain of oxygen, eventually causing brain death within just a few minutes. As a result, ER personnel and first responders dealing with opioid overdoses found themselves in highly problematic situations where every second counted in preventing brain damage or death after an overdose.* They found a solution in the drug naloxone, a generic injectable better known as the "overdose drug" for its fast action in blocking the effects of opioids.

NALOXONE ON THE FRONT LINES OF THE CRISIS

Under the brand name Narcan, naloxone had been approved by the FDA in 1971. A naloxone injection administered before the death of brain tissue reversed the effect: just seconds later, the person who had overdosed would be wide awake and breathing. (In my interviews with first responders for this book, I heard stories about people coming out of overdoses angry at having been ripped out of opioid bliss and ready to fight. Other first responders dismissed these "war stories" and complained that the more common response when people wake up after naloxone is vomiting from the administration happening too quickly.)

---

* Even in cases where patients who have overdosed arrive in the ER with stable breathing, doctors and nurses cannot afford to wait hours for the drugs in the person's system to metabolize, because the overdose may be masking another health problem and the risk of irreversible damage. For example, an unconscious person who injected heroin may also have been hit over the head and have a brain bleed. Health professionals also use naloxone to wake patients so the professionals can diagnose what's wrong, ascertain which drug(s) the person has taken, and ensure they haven't missed something life-threatening.

While injectable naloxone continues to be widely used in hospitals, for first responders such as police officers and other law enforcement, an intranasal form of the drug became popular after FDA approval in 2015. Administering naloxone was a new role for police officers. In the past, they would call paramedics and wait for them to arrive—not administering any medication directly. The urgent need to respond quickly opioid overdoses forced law enforcement into a healthcare role. Many states passed laws authorizing or requiring officers to carry naloxone for fast response.

Similarly, while in the past only some specialized first responders like paramedics and advanced EMTs were expected to utilize medications on the scene, the opioid crisis led some states to require more personnel, such as emergency medical responders (EMRs) and EMTs, to administer naloxone.

Families and Patients Enter the Naloxone Zone

In recent years, the push to expand access to naloxone has extended to patients and their families—in effect, creating a third front-line group of first responders. Many states have authorized standing orders to bypass prescription requirements and make it easier to distribute naloxone to patients taking opioids and their family and friends, subject to completion of training on opioid overdose prevention, recognition and response. The vast majority of states have gone further to permit the sale of naloxone over the counter (OTC) in pharmacies.

As naloxone has proliferated, the biggest issues have been cost and supply. Naloxone is an expensive and short-term solution. While pricing varies widely, naloxone often sells in the range of $75 per unit, with two to four units required to counteract many overdoses. Millions of dollars of state and federal funding flowed into making naloxone available as widely as possible, but far more is needed. Meanwhile, people spared from an overdose death by naloxone need access to addiction treatment, or they remain at risk of future overdoses calling for more naloxone.

According law enforcement personnel, the problem in many communities is that the drug works

Naloxone is an expensive and short-term solution. While pricing varies widely, naloxone often sells in the range of $75 per unit, with two to four units required to counteract many overdoses.

so well that many people with hardcore opioid addictions have come to treat it as a "safety net," repeatedly overdosing, calling 911, and counting on getting Narcan from first responders to bring them back from the brink.[14] This, in turn, has given rise to the question of how to prevent repeat overdosers from taking advantage of an expensive and limited resource to sustain continued opioid abuse.

ENDING THE SECONDARY STATUS OF ADDICTION TREATMENT

Another reaction to the opioid crisis has been the growing recognition that addiction treatment must be an integral part of our healthcare delivery system. In 1999, when the first wave of the opioid crisis began, the vast majority of American health insurance plans did not cover addiction treatment for substance use disorders (SUDs) or the subcategory of opioid use disorders (OUDs).

This was a historical legacy of our system differentiating between insurance coverage for medical conditions and behavioral health conditions. In other words, from its inception, health insurance covered doctor visits, medications, and surgery to treat "medical" conditions—such as heart disease, diabetes, and cancer. By contrast, for decades, mental health and behavioral conditions—such as addiction, autism, and depression—were categorized as a nonmedical "other" category, which to insurers justified their noncoverage. Addiction was treated as a moral issue, rather than a healthcare issue. Even where behavioral health coverage was available, it tended to be extremely limited and excluded addiction treatment.

At a national level, the first major legal shift came in 2008, when the federal government enacted the 2008 Mental Health Parity and Addiction Equity Act (MHPAEA). The law ordered an end to the double standards that had denied people access to addiction treatment and mental health resources. For the first time, the government had the power to go after insurance companies that discriminated against coverage for addiction treatment and mental health. It is no accident that parity became a more pressing in the wake of the opioid crisis. The crisis called attention to the lack of access to insurance coverage to treat addiction, and launched the slow process of forcing parity between coverage for medical care and for addiction and mental health.

The second shift came in 2010, when the Affordable Care Act (ACA) went further—mandating insurance companies to include coverage in all health plans to treat substance use disorders (SUDs). The law included SUDs in the definition of minimum essential health benefits that insurers were required to cover. This requirement kicked in as of 2012, with all health plans—commercial insurers, self-funded employer plans, and Medicaid—required to provide resources to screen people at risk, and direct them to appropriate resources, as well as ensure access to detoxification and ongoing treatment.

This, in turn, led to the expansion of access to addiction treatment resources in the Medicaid program, which funds health-care for people living near or below national poverty level.* While the Affordable Care Act expansion of Medicaid was politically divisive, Congressional Republican efforts to roll back the Medicaid

---

* In *From ObamaCare to TrumpCare: Why You Should Care* (2017), my coauthor, Rob Fuller, and I dealt at greater length with the underlying conflict over healthcare policy and poverty reflected in the evolution of the Medicaid Program over the past fifty years.

expansion in 2017 foundered on the popularity of the funding for opioid treatment. Even several of the Republican-led states that declined to participate in the broader ACA Medicaid expansion, such as Virginia, nonetheless took advantage of federal funds for the limited purpose of expanding Medicaid opioid treatment resources.

Beyond the extension of Medicaid to cover more people in response to the opioid crisis, the range of services expanded dramatically. In 1965, when Medicaid was first enacted, Congress limited financing for most residential addiction treatment (as well as mental health) through a law known as the Institutions for Mental Diseases (IMD) Exclusion that barred funding for some residential addiction treatment until it was partially repealed in the fall of 2018.

The opioid crisis and the growing need for resources to treat addiction called attention to impediments to providing care for the 12 percent of Medicaid beneficiaries over age eighteen with an SUD.* For the first time in fifty years, bipartisan support emerged for overcoming this funding prohibition and even repealing it. The Centers for Medicare and Medicaid Services (CMS) developed strategies to fund the states in expanding the continuum of addiction treatment services, including both overdose prevention and the provision medication-assisted treatment (MAT) to address and treat opioid addiction as a chronic condition. The Medicaid funding focus extended to hard-hit rural areas and Native American tribal communities struggling with these issues.

---

* The 12 percent statistic was reported in a 2011 SAMHSA National Survey of Medicaid beneficiaries over 18 with a substance use disorder. Also reported in Center on Budget & Policy Priorities, "Medicaid Works for People with Substance Use Disorders," January 19, 2018.

GROWING FURY AND LAWSUITS AGAINST BIG PHARMA

A third reaction to the opioid crisis was the dawning realization that it was self-inflicted—caused in large part by the companies manufacturing and marketing opioids. Filing lawsuits is one thing Americans know how to do better than almost anyone else in the world. In a country known for being litigious, it should come as no surprise that one American response to the opioid crisis has been to sue.

The epicenter of the lawsuits? Cleveland, Ohio. Remember "If you build it, they will come?" In the movie *Field of Dreams,* Kevin Costner hears these words and builds a baseball field in the cornfields of Iowa. The movie ends with an unending line of cars coming through the darkness to his baseball diamond. In Cleveland, they are coming—cities, counties, states, Native American tribes, victims of the opioid crisis—not to a baseball field, but to a federal courthouse. They have filed lawsuits by the hundreds against the makers and distributors of prescription painkillers. These cases are all being consolidated before Judge Dan Polster.

In filing these cases, the plaintiffs are taking a page out of the playbook of the cases against Big Tobacco twenty years ago, when local and state governments sued tobacco companies for the damages incurred by the companies' misrepresentation of the dangers of smoking, in the name of profits. Those cases settled for billions of dollars, which were used to combat nicotine addiction and treat patients for lung cancer and other tobacco-related ailments. This model of "multidistrict" litigation has been used in other nationwide complex cases, such as the cases by NFL players alleging the NFL misled them about the dangers of repeated concussions and chronic traumatic encephalopathy (CTE).

The Cleveland lawsuits claims allege that drug companies misled doctors and patients with lies about the harms and addictive nature

24

of opioids. (In Chapter 4, we'll take a closer look at this issue.) One of the main theories in the Cleveland lawsuits is that drug companies violated the Racketeer Influenced and Corrupt Organizations (RICO) Act, a law enacted in 1970 to take on organized crime. The law offers an effective way to allege a conspiracy for fraudulent conduct and bring together separate acts by different companies and individuals across the industry in a single case. This allows plaintiffs to show that these acts of misconduct did not occur in isolation, but rather were part of a larger scheme. The case also alleges violations of other federal laws, like the Controlled Substances Act (also enacted in 1970), outright fraud, and public nuisance.

Many people are closely watching the opioid litigation to see how much money is actually extracted from Big Pharma, and what other limits may be imposed on pharmaceutical companies.

CLAMPING DOWN ON PHYSICIAN OVERPRESCRIBING AND PRESCRIPTION DRUG MONITORING PROGRAMS (PDMPS)

Beyond the role of drug companies, the opioid crisis shone a light on the need to address the problems with physician prescribing. This has accelerated the fourth reaction to the crisis: acknowledging and acting on the need for real-time tracking of opioid prescribing, to identify both doctors who are overprescribing and patients who are gaming the system by obtaining multiple prescriptions from different doctors. PDMPs allow providers to analyze a particular patient's past and present prescription drug use before they write prescriptions for opioids or other drugs with high rates of addiction.

In 1971, the DEA had built a national database to track the movement of controlled substances, but it did not track the flow from physicians to patients. The Automation of Reports and Consolidated Orders System (ARCOS) focused only on shipments of drugs from manufacturers to distributors, and then on to pharmacies and physicians. The ARCOS database did not seek to capture data about the physician—patient or pharmacy—patient encounter or flow of drugs. The DEA regulations only required that doctors and pharmacies keep these records onsite in the form of dispensation logs that could be audited upon request.

Whether this was an oversight or a function of the limits of technology when the system was built, it created a significant data gap. As the opioid crisis worsened, pressure grew to track the "last mile" of prescribing and dispensing practices to flag overprescribing.

To fill the gap, the states developed prescription drug monitoring programs (PDMPs), electronic databases that track controlled substance prescriptions. Because states have been forced to develop their PDMPs individually, there was no national system. This meant that each state maintained its own data and information systems, making it harder to share information about patients or doctors across multiple states. Another challenge was that PDMPs were largely left to the states to fund, without any central federal support.

California provides a revealing example of this dynamic. Although the state initially implemented its own PDMP database in 1996, the system, known as the Controlled Substance Utilization Review and Evaluation System (CURES), was badly underfunded for its first fifteen years in existence, and frequently didn't work. In essence, the state had created a database and assigned responsibility to a state Bureau of Narcotics Enforcement, but provided little to no money for personnel or technology to make it functional.

Despite the early challenges faced by PDMPs, one perceptible response to the opioid crisis has been an expanded focus by states on establishing and improving their PDMPs. In 2013, California finally provided funding by charging doctors a $6 fee when they underwent relicensing. Still, checking the system before prescribing or dispensing remained optional. In 2016, California passed two key requirements to address this problem. First, to ensure that the database was current, one new law requires that pharmacies and physicians report controlled substance prescriptions "as soon as reasonably possible" but no later than seven days after prescribing or dispensing.[15]

Second, to make sure that doctors actually checked it, the law requires practitioners to review a patient's controlled substance prescribing history no *earlier* than twenty-four hours or the previous business day before prescribing a controlled substance to the patient for the first time.[*]

Doctors are expected to be on the lookout for patients who are seeking drugs by going to multiple physicians for the same problems. On an ongoing basis, doctors are now required to check the records at least every four months, with failure to check mandating investigation by the medical board for potential imposition of discipline. Similar laws have passed or are under consideration in other states.

As we'll explore in Chapter 9, we remain a disturbingly long way from a shared interstate database to track prescribing and dispensing patterns. For now, the immediate focus is on the less-ambitious goal of integrating PDMP data into health information technology (HIT) systems, so that doctors and health facilities can query PDMP databases within the native electronic health record (EHR) systems environment, bypassing the clunky process of needing to check PDMPs separately. For now, doctors continue to complain about the lack of integration between EHR and PDMP databases, which makes the review and verification process more burdensome.

---

* CA Health and Safety Code § 11165.4. The law included exemptions for veterinarians and pharmacists, and prescriptions for fewer than five days post-surgery, prescriptions to hospice patients, inpatient prescribing and in surgery centers and dental offices, all of which were permitted to consult the database on the next prescription to the same patient.

PHYSICIAN OVERPRESCRIBING
OVERRIDES PRIVACY CONCERNS

Beyond the pressure to expand the use of PDMPs to monitor physician prescribing of opioids and other controlled substances, a fifth reaction to the crisis has been a growing perception that things are so bad that it is time to roll back medical privacy concerns.

A fifth reaction to the crisis has been a growing perception that things are so bad that it is time to roll back medical privacy concerns.

I got a close look at this emerging trend when our firm represented Alvin Lewis, MD, a doctor whose case tested the bounds of patient privacy. The medical board searched the CURES PDMP database, found prescriptions that it regarded as excessive, and used that information to file disciplinary charges. One of my former partners appealed, arguing that the lack of a search warrant meant the PDMP search had inappropriately invaded patient privacy. The case went to the California Supreme Court, which disagreed with the appeal, finding that, while the search encroached on the privacy interest of the patient in prescription records, it was justified when balanced against the government's interest in protecting the public from the unlawful use of dangerous prescription drugs and protecting patients from negligent physicians.[16] In other words, the opioid crisis outweighed patient privacy.

The *Lewis* decision established that the government's interest in detecting overprescribing trumped medical privacy. In 2015, the medical board and the California Department of Public Health launched an interagency review of death certificates for thousands of patients, cross-checking causes of death that were suggestive of possible overdoses (such as heart attacks) with medical records from doctors, hospitals, and coroners. The review was the broadest review of physician prescribing in state history, encompassing more than two thousand cases to date and leading to investigations of hundreds of physicians.

Pressure to roll back privacy has also come up in the physician-patient context to ensure that doctors have the data they need. In 2017, the US Senate voted to pass "Jessie's Law," a bill introduced after Jessie Grubb, a thirty-year-old woman living in Ann Arbor, Michigan, died as a result of an OxyContin overdose. Grubb's surgeon had prescribed the opioid for acute, post-surgical pain, without any idea that she was in recovery from heroin addiction. After being reintroduced to opioids, Jessie ground up the pills to avoid the time-release and overdosed. Had her doctor known of her heroin addiction, he would not have prescribed OxyContin. But at the present time, two federal laws, the Health Insurance Portability and Accountability Act (HIPAA) and Title 42, Code of Federal Regulations (CFR), Part 2, prevented Grubb's doctors from accessing records relating to Jessie's substance abuse treatment history and made it difficult to talk to her family about it. (The latter regulations are specific to substance abuse treatment records, and require specific patient consent for any information sharing, reflecting the view that we need to keep substance abuse treatment secret so that people are not deterred from seeking treatment due the stigma associated with it.)

While Jessie's Law did not advance to a vote in the House of Representatives, its passage in the Senate signals that we may have hit a "high watermark" on privacy considerations. The bill's focus on revising privacy rules to enable more information-sharing among care providers and families—overriding HIPAA and Title 42 CFR, Part 2—reflects a growing view that privacy protection has gone too far and conflicts with the pressing need to prevent more opioid-related tragedies by ensuring that doctors can see records of past treatment of SUDs and talk to families and other doctors who treated the SUD.

While compliance with healthcare privacy and data security requirements remains a significant issue, a growing number of healthcare organizations—health systems, payers (insurance companies), and medical groups— have decided that it is essential to review proactively their patient data for signs of substance abuse, and to think about intervention strategies. A decade ago, many organizations now conducting such patient data reviews would have hesitated for fear of running afoul of patient privacy concerns. The opioid crisis is the direct pressure point leading to this change.

CRIMINAL PROSECUTIONS OF DOCTORS AND PHARMACISTS

A sixth reaction to the crisis has been criminal prosecutions of doctors and, more recently, pharmacists. As a lawyer working on prescribing issues, I have seen a significant swing of the pendulum on this issue. Just a decade ago, doctors would be prosecuted for failing to provide sufficient pain medication. These days, more and more doctors find themselves under investigation for overprescribing.

The other notable shift has been from medical board investigations of overprescribing to criminal investigations. Each state has physician and pharmacy licensing boards that are responsible for investigations of licensees and imposition of civil disciplinary actions such as license revocations, suspensions, and probations. For many years, overprescribing cases would be investigated by licensing boards for disciplinary charges for excessive prescribing, prescribing without appropriate physical exams, or other deficiencies. But throughout the 2000s, we began to see a growing trend of criminalization: district attorneys (DAs) launched criminal investigations of doctors for overprescribing, not waiting for medical boards to take action.

In addition to local DAs, the opioid crisis has driven increasing criminal enforcement efforts by the DEA to stop doctors from overprescribing. Across the country, prosecutors took on "pill mill" doctors, who were accused of prescribing vast amounts of opioids without providing serious patient examinations or other medical treatment.* Even today, the DEA continues to characterize the opioid crisis as flowing from doctors operating "candy stores for addicts," giving out way too much medication, too easily, to too many people who are asked for minimal explanation with little to no examination.**

> Even today, the DEA continues to characterize the opioid crisis as flowing from doctors operating "candy stores for addicts," giving out way too much medication, too easily, to too many people who are asked for minimal explanation with little to no examination.

From my vantage point, the reality on the ground is more complicated. The vast majority of pill mills have been shut down and their operators prosecuted. The primary sources of easy access to prescription drugs these days are increasingly online e-commerce options located in China and elsewhere, out of the reach of US law enforcement. Few American doctors and pharmacists are knowingly taking the risk of prescribing in ways that are flagrantly illegal and likely to draw the interest of criminal investigators. Many more of the doctors and pharmacists I encounter in criminal prosecutions have a "deer in

---

* The most highly publicized pill mill case in California involved Lisa Tseng, MD, who was convicted of second-degree murder charges in three patient overdose deaths and is now serving a sentence of thirty years to life. Another famous California pill mill doctor, Julio Diaz, MD, the "Candy Man," was sentenced to twenty-seven years following seventy-nine convictions after twenty overdose deaths. These were just two of the biggest of a long string of prosecutions of doctors for giving patients unscrupulously easy access to opioids.

** Throughout this book, with the exception of a handful of examples of quoting resources and describing specific perspectives, I have tried to avoid labeling people as "addicts" and instead refer to people as being addicted or in recovery from addiction. The use of person-centered language, emphasizing the person and not the disability, is a valuable step towards eliminating stigma and shame.

the headlights" reaction: it was not until law enforcement raided their clinics that they realized that they were being manipulated by patients and, in many cases, by nonphysician practice managers looking to cash in on the easy money of selling drugs with a high street value.

When physicians fail to keep up with changing standards and haven't retrained to meet prescribing standards, both the doctors and their patients are at significant risk.

When physicians fail to keep up with changing standards and haven't retrained to meet prescribing standards, both the doctors and their patients are at significant risk.

Working on these issues in Southern California added a unique facet. Los Angeles has so many celebrities that every third physician I work with seems to have famous patients. After I first moved here in the early 2000s, I got involved in the defense and crisis response of a number of cases involving overprescribing to well-known Hollywood figures.

In February 2007, for example, thirty-nine-year-old former model and reality television star Anna Nicole Smith overdosed in a Florida hotel, with nine medications in her bloodstream, including opioids and benzodiazepines. After criminal charges were filed against several of her doctors, one of her doctors asked me to advise on prescribing practices: Where might things have been done differently and how should they be handled going forward? Ultimately, one of her doctors was convicted; the other was acquitted of any wrongdoing.

Among other allegations in the Anna Nicole Smith case was that her doctors had protected her privacy by falsifying the patient name on the prescription. Even though it is clearly an illegal practice to write a prescription in the wrong name, I've seen more than a few doctors guilty of this misjudgment at the request of celebrities or wealthy people worried about their privacy. I vividly recall the disappointment of one doctor—who specialized in ketamine parties for Hollywood celebrities—when I explained in the investigation that the board would not be swayed by the number of A-list movie stars willing to testify on his behalf about the benefits of his methods. It's easy to blame the doctors involved for being enablers by treating people with celebrity, money, and power more indulgently. The reality is that the profound level of entitlement in our celebrity culture presents a huge challenge for the doctors who treat them.

The prosecution of Michael Jackson's doctor in 2009 highlighted the danger in succumbing to pressure from famous clients. Public outrage over the death of the beloved pop star meant that the LA District Attorney was motivated to move quickly and decisively. Conrad Murray, MD, was convicted of manslaughter.

THE NATIONAL OPIOID COMMISSION REPORT

In the seventh, most recent reaction to the opioid crisis, in 2017 President Donald Trump appointed the President's Commission on Combating Drug Addiction and the Opioid Crisis. He named former New Jersey governor Chris Christie as commission chair in this bipartisan group that included Patrick Kennedy, the former Rhode Island congressman, who has been outspoken about the crisis.

The commission produced a 2017 report that led to the declaration of a national public health emergency—albeit not a national emergency for federal funding purposes under the National Emergencies Act.[17] The report offers a useful snapshot of the various policy recommendations currently on the table, including the need to increase access to naloxone and improve PDMPs. The report also called for more federal funding, prevention efforts, prescriber education, efforts to reduce the supply of illegal drugs, and more research and development on non-opioid medications and therapies. Other government agencies and public policy think tanks have similar lists of action items, but this one is a logical reference for an official government roadmap for addressing the crisis. The suggestions, as we will see, are all positive—but they fall short of getting to the heart of the crisis.

KEY TAKEAWAYS | CHAPTER I

· ·

The opioid crisis is really three separate, ongoing crises that have unfolded in succession:

- A wave of physician overprescribing of pain medication that began in the late 1990s with OxyContin

- A wave of black tar heroin that filled the void after government crackdowns on doctors made it difficult to get prescriptions

- A wave of illegal and extremely deadly fentanyl, often mailed in small, hard-to-detect packets from China and frequently used as a counterfeit for other prescription opioids or laced into other drugs, such as heroin and cocaine, because of its low price

While prescription opioid and heroin remain significant sources of overdose deaths, fentanyl has become the leading killer, with a steeply rising death toll increasing year over year.

The explosion of the opioid crisis since 1999 gradually has led to a series of legal responses:

- A focus on increasing access to and use of naloxone, the overdose drug, by first responders such as EMTs, police, and emergency personnel

- A steadily increasing crackdown on physician overprescribing by state licensing boards, local law enforcement, and the DEA

- Making addiction treatment a covered benefit under health insurance plans

- Increasing the use of prescription drug monitoring programs to allow tracking of patients who engage in drug seeking from multiple sources, and physicians who overprescribe

THE HISTORY AND SCIENCE OF OPIOIDS

"If we could sniff or swallow something that would, for five or six hours each day, abolish our solitude as individuals, atone us with our fellows in a glowing exaltation of affection and make life in all its aspects seem not only worth living, but divinely beautiful and significant, and if this heavenly, world-transfiguring drug were of such a kind that we could wake up next morning with a clear head and an undamaged constitution—then, it seems to me, all our problems (and not merely the one small problem of discovering a novel pleasure) would be wholly solved and earth would become paradise."

ALDOUS HUXLEY (1894-1964)

THE OPIOID CRISIS HAS CHANGED the American landscape, presenting a singular threat and demanding a response. Before we look deeper at the questions of what created this crisis or how we address it going forward, it's useful to understand the history and science behind the allure of opioids, and their addictiveness.

OPIATES VERSUS OPIOIDS

We sometimes use the words "opioid" and "opiates" interchangeably. Both refer to chemical compounds that interact with receptors in our neurons and our nervous systems to produce pleasure and relieve pain. The big difference is that "opiates" refers only to the compounds (alkaloids) that develop naturally in and are derived from the opium poppy plant, while "opioids" refers to a much broader class of things: opiates and various semi-synthetic and wholly synthetic medications that are the focal point of this book.

Opium poppy (*Papaver somniferum*) is an ancient plant. It contains numerous alkaloids (nitrogen-based chemical compounds), of which the best known derivatives are morphine and codeine. These are extracted from the resin of the opium plant's unripe seed pods.

> The big difference is that "opiates" refers only to the compounds (alkaloids) that develop naturally in and are derived from the opium poppy plant, while "opioids" refers to a much broader class of things: opiates and various semisynthetic and wholly synthetic medications that are the focal point of this book.

I saw opium production up close in 1994. I had flown to Southeast Asia and made my way up to Pai, a city in northern Thailand near the border of Laos and Myanmar. Over a few days, I hiked with a guide into a mountainous area to visit several small communities of indigenous hill tribe slash-and-burn farmers who grow, among other things, opium poppies. These "villages" consisted of a few communal huts, without electricity or running water.

After I turned down the offer of a snack of some worms that had been pulled off some of their plants, I asked (through Pik, my translating guide, who had grown up in one of the local villages) about opium. One older farmer showed me how he scraped a brown gummy substance out of seed pod and then put it out to dry in the sun.

Later that evening, I watched the senior members of the extended family passing around a long pipe to smoke the end product. Smoking homegrown opium was a nightly occurrence among these farmers. They invited me to try it. What I remember is that it put me to sleep; I had been sleeping lightly in these communal hill tribe homes, with everybody in the same room, but that night I was out like a light. I wish I had vivid dreams to report, but all I recall is waking up the next morning, feeling good. It was strange to reconcile the seemingly innocuous, small-scale ramshackle operation with the massive crime establishment that we'll talk about later in this book.

A BRIEF HISTORY OF OPIOIDS

"Modern pharmacology," wrote Aldous Huxley, "has given us a host of new synthetics, but in the field of the naturally occurring mind changers it has made no radical discoveries. All the botanical sedatives, stimulants, vision revealers, happiness promoters and cosmic-consciousness arousers were found out thousands of years ago, before the dawn of history."[1]

Prehistoric evidence suggests that opium use may date as far back as fifty thousand years ago, based on residue of opioids in Neanderthal settlements. Evidence of opium poppy cultivation stretches back as far as five thousand years ago. Opium was revered not only for its pain relief but for a range of purposes: relaxation, mood elevation, anxiety and stress reduction, sleep promotion, or easing an inevitable death. We can only imagine that there were more than a few casualties of experimentation along the way.

Archaeologists have found evidence of opium use across numerous ancient societies, from the Greeks to the Persians and across the Middle East. The Sumerians included references on clay tablets on how to prepare opium. In ancient Mesopotamia, the name for opium poppies, *hul gil*, means "the joy plant." Assyrian medical tablets discovered by archaeologists reference it as *arat pa pa*, "juice of the poppy."

Pharaohs in Egypt, going back to King Tutankhamen twenty-four hundred years ago, were buried with opium jugs. The Greek poet Homer wrote about opium (an element of "nepenthes," the "drug of forgetfulness") in *The Odyssey* and *The Iliad*. In *The Odyssey*, Helen of Troy, daughter of Zeus, takes the opium-laden nepenthes she obtained in Egypt and mixes it into the wine for her banquet guests to "lull all pain and anger, and bring forgetfulness to every sorrow."

Roman merchants sold opium in the marketplaces, where it was regarded simultaneously as a symbol of sleep and death. Even after the rise of Islam led to prohibitions of alcohol, opium use continued in the Arabian Peninsula.

Throughout the last two thousand years, opium played a central role across numerous cultures as both a way to provide a painless death and also as a medical treatment for pain, sleeplessness, headaches, or diarrhea. When we think of how much we know now about the dangerous chemical compounds that were used medicinally alongside opium before the twentieth century, such as mercury and arsenic—both of which we now recognize as actively harmful to human health—opium has played an important role in providing legitimate medical benefits.

SEMISYNTHETIC AND SYNTHETIC OPIOIDS

Recall that the term "opiates" refers not only to the opium poppy itself, but also to the chemical compounds it contains and the derivatives, including morphine, codeine, and thebaine. These natural opiates were first identified as separate compounds within the opium plant in the 1800s.

When we talk about *opioids,* we have to add two additional categories beyond natural opiates: semisynthetics and synthetics. Semisynthetic opioids are further chemically derived in laboratories from the natural opiates. The semisynthetic category includes

- heroin, an illegal morphine derivative;

- hydromorphone, a morphine derivative;

- hydrocodone, a codeine derivative; and

- oxycodone, a thebaine derivative best known by the brand name OxyContin.

As a result of their chemical processing, the semisynthetics are more powerful than pure opiates, such as morphine and codeine. Let's take heroin as an example of how semisynthetic opioids come into being. First produced in the 1870s, heroin is the byproduct of a simple chemical reaction between morphine and acetic acid. When the two are baked together, the morphine dissolves into the acetic acid and bonds with it chemically. In some varieties of heroin, the product is purified into a smokable whitish or brownish powder, or an injectable form.

What we call "black tar" heroin is an impure mixture where the acetylation is stopped quickly, leaving a crude black resin (tacky) form. It's the only type of heroin that comes in solid form, which users typically melt down and inject or smoke. Black tar heroin can also be purified with substances like hydrochloric acid, ammonium hydroxide, and sodium carbonate to dissolve, separate out, and remove contaminants.

The third type, purely synthetic opioids, are pharmaceutical creations made from scratch in laboratories. These are, essentially, manmade replicas of the semisynthetics. Examples of synthetic opioids include

- methadone (developed by German scientists Gustav Ehrhart and Max Bockmühl in the late 1930s);

- pethidine (developed by German chemist Otto Eisleb in 1939);

- levorphanol (developed in Germany in 1948);

- dextropropoxyphene (developed by Eli Lilly in 1955);

- fentanyl (developed by Janssen Pharmaceutica in 1959);

- tramadol (developed by Grünenthal GmbH in 1962);

- carfentanil (developed by Jannsen in 1974); and

- sufentanil (developed by Jannsen in 1974).

Synthetic manufacture opens up all kinds of possibilities for chemists with access to various precursor chemicals. While fentanyl and carfentanil were originally developed as approved legal drugs, illegal manufacturers have used precursor chemicals in labs

While fentanyl and carfentanil were originally developed as approved legal drugs, illegal manufacturers have used precursor chemicals in labs across China, Mexico, and other countries to flood the US with illegal versions.

across China, Mexico, and other countries to flood the US with illegal versions. The explosion of synthetics like fentanyl and its analogs may well be the scariest part of the opioid crisis.

THE SCIENCE BEHIND OPIUM'S ALLURE

What was it that made opium so powerful so early in human history? Our brains are wired with neuropathways that respond to chemicals—neurotransmitters—produced by our pituitary glands and our central nervous system. When we experience pleasure—such as through food, sex, or music—or are placed under physical stress, such as through exercise, our bodies release endogenous (naturally occurring) chemicals, such as endorphins, dopamine, and norepinephrine, which are closely associated with substance-use disorders. These chemicals are released at the end of nerve impulses and spread across the synapse, arriving at neuroreceptors in different sectors of our brains, nervous system, and gastrointestinal tract. The immediate result is that we feel better: we feel less pain and are calmer, and more at ease. Our breathing slows. We feel happy.

Similarly, when dopamine reaches our neuroreceptors, it enables us to move and feel pleasure. Similarly, the norepinephrine mobilizes our brains and bodies for action. These chemicals stimulate different parts of our brain that regulate our emotions, cognition, and motivation. What we experience as pleasure is often the byproduct of the right levels of chemicals in our system. For the past thirty years, I have exercised most days of the week for the endorphin rush; I know that my anxiety and stress will lift as soon as I work up a good sweat.

The power of opium and its derivatives, both natural and manmade, is that they are alkaloids that essentially trick our bodies with a chemical structure that mimics endorphins and dopamine, and activates the same neurotransmitters. These drugs send out an intense wave of pleasure through our reward centers and reduce our experience of pain.

While more pleasure and less pain sounds good, there is a big risk in the way that opioids induce that easy, calm feeling, because it is linked to your respiratory system. Your breathing slows. The respiratory system in your brain relaxes. You breathe more slowly, taking fewer inhalations of oxygen. You take shallower breaths. While these things are not dangerous when they happen naturally, opioids can slow your breathing too much.

If a healthy person ordinarily draws twelve to fifteen breaths per minute, the rate for a person who has overdosed on opioids slows: ten, eight, six, four, two—and ultimately zero breaths per minute. Anoxic encephalopathy occurs when the deprivation of oxygen to brain tissue causes the tissue to die. Brain death can occur in as little as a minute or two. Whether in pursuit of euphoria or pain relief, a person who takes too high a dose of opioids—and that could be a microscopic amount given the extreme potency of many synthetic opioids—depresses their respiratory system into asphyxiation. They stop breathing, and they die.

> **Whether in pursuit of euphoria or pain relief, a person who takes too high a dose of opioids—and that could be a microscopic amount given the extreme potency of many synthetic opioids—depresses their respiratory system into asphyxiation. They stop breathing, and they die.**

THE PROBLEM OF TOLERANCE

Beyond the risky nature of opioid dosing, the other reason that so many people have died from opioids has to do with the science of addiction. When opioids first take over our neurotransmitters, a doctor-recommended dose may be sufficient. But the body begins to build up a tolerance to repeated use of the drugs, and the effect dulls over time. The user no longer gets the same blissful feeling and must raise the dose to achieve the same level of response. The reason is biological adaptation: as opioids bond to the receptors in our brains, our brains adjust, producing fewer neurotransmitters in order to adjust for the overstimulation from the opioids. In essence, the effect is muted because our bodies compensate for the effect of the drug.

This sets off a cycle of dependency: the opioid user must take higher and higher doses to get a reaction. This phenomenon is almost inevitable with repeated administration of any opioid.[2]

Put these two problems together—a high risk of over-suppressing respiration and a need to increase the dosage to make up for the diminishing effect—and you have a recipe for disaster. As we see in overdose deaths, people who get addicted self-administer larger and larger quantities of opioids as a result of developed tolerance. In some cases, overdoses occur because dosing reaches a level of respiratory suppression and people stop breathing. In other cases, overdoses occur when people who stopped taking opioids restart, and are undone by the dose that they might have been able to survive when their tolerance was higher.

If tolerance wasn't enough of a problem, many people who take opioids on a long-term basis experience a different problem, opioid-induced hyperalgesia (OIH). Their sensitivity to pain increases as a result of changes in certain neuroreceptors. For people with OIH, the intensity of the pain experienced feels worse over time. Sometimes, it spreads to more locations in the body. While raising the dosage of opioids helps someone developing tolerance to feel relief, for people with OIH, increasing the dosage makes them feel worse.

THE SCIENCE OF ADDICTION

Tolerance and dependence—fairly typical physiological reactions to consistent opioid use—affect most people who use these drugs. It's simply what happens when your body habituates to the drug. When you are opioid-dependent, your body has become accustomed to the drug and is expecting the next dose. Abrupt discontinuation (or substantial lowering) of the dose causes highly unpleasant withdrawal symptoms.

On the mildest side, symptoms look a lot like a bad flu—fever, chills, muscle aches, sweats, racing heart, diarrhea, nausea, and vomiting. Severe withdrawal from opioids can last a week or more, complete with intense, unremitting drug cravings, nausea and vomiting, depression, and insomnia.

While dependence reflects the way our bodies adapt to the drug, addiction refers to a pattern of substance use and behavior that moves beyond abuse to dependence, through brain and behavioral developments in which the drug use becomes compulsive, despite harmful consequences. The etymology of "addiction" comes from the Roman legal term *addictus*, meaning a person enslaved to repay debts. The American Society of Addiction Medicine defines addiction as a primary, chronic disease of brain reward, motivation, memory, and related circuitry that manifests biological, psychological, social, and spiritual dysfunction. In other words, a person becomes "enslaved" to the pathological pursuit of reward or relief, with impaired behavioral control, craving, diminished recognition of significant problems with behaviors, interpersonal relationships, and emotional response. Without treatment, addiction leads progressively toward disability or death.

In other words, an addicted person can't stop using the thing to which he or she is addicted despite the negative consequences. Addiction impairs the person's ability to meet work and social obligations, and to maintain relationships with friends and family. In the addicted brain, neural pathways that once experienced a sense of pleasure and reward for normal, healthy activities, such as work, school, time with family and friends, and sleep, get rewired to prioritize the drugs.

Addiction impairs the person's ability to meet work and social obligations, and to maintain relationships with friends and family.

As we'll explore more in Chapter 7, our understanding of addiction has advanced dramatically in recent decades, yet the treatment of addiction in an evidence-based manner is only in its infancy.

KEY TAKEAWAYS | CHAPTER 2

Opioids include

- opiate compounds extracted from the opium plant, like morphine and codeine;

- semisynthetic compounds developed by chemical processing of opiate compounds, like heroin; and

- purely synthetic creations that mimic opiate compounds and are manufactured with precursor chemicals in laboratories, like fentanyl.

Human opium cultivation dates back at least five thousand years. The power of opioids is that they that interact with receptors in our brain nerve cells and our nervous systems to produce euphoric pleasure and relieve pain. Popular uses of opioids since ancient times have included relaxation, mood elevation, treating diarrhea, reducing anxiety and stress, inducing sleep, or easing an inevitable death.

Opioid dependency is byproduct of tolerance as people require higher doses over time to get the same pleasurable and pain-relieving effect on brain chemistry. A person dependent on opioids is deemed to have an opioid use disorder (OUD). The challenge for a person with an OUD is that reducing the dose can lead to uncomfortable withdrawal symptoms and cravings. The point where an OUD is sufficiently severe to constitute an addiction is when a person's continued opioid use becomes compulsive despite harmful consequences on work, social obligations, and relationships with friends and family.

CHAPTER 3

THE SHIFT TO A REGULATED SYSTEM OF OPIOIDS

"[W]hat is here charged is that the defendant physician, by means of prescriptions, has enabled one known by him to be an addict to obtain from a pharmacist the enormous number of doses contained in 150 grains of heroin, 360 grains of morphine, and 210 grains of cocaine—3,000 ordinary doses! This opinion related to definitely alleged facts, and must be so understood. The enormous quantity of drugs ordered, considered in connection with the recipient's character, without explanation, seemed enough to show prohibited sales and to exclude the idea of bona fide professional action in the ordinary course."

SUPREME COURT OF THE UNITED STATES IN
***LINDER V. UNITED STATES* (1925)**

WHILE THE STORY OF the medicinal use of opiates in Chapter 2 is an ancient one, the predominant story over the past two hundred years has been one of balancing medicinal use against the danger of opium's addictiveness.

Opium's history in America goes back to the founding of the country. During the Revolutionary War, both the British and our own Continental armies used opium to treat wounded soldiers. Our third president, Thomas Jefferson, cultivated opium poppies at Monticello. And while Lin-Manuel Miranda didn't include it in his musical, *Hamilton*, doctors taking care of a dying Alexander Hamilton after his duel with Aaron Burr in 1804 administered laudanum, a popular alcohol-based opium tincture.

In those days, opium was unregulated by government. In fact, laudanum, developed in the 1500s, was popular precisely because—in contrast to alcohol—it was a medicine and therefore not taxed, making it more affordable. It had been around since the late 1600s, as European physicians mixed opium with brandy, wine, whisky, and other drinks as treatment for pain and many other conditions. Among famous people with laudanum addictions was President Abraham Lincoln's wife, Mary Todd Lincoln.

> Among famous people with laudanum addictions was President Abraham Lincoln's wife, Mary Todd Lincoln.

Perhaps the most relevant place to begin the story of opium regulation in America is the mid-nineteenth century. After Chinese immigrants chasing the Gold Rush came to San Francisco in the 1850s, opium dens proliferated, leading the city to enact the first opium den ban in the country.*

---

* While opium in America had been managed as both a form of medicine and as a vice since the eighteenth century, China had prohibited opium a century earlier, leading to the Opium Wars, two British–Chinese disputes. The source of the conflict was the British East India Company's smuggling of opium from India into China, which may have

The talent of some of the most famous people suffering from opium addiction—Charles Dickens, Edgar Allan Poe, and Samuel Taylor Coleridge—lent a certain seedy glorification to the drug, despite awareness of its addictive qualities. It developed an association with other vices, such as gambling and prostitution.

The Civil War played a central role in opium's growing use, with the Union and Confederate Armies supplying opium pills, powders, and tinctures to soldiers for battlefield injuries. The Union Army alone issued nearly ten million opium pills and 2.8 million ounces of opium powders and tinctures to its soldiers.

ADDICTION IN THE UNITED STATES

By the late nineteenth century, addiction was an acknowledged problem in America as well. The US had as many as two hundred thousand people with opium addictions by then, a disproportionate share being women, based on prescribing patterns for menstrual pain and "hysteria," among other things.[1] This was also the beginning of the shift from the use of opium to the more purified derivatives, morphine and heroin, which were injectable through a hypodermic syringe. Opium in all of its forms, including heroin, was a central part of American medicine,

---

represented as much as 20 percent of the revenue of the British Empire at the time. In 1839, the Chinese Emperor demanded an end to British importation based on the resulting problem of addiction in China, ultimately leading to violent confrontations, confiscation of imported barrels, and detention of British traders. An outraged Britain went to war, attacking the city of Canton (today, Guangzhou) and defeating China, requiring in the 1842 Treaty of Nanjing that China cede control over Hong Kong, open five new ports to trade, pay damages, and permit the opium trade to continue—perhaps the biggest victory for drug traffickers over a sovereign nation in history. In 1856, the British and Chinese fought a second Opium War, sparked by Chinese resistance to Western demands to expand the opium trade, which again led to British victory in 1860, with the humiliation of legalized opium forced onto China. By 1890, estimates were that a quarter of all Chinese men were addicted to opium. It is no small irony that China is today one of the primary exporters of illegal opioids, ordered online and mailed into the US.

available with no formal regulatory oversight structure.

This began to change in the late 1890s, as states enacted laws requiring valid physician-issued prescriptions for patients to procure opioids. The

> **Opium in all of its forms, including heroin, was a central part of American medicine, available with no formal regulatory oversight structure.**

enactment of the Pure Food and Drug Act in 1906 also marked an important shift. For the first time, medications containing morphine, heroin, or cocaine were required to be labeled with identification of their contents.

In 1908, President Theodore Roosevelt appointed a physician, Hamilton Wright, MD, as the first US Opium Commissioner.[2] In 1909, Dr. Wright led the American delegation to the First International Opium Commission in Shanghai, the same year that Congress passed the Opium Exclusion Act, banning its importation for smoking. As Opium Commissioner, Wright's words in 1911 might as well have been uttered today:

> Of all the nations of the world, the United States consumes most habit-forming drugs per capita. Opium, the most pernicious drug known to humanity, is surrounded, in this country, with far fewer safeguards than any other nation in Europe fences it with. China now guards it with much greater care than we do; Japan preserves her people from it far more intelligently than we do ours, who can buy it, in almost any form, in every tenth one of our drug stores. Our physicians use it recklessly in remedies and thus become responsible for making numberless "dope fiends," and in uncounted nostrums offered everywhere for sale it figures, in habit-forming quantities without restriction. Even in Russia medical practitioners ... have guarded it as one might guard

a pearl, for use and against abuse. A physician there would no more think of giving it at an ordinary time of physical or mental stress than he would think of taking it himself because he had a trifling pain or felt a little worry. Here physicians often are addicted to the habit, and they continually prescribe opium for insufficient causes or without any real excuse. The contrast between European and American professional ethics in this matter is deplorable, and the dark side of the picture is America's. A proportion of our doctors and a much larger ratio of our druggists regard their liberty to prescribe and sell as a license to advise and furnish to its victims the narcotic curse on demand.[3]

In 1914, the United States joined thirty-three other nations in sharply limiting the importation and production of opium and opium derivatives via the International Opium Commission. This year was the same year the US passed the Harrison Narcotics Tax Act, a key tax measure on drugs that effectively eliminated opium and heroin from widespread use. The act required those involved in importing, exporting, manufacturing and distributing opium or cocaine to register with the federal government and pay the related tax levies.

FEDERAL-STATE TENSION OVER OPIOID PRESCRIBING

While the Harrison Act marked the beginning of federal recognition of the need to limit illegal opioid access, one of the law's provisions exempted doctors prescribing the drugs "in professional practice" from requiring to register and pay taxes. This meant that law enforcement could neither go after doctors who were prescribing dangerously nor their addicted patients who were abusing access to opioids. It's important to remember that, in addition to believing that they were fulfilling their responsibilities by giving opioid maintenance doses to prevent people from going through withdrawal, many doctors were addicted themselves. Most famously, in *Genius on the Edge: The Bizarre Double Life of Dr. William Stewart Halsted,* Gerald Imber, MD, tells the story of Dr. Halsted (1852–1922), one of the "Big Four" founding professors at the Johns Hopkins Hospital and so-called Father of Modern Surgery, who took prolific amounts of morphine, along with cocaine.

This exemption of doctors led to a series of Supreme Court decisions that illuminate the tension surrounding opioids and medical practice. First, in 1919, the Supreme Court issued two decisions challenging the Harrison Act. The *United States v. Doremus*[4] case rejected a challenge to the Harrison Act based on the argument that it was an illegal tax, with its true purpose not being to raise revenue, but to eliminate opium and heroin from use. The case of *Webb v. United States* raised the question of the ability to regulate doctors.[5] Dr. Webb was a physician who sold prescriptions for morphine. At a price of 50 cents per patient, he was enormously popular and had thousands of "patients."

Examining Dr. Webb's practice, the Supreme Court rejected the concept that supplying morphine to addicted people without actually assessing, diagnosing, or treating them in any other way constituted the practice of medicine. The Supreme Court distinguished between professional treatment of patients and merely keeping addicted people comfortable by maintaining their use.

The following year, 1920, the Supreme Court refined its analysis of the issue in the case of *Jin Fuey Moy v. United States,* clarifying that physician immunity for prescribing morphine was limited to "the bounds of a physician's professional practice" and did not extend to a "sale to a dealer or a distribution intended to cater to the appetite or satisfy the craving of one addicted to the use of the drug."[6] Such a prescription, said the Supreme Court, "protects neither the physician who issues it nor the dealer who knowingly accepts and fills it."

In 1922, the Supreme Court ruled in *United States v. Behrman* that the doctor's intention did not matter. In other words, violation of the Harrison Act was a strict liability crime.[7] Dr. Behrman, like Drs. Webb and Moy, had prescribed huge amounts of opioids (heroin and morphine, along with the non-opioid stimulant cocaine), but the court dismissed the indictment because Dr. Behrman claimed that his intention was to cure the addiction. The Supreme Court ruled that, good intentions or not, he had violated the law by his prescribing practices. Notably, Justices Oliver Wendell Holmes and Louis Brandeis, two of our greatest jurists, dissented on the basis that if Dr. Behrman had prescribed in good faith and with reasonable care, then he should have a defense to prosecution.

THE FIRST OPIOID CRISIS?

Following the *Behrman* decision, the federal government, through federal narcotics officers associated with the US Department of Treasury, began to crack down on doctors who treated drug addiction, filing criminal charges

By the 1930s, more than twenty-five thousand physicians were charged, and thousands served jail time for prescribing narcotics.

and sending doctors and drug offenders to jail in rising numbers. By the 1930s, more than twenty-five thousand physicians were charged, and thousands served jail time for prescribing narcotics.[8]

This, in turn, prompted the Federal Bureau of Narcotics and Department of Treasury to focus their energy on stopping doctors from being the "leak" in the bucket of opioid and narcotics control. From the perspective of doctors trying to treat people struggling with pain and addiction—and the patients themselves—federal agencies were a source of terror.

The *Behrman* decision itself did not last. In 1925, the Supreme Court ruled unanimously in *Linder v. United States*[9]—in a decision written by Justice James McReynolds, who had joined Justices Holmes and Brandeis in the *Behrman* dissent—that it was up to the individual states, not the federal government, to decide what constituted bona fide medical practice in the treatment of addiction. The *Linder* case involved a physician, Charles Linder, MD, who had been tricked into prescribing cocaine and morphine by a patient complaining of stomach pains, who insisted she only needed a prescription one time in the absence of her regular doctor. She turned out to be addicted and working as an undercover agent provocateur for the Department of Treasury. While Dr. Linder was not regularly in the business of prescribing to addicted patients, government agents raided his office, arrested him, indicted him under the *Behrman* rule, and convicted him. The Supreme Court reversed his conviction, returning to the earlier rule in *Webb* and *Jin Fuey Moy* that the determination of the legitimacy of prescribing had to be made on a case-by-case basis and at the state level, not by federal policy. "Obviously," stated the decision, "direct control of medical practice in the states is beyond the power of the federal government."

From 1925 on, jurisdiction over prescribing moved to the states, leading to the tension described in Chapter 1 between medical board regulation and local district attorney criminal enforcement. In 1930, the Federal Bureau of Narcotics was formed, subsequently leading to other federal agencies, including the National Institute of Mental Health (NIMH, formed in 1946), the Alcohol, Drug Abuse, and Mental Health Agency (ADAMHA, formed in 1973), and finally the Substance Abuse and Mental Health Services Administration (SAMHSA, formed in 1992).

This conflict also had significant reverberations on the ground for both pain medicine and addiction treatment. A whole generation of physicians, traumatized by the post-*Behrman* aggression of federal law enforcement, remained reluctant to get involved with opioid prescribing—something echoed nearly a century later in the current tense environment around opioids. This early tension had significant implications more broadly for the status of addiction treatment. When we look for explanations of how and why addiction treatment became such a siloed activity, separated from the rest of our healthcare system, the post-*Behrman* crackdown on physicians is undoubtedly a key part of the picture.

When we look for explanations of how and why addiction treatment became such a siloed activity, separated from the rest of our healthcare system, the post-*Behrman* crackdown on physicians is undoubtedly a key part of the picture.

THE CONTROLLED SUBSTANCES ACT

The Harrison Act was ultimately replaced in 1961, when the US signed on to the United Nations Single Convention on Narcotic Drugs, an international treaty to create worldwide prohibitions on the manufacturing, importation, possession, use, and distribution of opioids and other substances. The Controlled Substances Act of 1970 (CSA), signed into law by US President Richard Nixon as part of a larger Comprehensive Drug Abuse and Prevention and Control Act, implemented the 1961 treaty. Essentially, the CSA consolidated the tangle of more than four dozen different federal drug laws into one overarching system focused simultaneously on managing prescription medicine and stopping the flow of illegal drugs.

Since the 1973 formation of the Drug Enforcement Administration (DEA) as a unit within the US Department of Justice, the DEA has enforced the CSA. The primary mechanisms of enforcement have included mandatory registrations of physicians, chain-of-custody tracking of drugs from manufacturers to distributors to physicians and pharmacies, as well as annual production quotas.

One evolution over the course of the past fifteen years has been the ability of the DEA to track prescribing data in real time. I remember a DEA agent's excitement in the early 2000s when he shared that, for the first time, he could get a real-time printout of the top prescribers in the state. Almost inevitably, when DEA agents visited physicians and pharmacies atop the prescribers list for medications like Vicodin and OxyContin, they were likely to find overprescribing and other compliance problems.

Under the CSA, controlled substances are assigned to five lists, depending on the perception of their risk of abuse:

Schedule I

Schedule I is reserved for substances that are deemed to be drugs of abuse not having any recognized medicinal benefits. Physicians may not prescribe and pharmacies may not dispense Schedule I controlled substances, which, as of this publication, continue to include cannabis. Inclusion on Schedule I of the CSA limits research significantly by requiring specific application and approval of a waiver from the DEA.

Heroin is the only opioid permanently designed as Schedule I. In 2017 and 2018, the DEA issued temporary scheduling orders placing on Schedule I various forms of fentanyl, which is ordinarily a Schedule II controlled substance. The temporary elevation reflects the central role of illegal fentanyl in the current death spiral. The 2018 order focused on chemical precursors being used by criminal manufacturers: "fentanyl-related substances that are not currently listed in any schedule" of the CSA "and their isomers, esters, ethers, salts and salts of isomers, esters, and ethers in Schedule I."

Schedule II

Schedule II controlled substances may be legally prescribed, but they are considered to have the highest risk of abuse and dependence. Schedule II drugs are subject to heightened restrictions on prescribing, including a thirty-day supply limit and a prohibition on giving refills with a prescription. The federal government is currently considering a three-day limit on new Schedule II opioid prescriptions for some kinds of acute onset pain.

Schedule II is the predominant schedule for opioids, including

- opium, and its natural derivatives, morphine and codeine;

- fentanyl (Duragesic, Sublimaze);

- semisynthetic opioids hydrocodone, hydromorphone (Dilaudid), and oxycodone (OxyContin);

- methadone, a longtime Schedule II medication, approved by the FDA as a replacement medication for heroin in 1971;

- meperidine, a synthetic opioid (Demerol); and

- carfentanil (Wildnil).

In 2014, hydrocodone-acetaminophen combinations (Vicodin, Norco, Lorcet) were moved from Schedule III to Schedule II in reflection of growing awareness of the risk of their abuse.

Schedule III

Schedule III controlled substances are deemed to be at moderate risk of abuse and dependence. This includes buprenorphine (Suboxone, Subutex), which was first scheduled on Schedule V in 1985 but was moved to Schedule III in 2002.

Schedule IV

Schedule IV controlled substances are deemed to be at low risk of abuse and dependence and include

- the synthetic opioid Tramadol, first scheduled as a Schedule IV controlled substance in 2015; and

- benzodiazepines, a non-opioid class of sedatives and anti-anxiety drugs discussed later in the book, including alprazolam (Xanax), clonazepam (Klonopin), diazepam (Valium), lorazepam (Ativan), midazolam (Versed), temazepam (Restoril), and triazolam (Halcion).

Schedule V

Schedule V controlled substances are deemed to be at the lowest risk of abuse. The only opioid-related medication on Schedule V is cough syrup with codeine (Robitussin AC, Phenergan with codeine).

CONTINUED FEDERAL-STATE TENSION

As we approach a half-century in which the CSA has regulated the status of opioids alongside state oversight of the practice of medicine, it is worth considering where our system is working and where it is breaking down.

Compared to the conflict between the DEA and the states over cannabis (where cannabis remains a Schedule I criminalized controlled substance for DEA purposes, even as the majority of states permit its medicinal use), there appears to be relative alignment in state and federal approaches to opioids.

In 2008, in response to the proliferation of websites on which consumers could order opioids without physician involvement, Congress passed and President George W. Bush signed into law the

Ryan Haight Online Pharmacy Consumer Protection Act. The Ryan Haight Act prohibited online prescribing without an "in-person medical evaluation" for controlled substances. While the *Linder* rule remains in place, leaving oversight of prescription to the states, the Ryan Haight Act brought the DEA and federal prosecutors closer to the oversight of prescribing without legitimate medical exams.

Compared to the conflict between the DEA and the states over cannabis (where cannabis remains a Schedule I criminalized controlled substance for DEA purposes, even as the majority of states permit its medicinal use), there appears to be relative alignment in state and federal approaches to opioids.

The increasing role of the DEA has been even more visible with respect to pharmacy dispensation of controlled substances. As the history of the *Webb, Jin Fuey Moy, Behrman,* and *Linder* cases highlight, historically, physician prescribers bore the brunt of the law enforcement and regulatory focus for overprescribing or otherwise inappropriate prescribing. However, in recent years, the DEA has been increasingly vocal about the expectation that pharmacies that receive prescriptions and dispense to patients serve as a key safeguard in the process. Pharmacies have also been named in lawsuits for negligence in filling prescriptions leading to overdose deaths.

DEA regulations refer to a "corresponding responsibility" that rests with pharmacists who dispense drugs to ensure compliance with controlled substance laws. In the view of the DEA, pharmacists are at risk if they fill prescriptions when they "either know of or have reason to know that the prescription was not written for a legitimate purpose." When prescriptions are not issued for a legitimate medical purpose, a "pharmacist may not intentionally close his eyes and thereby avoid [actual] knowledge of the real purpose of the prescription."

Beyond physician irresponsibility, what are the DEA and pharmacy boards looking for? They are looking for drug-seeking patients trying to utilize forged prescriptions. The DEA and state pharmacy boards do this by regularly reviewing prescription drug monitoring program (PDMP) compliance, and taking enforcement action against noncompliant pharmacies that fail to review and input PDMP data. Both DEA and state pharmacy boards are increasingly auditing (in the case of the DEA) and taking enforcement action (in the case of state pharmacy boards) for failure to verify prescriber's medical licenses (and right to prescribe), as well as ensuring the correct DEA numbers.

While pharmacies are not expected to second-guess physician prescribing decisions, there is a growing list of red flags expected to be identified, such as prescribing practices that are, on their face, concerning (such as excessive prescribing), as well as drug-seeking behavior by patients. Particular concerns identified in the DEA's 2010 "East Main Street Pharmacy" decision identified these examples of practices the Columbus, Ohio, pharmacy should have red-flagged:

- Doctors who dispense in a "cocktailed" combination manner suggestive of abuse

- No individualization of dosing by the prescribing physician

- Multiple prescriptions for the strongest formulations of abused drugs, such as hydrocodone (Vicodin's main ingredient, among other brand names) and alprazolam (Xanax, a benzodiazepine)

- Requests for early dispensing of refills

- Refills sought when patients or doctors are based at a significant distance to the pharmacy

- Disproportionate prescribing of controlled substances

- Patients appearing in groups

- A significant percentage of cash prescriptions

On one level, the additional focus on the point where medication is dispensed as an additional layer of protection, in the face of the opioid crisis, makes perfect sense. Pharmacies offer a final chance to double-check and avoid physician errors, manipulation by drug-seekers, and other bad behavior.

However, if you talk to any patient who depends upon opioids to manage chronic pain, the rising expectations of pharmacies and physicians alike have created enormous barriers to obtaining legitimate opioid pain medication. Many pharmacies are now protecting themselves by simply declining to fill any prescriptions for opioids. In other cases, pharmacies will not fill prescriptions until confirmation that the doctor has provided documentation of the prescription to the patient's health plan. These hurdles, intended to prevent abuse, make the process of getting medications miserable for patients who are legitimately in need.

Many pharmacies are now protecting themselves by simply declining to fill any prescriptions for opioids. In other cases, pharmacies will not fill prescriptions until confirmation that the doctor has provided documentation of the prescription to the patient's health plan.

Even worse for patients, many doctors have elected to stop prescribing opioids to avoid the regulatory hurdles and risk, adding to the challenge for people living with chronic pain. One of the big ongoing challenges is creating a system that works for everyone: law enforcement, regulators, doctors, pharmacies—and, of course, patients.

KEY TAKEAWAYS | CHAPTER 3

• •

- As a result of pervasive medical and recreational use of opioids, dependency and addiction began to be recognized worldwide as a problem by the late nineteenth century, culminating in US federal regulation of opioids in 1914 with the Harrison Narcotics Tax Act, a tax that made opium and heroin cost-prohibitive.

- Since physician prescribing was exempted from the 1914 law, thousands of people dependent on heroin, morphine, and other opioids flocked to doctors after the enactment of the Harrison Act. This led to accusations of physician overprescribing and a series of 1920s Supreme Court decisions culminating in a federal crackdown in the 1920s and 1930s that sent thousands of physicians to jail. There are many parallels and important context to be drawn from this original American opioid crisis.

- While the federal regulatory system for opioids was overhauled in the 1970s with the creation of the Drug Enforcement Administration (DEA), they carried on the legacy concern that physicians were the "leak" in the system of control enabling easy and inappropriate patient access to opioids. In recent years, pharmacies have increasingly been viewed as an additional checkpoint, expected to police suspicious prescriptions before dispensing. This pressure has led many doctors and pharmacies to decline to prescribe and fill prescriptions for opioids, creating challenges for many patients with legitimate needs for opioids.

IS PHARMA TO BLAME?

"There's going to be a jury somewhere, someplace, that's going to hit [the Sackler Family, owners of Purdue Pharma] with the largest judgment in the nation's history."

FORMER MISSISSIPPI ATTORNEY GENERAL MIKE MOORE

IN MANY RESPECTS, THE OPIOID CRISIS

is unique among public health crises insofar as it emerged from mistakes inside the healthcare community. By contrast, the Zika and Ebola viruses and mad cow disease are examples of public health crises that originated from outside our healthcare system.

Opioids present the rare—and possibly only—case where our healthcare system also played a causative role: Drug companies marketed opioids. Doctors prescribed them. Pharmacies put them in patients' hands. And patients overdosed or became addicted.

In this chapter, we'll take a look at the drug companies, and one in particular, Purdue Pharma. While I have little patience for long conversations about who's to blame, in this case, such a discussion offers a useful prelude to the question of what needs to change.

It was less than forty years ago, in the 1980s, that the prevailing belief in the healthcare community was that opioids did not pose a high risk for addiction.[1] Back then, there was an open debate in the medical community over how much opioids should be used for treating chronic pain. How did we get to a place where doctors began to prescribe so freely?

I'm sure that other villains in other drug companies will surface as more of the opioid story is written, but it's hard to see how they could compete with the story of three brothers born in Brooklyn, New York, to immigrant parents. The story of how Arthur, Mortimer, and Raymond Sackler grew Purdue Pharma into an opioid-selling behemoth and became one of America's richest families manages to be at once colorful and chilling.[*]

> The story of how Arthur, Mortimer, and Raymond Sackler grew Purdue Pharma into an opioid-selling behemoth and became one of America's richest families manages to be at once colorful and chilling.

---

[*] Perhaps the best telling of the story is the October 2017 *New Yorker* article, "The Family That Built an Empire of Pain," by Patrick Radden Keefe.

ARTIE SACKLER: HEALTHCARE MARKETING GENIUS

Arthur (1914–87), Mortimer (1917–2010), and Raymond (1920–2017) were physicians who focused on psychobiology, meaning the physical manifestation of psychiatric disorders—how changes in body function with pharmaceuticals could be alternatives to prevailing practices in psychiatry at the time, like electroconvulsive shock therapy, lobotomies, and psychoanalysis. They focused on the conditions of schizophrenia and bipolar disorder.

As children of the Great Depression, the Sackler brothers brought a unique sensibility as hustling entrepreneurs and rule-breakers to their work as doctors. The oldest brother, known to friends as Artie, paid his way through medical school by writing advertising copy for an ad agency. He was so successful as a marketer that he ended up buying and taking over the agency, and blazing a trail as a brilliant advertiser. This skill would ultimately make billions for Purdue Pharma and light the flame that sparked the opioid crisis—the promotion of the drug known as OxyContin. Artie Sackler's skill as a marketer was so legendary that, ten years after his death, he was inducted posthumously into the Medical Advertising Hall of Fame in 1997—a bitter irony two decades later, given the trail of his company's victims.

Sackler Success with Librium and Valium

In the 1950s, the Sackler brothers began looking for failed or distressed pharmaceutical companies that they could buy and turn around. They put Artie's advertising skills to work for a variety of medications, including Betadine, an antiseptic; the anti-anxiety drug Librium; and the sedative Valium. The latter two drugs were a huge success for the brothers, who made a fortune based on Artie's slick ads in physician journals and leave-behind marketing for doctor offices.

Artie had a knack for making his sales pitches sound serious and clinically focused, no matter how little evidence supported them. In the late 1950s he got caught fabricating fictitious doctors as product endorsers, but he didn't suffer any lasting consequence for the fraud. One campaign for the benzodiazepine Valium exemplified his careless approach: promoting the drug to doctors for patients who had no psychiatric symptoms. Artie was so successful that Valium addiction became a crisis in miniature of its own, long before opioids. Between 1969 and 1982, Valium was the most prescribed drug in the US, with more than 2.3 billion pills sold in its peak year, 1978.[2]

Among Artie's brilliant, if conflict-ridden, moves was moving from advertising to publishing his own newspaper, *The Medical Tribune*. At its peak, the newspaper reached more than six hundred thousand doctors, giving Artie a powerful platform from which to sell his drugs. In the late 1950s, Artie was found to have the head of the FDA Antibiotics Division, Henry Welch, PhD, on the take, paying him to promote products in his speaking gigs. But still, Artie didn't suffer any lasting consequences.

In 1962, he was called to testify before a US Senate Committee chaired by Tennessee Senator Estes Kefauver, who was troubled by the process that allowed the Sackler brothers to develop a new drug, test it, "secure favorable reports" from hospitals they were connected to, develop a marketing campaign, and publish articles and advertising to sell their creation. Kefauver, who had previously investigated the Mafia, clearly saw the dark side of the Sackler empire, but ultimately he couldn't slow it down, let alone stop the coming drug-fueled train wreck.

PURDUE PHARMA AND OXYCONTIN

All of these adventures laid the groundwork for the Sackler coup de grace, Purdue Pharma. In 1952, the brothers bought Purdue Frederick, a small drug company known for making laxatives. Artie took a backseat and let Ray and Morty run the company. They changed the company name to Purdue Pharma. In 1987, Ray and Morty began a great run with the popular opioid painkiller MS Contin. MS stood for morphine sulfate and Contin for continuous; MS Contin offered a controlled morphine release as the pill dissolved in the blood stream.

Looking for a follow-up to MS Contin before its patent expired, the Sacklers settled on a controlled-release dose of oxycodone, which they called OxyContin. In 1995 the FDA approved the drug.[*] By 1996, Purdue Pharma already had ample evidence that OxyContin was being abused, and concealed that information, while continuing to market the drug as less addictive than other opioids, according to federal prosecutors in 2006.

> **Looking for a follow-up to MS Contin before its patent expired, the Sacklers settled on a controlled-release dose of oxycodone, which they called OxyContin.**

Purdue and the Sackler advertising and media arms had hailed their new products as a major breakthrough—a long-lasting painkiller with a delayed release mechanism. The big idea was that patients could take a single dose every twelve hours, meaning they could sleep through the night, unlike other drugs that required more frequent doses. The problem was that this turned out to be false marketing. Many patients started complaining that the effects wore off sooner than twelve hours, requiring more medication sooner and sooner. Moreover, patients developed tolerance and began to experience withdrawal symptoms like nausea, shaking, and itchiness if they waited the recommended time between doses.

Unsated by their previous marketing successes, the Sacklers ignored the problems patients were experiencing and ramped up

---

* For more on the marketing campaigns, see Keefe, "The Family That Built the Empire of Pain," www.newyorker.com/magazine/2017/10/30/the-family-that-built-an-empire-of-pain.

OxyContin sales with an unprecedented marketing effort. Pulling out all the stops, they fabricated "opiophobia," a fictional problem of physician fear of prescribing painkillers. This fabricated concept helped marketers pressure resistant doctors to prescribe for a broader range of conditions: cancer pain, acute short-term post-surgical pain, back pain, fibromyalgia. There was no apparent limit to the range of conditions OxyContin could treat.

The Sackler brothers paid prominent doctors not merely to pitch OxyContin but to deny that it was addictive. When doctors shared patient complaints that they were experiencing withdrawal symptoms, Purdue taught its thousand-plus marketers to lie, telling doctors OxyContin was less addictive than other products. The company fabricated statistics in an effort to hide how addictive OxyContin was, and the marketing team created fake scientific charts distributed to doctors, which spread the false marketing campaign far and wide.[3]

> **The company fabricated statistics in an effort to hide how addictive OxyContin was, and the marketing team created fake scientific charts distributed to doctors, which spread the false marketing campaign far and wide.**

Purdue conducted no studies on the risk of addiction. Instead, the company exploited a misperception by doctors that oxycodone was less potent than morphine. Denying that OxyContin was addictive, Purdue trained its sales reps to tell doctors that concerned patients might be experiencing "pseudo-addiction," meaning that their addiction symptoms, such as having the shakes, were in fact pain signals being falsely perceived as addiction.[4] The solution for this made-up condition? More OxyContin, of course.

Purdue supplied its army of marketers with swag, video testimonials from patients, and other goodies. It flew several thousand doctors to conferences to deliver presentations about OxyContin—

such a big undertaking that Purdue ran its own speakers bureau. The company also flew doctors to seminars in resort cities as a thank-you for prescribing OxyContin, and enlisted well-regarded doctors on its payroll to speak out about the problems of "opiophobia" and physician under-treatment of pain—and the need to prescribe more opioids. Not surprisingly, OxyContin became a billion-dollar-a-year product for Purdue Pharma.

Purdue's largesse went far beyond doctors. After persuading the FDA to include a product insert claiming, without factual basis, that OxyContin was safer than rival products because of its delayed absorption mechanism, Purdue offered a job to the outgoing FDA examiner who approved the statement. With this full-court press, OxyContin was the epicenter of the first wave of the opioid crisis: physician overprescribing.

THE UNRAVELING OF OXY

Throughout the late 1990s, the signs of a problem were already there. For all of the positive publicity and profits, Oxy, as it was known, had become an abused street drug. Some patients sold the pills for profits, and people were grinding up and snorting them, or dissolving pills in liquid to inject them, overcoming the slow-release mechanism. And, sure enough, patients were dying in their sleep of overdoses.

In 1999, some four hundred thousand people admitted to misusing OxyContin for nonmedical purposes to get high. By 2002, the number was up to 1.9 million people. By 2003, it was 2.8 million. That year, the DEA had identified Purdue's "aggressive methods" as a source of OxyContin's "widespread abuse."[5]

None of the bad news slowed down Purdue's marketing; Purdue Pharma was itself so addicted to sales that it couldn't stop even in the face of evidence that its drug was killing people. Based on sales patterns, Purdue knew full well the pill mill locations where unscrupulous providers doled out huge numbers of prescriptions, but it did nothing to stop the abuse. Despite the mounting overdose death toll, the Sackler fortune continued to grow, and the company continued its aggressive sales efforts. While Purdue dropped some of its original marketing claims under pressure in 2001, by 2003 the FDA was still warning the company of ads that "grossly overstate[d]" the safety of OxyContin. Was the fix In?

Even as lawsuits began to mount, Purdue continued to market OxyContin aggressively. One of the most shocking pieces of the story occurred in 2007, during the federal prosecution of Purdue Pharma for alleged fraud. Purdue hired former New York Mayor Rudy Giuliani to try to kill the case. His work stands as a case study in the effective use of power.

Just six years after 9/11 and long before his odd appearance on behalf of the Trump administration, Giuliani was still regarded at the time as "America's Mayor." Wielding his celebrity, Giuliani persuaded key legislators like Congressman Curt Weldon, who has taken on Purdue, to back off. Giuliani used his status as a cancer survivor to make the outrageous claim that Purdue had good motives: "I understand the pain and distress that accompanies illness," he said. "I know that proper medications are necessary for people to treat their sickness and improve their quality of life."[6] Giuliani's firm organized the "Rx Action Alliance," a consortium of drug makers, physicians, and law enforcement authorities against drug abuse.

The case may have been too big to be scuttled altogether, but what Giuliani achieved was incredible for Purdue and bad for America: What was arguably the worst episode of abuse in pharmaceutical industry history settled for what amounted to a minor slap on the wrist. The company settled charges of FDA violations for $600 million in fines.

Three executives, president Michael Friedman, attorney Howard Udell, and medical director Paul Goldenheim, MD, pled guilty to criminal misdemeanors, paying less than $35 million in fines.

If $635 million sounds like a lot, consider that, in 2009, Pfizer

What Giuliani achieved was incredible for Purdue and bad for America: What was arguably the worst episode of abuse in pharmaceutical industry history settled for what amounted to a minor slap on the wrist.

paid $2.3 billion to settle much more mild charges that it paid kickbacks and engaged in off-label (unapproved) promotion of Lyrica, a diabetes/nerve pain drug; Bextra, an osteoarthritis drug; Geodon, an antipsychotic; and Zyvox, an antibiotic. In a nutshell, Pfizer had engaged in some of the same tactics as Purdue, with much less deadly results. They had pushed sales reps to promote the drugs to doctors for purposes that were not FDA-approved. Pfizer had flown doctors to all-expense paid resorts.

In 2012, GlaxoSmithKline paid $3 billion for failing to disclose safety data on Avandia, a diabetes drug, and for improperly promoting antidepressants Paxil, Wellbutrin, and a handful of other drugs. GlaxoSmithKline had inappropriately pushed Paxil as a pediatric drug, a use for which it wasn't approved. They had pushed Wellbutrin for weight loss, ADHD, and other conditions. And they had paid for fancy restaurants and trips for their doctors.

So why did these two drug companies pay $5.3 billion between them and Purdue get away with a $600 million fine for behavior that left victims dead by the thousands? Credit Giuliani. The minimal nature of the fines and sentences was an outrage for what was arguably the worst fraud in pharmaceutical industry fraud, and certainly the most damaging in terms of the loss of life. Tens, if not hundreds, of thousands of Americans have died at the hands of Purdue Pharma,

THE UNITED STATES OF OPIOIDS

and the executives received only criminal misdemeanors. Friedman, Udell, and Goldenheim—and the Sacklers themselves—deserved to be behind bars for life.

Giuliani earned his fee with that shockingly light sentence for Purdue's execs. The sentences enabled Purdue to minimize the conduct with lawyerly verbiage, painting it as ancient history. A Purdue Pharma press release issued at the time offered the minimal conceivable admission: "Nearly six years and longer ago, some employees made, or told other employees to make, certain statements about OxyContin to some healthcare professionals that were inconsistent with the FDA-approved prescribing information for OxyContin and the express warnings it contained about risks associated with the medicine."[7]

Perhaps the biggest outrage of the press release was that Purdue was permitted to whitewash the wrongdoing, declaring that "Mr. Friedman, Dr. Goldenheim (while at Purdue) and Mr. Udell neither engaged in nor tolerated the misconduct at issue in this investigation. To the contrary, they took steps to prevent any misstatements in the marketing or promotion of OxyContin and to correct any such misstatements of which they became aware." In other words, Purdue was permitted to pay a relatively minuscule amount and dismiss its own wrongdoing. And as the fraud was unveiled in the United States, Purdue simply shifted its marketing efforts to other parts of the world.

> Purdue was permitted to pay a relatively minuscule amount and dismiss its own wrongdoing. And as the fraud was unveiled in the United States, Purdue simply shifted its marketing efforts to other parts of the world.

INSYS CHARGED WITH FRAUD

While no other opioid manufacturer approaches the level of villainy of Purdue Pharma, the other drug maker whose leadership has been charged criminally is Insys Therapeutics, the maker of Subsys, an under-the-tongue fentanyl spray intended for managing pain in cancer patients.[8]

In December 2016, federal prosecutors charged the billionaire founder of Insys, John Kapoor, along with CEO Michael Babich and former company executives, with fraud. Kapoor and Insys executives were charged with misconduct including paying bribes to doctors to encourage them to prescribe the drug, fueling the opioid crisis in the process. Doctors prescribed for patients who did not have cancer, and did not need such a powerful drug.

In the summer of 2018, Insys settled charges against the company itself for payment of $150 million.[9] While charges against Kapoor and other senior executives were pending as of the fall of 2018, numerous company employees have pleaded guilty to participating in the kickback schemes, resulting in prison sentences.

The contrast between the slap on the wrist for Purdue executives and the sentencing of Insys employees reflects how much the political environment changed between 2007 and 2018. Opioid manufacturers who thought their inclusion in the civil litigation was bad enough may be surprised to learn that they are next in line for criminal investigation.

PHARMA FRAUD BEYOND PURDUE AND INSYS

While Purdue Pharma may have been the single worst actor in the pharmaceutical industry and Insys is thus far the only other opioid maker whose executives have been charged criminally, they were far from alone. After significant attention to the problem of pills being crushed and abused, Endo Pharmaceuticals marketed its Opana ER (oxymorphone) as crush resistant, a claim that was ultimately contradicted by the FDA, which took the step of requesting removal of the drug from the market. Endo also promoted Percocet, Percodan, and Zydone. It also sponsored a website, PainKnowledge.com, claiming that people who took opioids as directed "usually do not become addicted."

Janssen Pharmaceuticals, a subsidiary of Johnson & Johnson, promoted Duragesic, the Fentanyl patch, and Nucynta ER, another opioid. Mallinckrodt Pharmaceuticals aggressively marketed its Exalgo hydrocodone combination products and Roxicodone oxycodone combination products. Cephalon, a subsidiary of Teva Pharmaceutical, marketed Actiq, a fentanyl lozenge, and Fentora, a fentanyl tablet. Allergan marketed Kadian (extended release morphine) and Norco, the hydrocodone combination product.

This list of unscrupulous marketing of dangerous opioids is far from exhaustive. The bottom line is that, while Purdue may be the "hog" of the group with its deadly promotion of OxyContin, there is blood on the hands of many other pharmaceutical manufacturers for misleading and aggressive marketing.

Purdue may have gotten off lightly in the 2007 criminal settlement, but the horrors it enabled have come to light. As we touched on in Chapter 2, a wave of litigation led by cities, counties, and state governments against Purdue and the other drug manufacturers, as well as against distributors (including McKesson, Cardinal Health, and Amerisource Bergen) is only getting started. While the drug makers face charges of deceptive marketing, the criticism of the drug distributors is that they turn a blind eye to evidence that drugs were being misused and misdirected, and take handsome profits while ignoring red flags that should have alerted them to suspicious transactions. To date, more than one thousand cases have been filed.

Some of the new cases also look to new targets beyond opioid manufacturers and distributors, such as pharmacies. The Cherokee Nation and State of Florida, for example, have filed lawsuits against national pharmacy chains Walgreens and CVS, alleging that they profited from overselling painkillers, flooded communities, and did too little to stop illegal sales.[10] Webb County, Texas, filed suits against pharmacy benefit managers (PBMs), including CVS and Express Scripts, arguing that PBMs had the ability to identify and prevent inappropriate prescribing, but conspired not to do so in order to increase their profits.[11] These cases raise a common question: who else, besides drug makers, profited by ignoring the disturbing signs of prescription drug abuse? Will health insurance companies be targets for their role in enabling overprescribing and turning a blind eye to the excessive prescriptions they were reimbursing? As the opioid litigation continues to expand, it may just be a matter of time.

KEY TAKEAWAYS | CHAPTER 4

• •

- The opioid crisis is unique among public health disasters and mass casualty events insofar as it was caused by multiple points of failure in our health system. Opioid manufacturers need to address their unique role in triggering the rising opioid overdose death toll by promoting misleading information to physicians and patients about their drugs.

- Long before the opioid crisis began in the late 1990s, Purdue Pharma and the Sackler family made a fortune through abusive drug marketing practices, including, in particular, the sedative Valium. Their deceptive promotion of OxyContin, hiding data on its true addictiveness and fabricating "opiophobia," a supposed physician fear of treating pain, played a unique role in sparking the opioid crisis. The timing of the spike in the opioid overdose death rate since 1999 is unmistakably tied to Purdue's promotion of OxyContin.

- Even after the federal government identified Purdue's abusive conduct and pursued criminal charges against company executives, the result was essentially a slap on the wrist in the 2007 settlement. There have been few criminal charges against other pharmaceutical executives. Instead, the primary reckoning is likely to be the resolution of hundreds of lawsuits (approaching one thousand) filed by cities, counties, and states against Purdue, other opioid manufacturers, and the major distributors for ignoring evidence that opioids were being misused and misdirected. These cases are likely to result in multibillion-dollar payouts to cover healthcare and other costs incurred as a result of the opioid crisis.

HOW OUR HEALTH SYSTEM ENABLED THE OPIOID CRISIS

"We [doctors] as a profession have caused an epidemic that is bigger than the HIV epidemic. We have more deaths from drug overdoses than occurred at the peak of the HIV/AIDS epidemic in 1995. That's how big this is. It's more deaths than in motor vehicle accidents. The cause in the opioid epidemic starts with getting a prescription of opioids from physicians."

ATUL GAWANDE, MD[1]

AS EASY AS IT IS to blame Purdue Pharma and other opioid manufacturers as the most flagrantly responsible party for sparking the opioid crisis, there were multiple other points of health system failure.

PHYSICIAN OVERPRESCRIBING

As we explored in Chapter 3, in America's first opioid crisis a century ago, physicians, not drug companies, were viewed by the government as the primary villains. At the time, physicians were seen as enablers of continued addiction through a loose approach to the requirements to prescribing heroin and morphine to patients. Little attention was paid to the role of drug companies like Bayer profiting from sales of heroin.

Fast forward a hundred years and little seems to have changed about the role of physicians in the current crisis. The specific opioids prescribed today are different, and our medical understanding of opioids has advanced, but physician overprescribing of painkillers remains a central part of understanding how the opioid crisis emerged. After all, drug company marketing may have encouraged physicians and created patient demand, but it took physicians to write prescriptions for every patient who overdosed or became addicted.

> Drug company marketing may have encouraged physicians and created patient demand, but it took physicians to write prescriptions for every patient who overdosed or became addicted.

The overarching problem when it comes to physician overprescribing has been insufficient training and education on how to prescribe opioids, how to treat pain through other means, and how to identify and manage dependency and addiction. Even without drug company deception, physicians were at a disadvantage based on the lack of medical school training on dealing with pain and addiction. One legacy of the crackdown on doctors in the 1920s was that doctors were better off avoiding these issues. It didn't help that, until the very recent past, addiction was seen as a moral rather than a medical issue that doctors needed to address.

This inattention to addiction and lack of understanding of how to treat pain set the stage by leaving doctors vulnerable to misinformation from drug makers and others. Perhaps the most famous "poster child" for physician confusion is Hershel Jick, MD. In 1980, the Boston University Medical Center professor wrote a now-infamous letter published in the *New England Journal of Medicine,* declaring as follows:

> Recently, we examined our current files to determine the incidence of narcotic addiction in 39,946 hospitalized medical patients who were monitored consecutively. Although there were 11,882 patients who received at least one narcotic preparation, there were only four cases of reasonably well documented addiction in patients who had no history of addiction. The addiction was considered major in only one instance. The drugs implicated were meperidine in two patients, Percodan in one, and hydromorphone in one. We conclude that despite widespread use of narcotic drugs in hospitals, the development of addiction is rare in medical patients with no history of addiction.[2]

Drug companies had a field day with this letter, which Dr. Jick subsequently acknowledged was flawed in failing to look at dosing, duration of opioid treatment, and other criteria used to define opioid addiction.

Jick was far from the only voice that was not attuned to the dangers of opioids. In a 1986 study that has been heavily criticized, an influential physician researcher of pain, Russell Portenoy, MD, summarized a study with a colleague of a retrospective review of thirty-eight patients taking various opioids. The study concluded that "opioid maintenance therapy can be a safe, salutary and more humane alternative to the options of surgery or no treatment in those patients with intractable nonmalignant pain and no history of drug abuse."[3]

Both of these examples highlight how slow doctors were to wake up to the risk of addiction in their prescribing practices; the more important point may be that physician training in safe prescribing practices, addiction prevention, and addiction management has been extremely limited. As we saw in Chapter 3, many early twentieth-century physicians saw it as appropriate medical care when they "maintained" people addicted to heroin and morphine to prevent them from going through withdrawal. While the medical community was pressured out of this position by federal agents, the physician community failed to develop an alternative. Almost a century later, we are only in the early stages of developing a thoughtful and nuanced position on how to prescribe for pain.

LACK OF PHYSICIAN TRAINING AND KNOWLEDGE

Atul Gawande, MD, MPH, my favorite writer about healthcare, put it more bluntly:

> I saw this all the time in my surgical training—that we did not treat pain, that we left people in terrible pain and suffering, and it was a kind of inhumanity that I thought was unacceptable. So I really keyed into the lessons from people like palliative care clinicians who said we have to measure pain, and we have to treat pain. But what we had not done was continue to measure what was happening

along the way … Basically, I was like: "More is better. Take some."[4]

Having worked with many physicians on issues around prescribing for pain, I can attest to the "take some" approach that Dr. Gawande describes. The problem is that pain arises in so many different contexts with so many different kinds of patients that it is impossible to offer doctors a simple solution. The problem is exacerbated because new medications and new research regularly change the standard of care and best practice, yet doctors are not retrained on new options. The overwhelming majority of doctors end up being easy targets for criticism and legal action as soon as their prescribing practices are examined, not because they are bad doctors but because the standard of care around treating pain changes significantly every few years.

THE EXPANDING ARRAY OF PAIN MANAGEMENT OPTIONS

Even in the early twentieth century, as medical journals were detailing advances in our understanding of the risks of opioid addiction and related issues, physician practices were slow to change. This was most often due to lack of information and lack of alternatives. Meanwhile, the options for doctors to consider and integrate into developing the most effective and safest approach kept getting more complicated. This is evident in the expanding array of non-opioid, alternative forms of pain relief that came on the markets over the past one hundred years, each with different mechanism of action, effectiveness, cost, and risks. It is useful to understand the landscape of options to treat pain for some context on why opioids are so popular.

Opioids

The centrality of opioids as a pain management medication has to do with their distinct biological effect. While other drugs block all sensory transmission, opioids act in a more nuanced way, selectively modulating pain perception while leaving intact

> While other drugs block all sensory transmission, opioids act in a more nuanced way, selectively modulating pain perception while leaving intact other sensations.

other sensations. In other words, beyond their appeal for the other effects detailed in Chapter 2, opioids are distinct in removing the perception of pain without interfering with basic sensations.

The array of opioids changed significantly over time. By 1924, heroin was phased out as a medication, converting over to an illegal street vice. It is interesting to think about how the most popular opioids today rolled out over the years:

1942: Demerol

1959: Fentanyl

1971: Methadone

1974: Percocet

1983: Vicodin

1984: Dilaudid

1987: MS Contin

1990: Duragesic Fentanyl Patch

1995: OxyContin

2012: Subsys Fentanyl Sublingual Spray

2018: Dsuvia Sufentanil Tablet

NSAIDs (Aspirin, Ibuprofen, and Naproxen)

Since the popular nineteenth-century opioids like heroin and laudanum are no longer with us, aspirin is technically the oldest pain-killer on the market, having debuted in America in 1899, marketed by the German drug maker Bayer. (Bayer covered its bases at the time by also purveying heroin.) As a nonsteroidal anti-inflammatory drug (NSAID), aspirin offered a new form of low-cost relief, less powerful but also safer than opioids, and able to be sold over the counter (OTC) for pain relief. Other NSAIDs, notably ibuprofen (Advil and Motrin) and naproxen (Aleve) came decades later, only gaining FDA approval in the 1970s. Ketorolac, best known for the brand Toradol, has been a popular alternative for short-term, severe pain.

1899: Aspirin
1974: Ibuprofen
1976: Naproxen
1989: Ketorolac

NSAIDs and opioids have very different mechanics that make NSAIDs more effective only for a limited range of types of pain, such as headaches and musculoskeletal pain. They cannot compete with opioids' effectiveness in treating a broader range of pain. In essence, the difference is that opioid analgesics act directly on the central nervous system, blocking the transmission of painful stimuli to the brain, while NSAIDs block production of an enzyme, cyclo-oxygenase (COX), that mediates pain at an injury site in the periphery of the nervous system.

Opioid analgesics act directly on the central nervous system, blocking the transmission of painful stimuli to the brain, while NSAIDs block production of an enzyme, cyclooxygenase (COX), that mediates pain at an injury site in the periphery of the nervous system.

NSAIDs decrease the transmission of pain and inhibiting the formation of fatty acid compounds (prostaglandins) that produce pain. In other words, opioids act much closer to the root of the central nervous system, while NSAID action occurs in the periphery.

The resulting pain relief is much milder. While many people assume NSAIDs are safe because today all are sold OTC, they also have multiple risks, including heart attack and stroke, ulcers, bleeding, and kidney failure. According to some estimates, as many as one hundred thousand people are hospitalized for gastrointestinal bleeding due to NSAIDs, with more than fifteen thousand deaths per year.[5]

Acetaminophen

Better known by the original brand Tylenol, acetaminophen is a non-addictive pain medicine that came on the market in the 1950s. Sold widely over the counter, acetaminophen is commonly used for headaches and other aches and pains. While its mechanism is distinct from NSAIDs, acetaminophen also operates by inhibiting the production of prostaglandins. Acetaminophen and hydrocodone have been an extremely popular combination drug (best known as the brand Vicodin). While acetaminophen does not present a risk of addiction, it does present a huge risk of liver damage. Exceeding the daily limit of 4 grams of acetaminophen causes several hundred Americans to die from liver failure each year.

Exceeding the daily limit of 4 grams of acetaminophen causes several hundred Americans to die from liver failure each year.

1955: Tylenol

Topical Agents

Topical creams and gels have been with us as a form of pain relief for more than a century. Bengay and Tiger Balm, two camphor and menthol-based creams with smells familiar to most people over a certain age, combine anesthetic numbing with analgesic pain relief, dulling the feeling of pain on the skin and in the muscles. There is no shortage of different topicals, including capsaicin, lidocaine, and diclofenac, all of which are nonsteroidal and anti-inflammatory. Topicals do not cross the blood-brain barrier, meaning that they have lower impact, fewer side effects, and do not lead to physical dependence. Their limited absorption into the body translates into having little to no effect on the underlying condition. Most topicals operate only to reduce or block pain peripherally for a limited range of conditions, such as arthritis or muscle strain or inflammation. Some topicals, like menthol, do even less, offering a pleasant sensation that counteracts pain, but not acting on inflammation.

1898: Ben-Gay (renamed Bengay)
1924: Tiger Balm

Nerve Blocks

For more than a century, doctors have used various anesthetic and steroid nerve block and trigger point injections to relieve pain and inflammation. These pain blocks and trigger point injections may be short-lasting (hours or days), but they present a nonaddictive solution to intense, localized pain.

Infusion Therapies for Pain

1948: Lidocaine
1970: Ketamine
1981: IVIG

There are numerous infusion therapies that can be used for very specific categories of pain, including immunoglobulin (IVIG), which can be effective in treating various forms of neuropathic pain.

Other infusion therapies for pain include lidocaine, stem cells, and ketamine. Lidocaine and ketamine are anesthetics, the latter known for producing a trancelike effect. Most infusion treatments tend to be condition-specific and offered by a more limited number of physicians, making them more expensive and a solution for a more limited range of patients.

Sedatives/Muscle Relaxants

Sedatives include muscle relaxants (such as Soma) and benzodiazepines (such as Valium), a highly addictive category of drug that often accompanies opioids in overdose cases, and may be even more challenging to wean patients off, as well as non-benzodiazepines (such as Flexeril and Robaxin). While their primary function is to reduce muscle tension by calming the central nervous system and suppressing reflexes, they are also used to treat certain kinds of pain, such as musculoskeletal pain and muscle spasms.

> 1959: Soma
> 1963: Valium
> 1974: Robaxin
> 1977: Flexeril (Cyclobenzaprine)

Other Drugs

There are other drug categories that are sometimes used to treat pain, including anticonvulsants, such as two drugs approved in 1993, gabapentin (Neurontin) and pregabalin (Lyrica), and carbamazepine (Tegretol), an earlier drug approved in 1953. These drugs target neuropathic pain (chronic pain caused by injury or neurologic disease) by stabilizing nerve cells. In addition, some physicians will attempt to address pain through antianxiety or antidepressant drug categories.

One pain therapy that has gained significant grassroots support in recent years among people living with pain is low-dose naltrexone (LDN). Naltrexone has become a significant form of medication-assisted treatment (MAT) for

> One pain therapy that has gained significant grassroots support in recent years among people living with pain is low-dose naltrexone.

opioid addiction because it blocks the effect of opiates and reduces cravings for opioids. At very low doses, LDN has a very different effect, functioning as an analgesic and anti-inflammatory, reducing the severity of pain symptoms in fibromyalgia, Crohn's disease, multiple sclerosis, complex regional pain syndrome (CPRS), and possibly for other auto-immune conditions.[6]

Reviewing these choices, it is apparent that opioids are, far and away, the most powerful category of painkiller, with the broadest and most direct effect on the nervous system. Unfortunately, the very thing that makes opioids powerful in treating pain—their action on receptors in the brain—also gives them a much higher potential to be deadlier than drugs that only operate on inflammation in the extremities.

As a consequence, opioids continue to play an important role for many kinds of pain, making it difficult to rule out their use entirely and creating an urgency to develop safer standards for their use. As we will see in Chapter 9, we are beginning to see guidelines such as those developed by the CDC for opioid prescribing in primary care. These guidelines are voluntary but point the direction of standard of care in the future, recommend that opioids not be the first choice for common pain problems, such as arthritis and back pain.

This makes sense, given their addictiveness. In a 2017 study by Bradley Martin of the CDC, the data showed that a five-day initial supply of opioids correlated to a 10 percent risk that the person would become a long-term user and would still be taking opioids a year later.[7] A ten-day supply of opioids increased that risk to 20 percent. With a thirty-day initial supply, the chance of being on opioids after a year climbed to 45 percent. With numbers like these, it's little wonder that the federal government is considering enacting a three-day limit on new opioid prescriptions.

NONMEDICATION APPROACHES TO PAIN

In addition to the various prescription medication options for treating pain, it is important to note that medication is not the only option for treating pain. In fact, there are numerous nonpharmacologic options for treating and managing pain that can be used as alternatives or in conjunction with medication, including these:

- Physical therapy, as well as stretching and other forms of gentle exercise, such as tai chi

- Acupuncture, accupressure, and other forms of neurostimulation

- Chiropractic care

- Massage

- Biofeedback and neurofeedback

- Occupational therapy

- Aquatherapy

- Hot/cold application

- Meditation, guided imagery, breathing exercises, and other relaxation techniques

- Comfort therapy (such as pet therapy, music, art, or drama therapy, or companionship)

The challenge with these nonpharmacologic therapies for pain is that the vast majority of physicians are not ordinarily trained or well-versed in utilizing these options. They also take much longer than prescriptions. In the words of one doctor I spoke with, "It takes thirty seconds to say yes [to a pain medicine prescription]. It takes thirty minutes to say no." The combination of a lack of

> The combination of a lack of physician training on alternatives with the difficulty of saying no to patients asking for a pain medication goes a long way to explaining why patients are likelier than not to get a prescription even when their first choice would be something else.

physician training on alternatives with the difficulty of saying no to patients asking for a pain medication goes a long way to explaining why patients are likelier than not to get a prescription even when their first choice would be something else.

In many cases, insurance companies decline to cover the cost of nonpharmacologic options on the basis that they are not evidence-based and don't have sufficient research to support their use. As a result, these options may only be available to a narrower subset of patients who have the time and resources to explore complementary and integrative health options that their doctors don't address. The vast majority of patients are likelier to be directed to pharmacologic options, meaning pills.

Many patients who look for nonpharmacologic options also consider supplements and herbal remedies, which are sold over the counter and much less lightly regulated in their ingredients and manufacturing than pharmaceuticals. While the majority of supplements are vitamins, minerals, and herbs that have been on the market for decades and are recognized as safe (such as ginger or turmeric), there are also many new lightly regulated substances, such as kratom, aconite, or germanium that are being used to treat pain despite reports of significant problems and danger associated with their use.

Several people who I interviewed described ongoing use of kratom, available over the counter without a prescription, after their doctors refused to continue prescribing opioids that they had used for pain. Kratom, extracted from the leaves of an evergreen tree that grows in Southeast Asia, has received attention as an opioid alternative for what the FDA has described as "opioid properties," meaning euphoric feelings, relief from pain, and decreased anxiety. Its availability as a supplement without prescription should not be taken as a sign of its safety: the FDA has expressed concerns at reports of over forty kratom-associated deaths from 2011 through 2018, leading to DEA consideration of designating it a Schedule I controlled substance.[8] While kratom may appear to be a solution based on its easier availability, it also appears to be a problem insofar as it seems to mimic opioids in having its own addictive properties and withdrawal symptoms.[9] In one study, for example, people who took kratom for more than six months experienced withdrawal symptoms similar opioid symptoms.[10] Kratom may also present overdose risks as well. In essence, kratom appears to be more accurately characterized as an alternative to opioids than a solution or means of treatment. With many people turning to it as a solution despite serious safety concerns, kratom stands as an example of the unique confusion about supplements as a solution for pain.

CONTINUED TENSIONS IN PRESCRIBING FOR PEOPLE WITH ADDICTION

While the therapeutic options for doctors have expanded dramatically with new medical advances and medications, the fundamental lines of conflict that emerged over opioids in the 1920s in many ways appear to be alive and well today.

On one side, doctors seek to be compassionate. Both the original Hippocratic Oath and its modern updates include a commitment by physicians to use treatment to help the sick and to keep the confidences of patients. My personal experience has been that the overwhelming majorities who treat chronic pain take this commitment seriously.

Meanwhile, law enforcement and regulators are trying to protect the public, addressing the public health safety and social problems of drugs getting into the wrong hands and drug dealers' opportunism, profiting off of putting people at risk. These are legitimate problems, sometimes enabled by doctors who don't take their obligations seriously and sometimes by doctors unaware of the consequences of their prescribing patterns.

In theory, it should be possible for both honest doctors and law enforcement to meet their responsibilities without getting in each others' way. The problem, evidenced in the Supreme Court cases cited in Chapter 4, is that the lines constantly blur. One person's Florence Nightingale, taking care of those in need, is another person's Dr. Feelgood, supplying a fix to a person with an addiction.

The battle lines between physician compassion and public health and safety can sometimes be gray. In the late 1920s, for example, the United States was in the thick of Prohibition. One of the exceptions to the ban on alcohol was an allowance that doctors could prescribe it for medicinal use. Patients rushed to doctors by the thousands. Were they all opportunists looking for a way to get around Prohibition? Or were some using alcohol as a form of medication? The defense offered by many doctors at the time was that they were motivated by sincere concern for their patients. While it would take the American Medical Association another three decades (until 1956) to declare alcoholism a form of illness, these doctors were responding to the impulse that patients would undergo withdrawal that would threaten their health—an approach to addiction that predominated at that time.

OPIOIDS SURPASSED BY OTHER ADDICTIVE MEDICATIONS

For much of the twentieth century, pain medicine languished as a casualty of the "first opioid crisis" culminating in the 1920s. Physicians were reluctant to prescribe opioids other than for cancer and end-of-life patients or for particularly acute pain. Other drugs, including sedatives and others on the list reviewed earlier in this chapter, filled the void. For many years doctors prescribed opioids sparingly, mostly reserving them for cancer patients. Pain medicine was not recognized as a distinct physician specialty until the relatively late date of 1983, when the American Academy of Pain Medicine (originally named the American Academy of Algology) was founded, recognizing pain medicine as a physician specialty. A change in physician and pain specialist attitudes was evident in the early 1990s. Dr. Russell Portenoy, the pain researcher who in 1986 had found opioid maintenance therapy to be a "safe, salutary and more humane alternative" to surgery, argued that patients with chronic pain could take opioids safely be taken for a period of months or years.[11] He is famously responsible for the 1996 statements that less than 1 percent of opioid users became addicted, the drugs were easy to discontinue, and overdoses were extremely rare in pain patients—statements that later proved to be based on extremely limited research.

The bottom line is that despite the political statements of the era, the medical community was not focused on the link between opioids and addiction. Why wasn't the medical community paying more attention? The simplest answer may be that, without people dropping dead all over the place, the issue was perceived as a limited issue.

THE JOINT COMMISSION'S PAIN CAMPAIGN

In looking at other parts of our healthcare system that contributed to the opioid crisis, I would be remiss if I did not talk about the role of national organizations, such as the Joint Commission on the Accreditation of Healthcare Organizations.

As an example of perspectives on pain treatment at the time, in 1990, a leading medical journal published an article recommending that doctors "ensure patients a place in the communications loop" of pain management, assessing patient satisfaction.[12] The article incorrectly claimed that "therapeutic use of opiate analgesics rarely results in addiction."

In 1995, the American Pain Society was promoting the notion of "pain as the 'fifth vital sign'" alongside the four longstanding vital signs: body temperature, pulse, respiratory rate, and blood pressure. The argument was that doctors were not assessing pain regularly, either at office visits or after surgery. In the words of APS president J. N. Mitchell in his annual address, "If pain were assessed with the same zeal as other vital signs are, it would have a much better chance of being treated properly. We need to train doctors and nurses to treat pain as a vital sign."[13] The Veteran's Health Administration, the largest government run healthcare system, joined the call to recognize pain as a fifth vital sign in 1999.

This approach gained sufficient traction that it was adopted by the Joint Commission in 2000–01, the leading body for accreditation of hospital and other healthcare organizations. The Joint Commission occupies such an important place in the healthcare landscape that the Centers for Medicare and Medicaid Services (CMS), the federal agency that oversees Medicare, has delegated to it the Medicare certification process for hospitals. In other words, as far as Medicare is concerned, hospitals are certified to participate if they meet the Joint

Commission's standards. It's hard to imagine a more powerful position than being the arbiter of standards not only for hospitals, but for virtually every type of healthcare facility under the sun.

In 2000–01, the Joint Commission revised its standards for pain assessment to address underassessment and undertreatment of pain, in response to complaints that doctors were not recognizing pain adequately.[14] Pain, the Joint Commission said, was a "fifth vital sign," an essential measurement that doctors and nurses were responsible for monitoring.

The problem was that, in making patient satisfaction with their pain medication part of the standard of evaluation of quality, the Joint Commission was putting pressure on doctors, nurses, and hospitals to keep patients happy, even if this meant ignoring negative side effects, like addiction. Pain surveys incentivized nurses to advocate and physicians to prescribe more medication to control and manage pain.

It turns out that when you ask patients to rate their pain in numeric terms, very few people will give low numbers. The consequences of asking patients to rate their pain subjectively are now apparent: few people underrate their pain; the norm is to overstate the pain, a positivity bias that leads to overprescribing. This also accompanied a progressively loosening standard for prescribing pain medicine, with doctors encouraged not just to prescribe for acute pain or cancer pain, but also for chronic pain. The ironic result is that hospitals, other health facilities, and physicians have been operating under a structure creating pressure to let patients, at risk of dependency and addiction, decide how much medication their doctors should prescribe. It is little surprise that CMS and the Joint Commission reversed course in 2016 on the use of pain survey. The Joint Commission has been named as a defendant in litigation as a result of its role in making the opioid crisis worse.[15] Unsurprisingly, the use of pain surveys is now in full retreat.

HOW REGULATORS ADD FUEL TO THE FIRE

One of the most insidious aspects of the opioid crisis is the way that government agencies attempting to police opioid prescriptions exacerbate the problem by driving people to illegal sources. When the DEA and state medical and pharmacy boards crack down on physician

One of the most insidious aspects of the opioid crisis is the way that government agencies attempting to police opioid prescriptions exacerbate the problem by driving people to illegal sources.

opioid prescribing and pharmacy dispensation, the natural reaction from many doctors and pharmacies has been simply to get out of the prescribing and dispensing of opioids altogether, leaving patients in pain with extremely limited options.

In this environment, those doctors who are still willing to prescribe opioids need to complete a rigorous series of steps to document their prescribing compliance:

- Checking the state Prescription Drug Monitoring Program (PDMP) database to see if anyone else is prescribing to the patient

- Periodically doing a urine drug screen (UDS) to see what the patient is taking

- Obtaining informed consent to ensure that patients understand the risks, benefits, and alternatives to opioid pain medication

- Entering into a physician-patient agreement to set requirements for the patient's good behavior, including using a single pharmacy and not acquiring drugs from other sources

- Documenting a thorough physical examination with objective findings (not just subjective complaints from the patient), considering any disease process and alternative medical explanations for symptoms

- Ordering any necessary diagnostic testing relevant to the diagnosis

- Developing a treatment plan that assesses goals for improvement in pain and function

- Considering whether to prescribe naloxone for potential overdose risk

- Reviewing reports of other doctors treating the same patient

- Performing an opiate risk assessment

- Limiting the dosage to relatively low amount (50–90 morphine milligram equivalents (MMEs))

- Developing a taper plan with a planned endpoint

- Recommending non-opioid therapies, such as physical therapy, acupuncture, aquatherapy, hypnotherapy, and psychosocial support, as may be appropriate

The net result of these steps is to rule out the majority of prospective patients based on signs that something else is going on (SEGO), usually suspicions that the person already has some kinds of drug problem and addiction. Doctors just can't afford to put their DEA registrations and medical licenses at risk by prescribing to patients in this category. I have written more patient termination letters than I can count for physician and medical groups to use when they encounter these patients. In the past few years, the challenge is that only a handful of pharmacies are willing to fill orders, in many cases only after doctors call and explain the nature of the prescription.

Of the patients who get turned away by doctors—who are protecting themselves from disciplinary actions of government agencies—only a handful find other, legal sources of help. Most of these patients are left to fend for themselves on the illegal market, where they encounter little difficulty getting fentanyl, heroin, and other drugs to fill the void. These patients are hardly the majority of illegal drug-seekers, but as we look for solutions to the opioid crisis, it's worth asking how we can do more to provide solutions for this population.

ESTABLISHING REALISTIC PATIENT GOALS

At the heart of the opioid crisis is a question about why this problem is so much worse in America than anywhere else in the world. The US consumes a disproportionate share of the world's opioids—quadruple the rate of prescriptions in the United Kingdom.[16] While the often-repeated claim that the US consumes 80 percent of the world's opioids is false, the actual figure—closer to 30 percent of the global total—is still disturbingly high.[17] Surely, patients everywhere want to be pain free, and doctors everywhere want to address their pain. But is there something different about the way that we approach pain in America?

In a 2017 article in *The Atlantic,* Olga Khazan drew on the experience of T. R. Reid, the author of *The Healing of America,* exploring the difference between the American approach to pain management and approaches in other countries.[18] Reid wanted to see how doctors in different countries would respond to his old shoulder injury. America was the only place where an expensive, radical surgery was proposed; elsewhere, the solutions focused on helping him adapt to living with the pain without using opioids. "Not only are our doctors more trigger-happy when it comes to treating pain," writes Khazan, but "we seem to find ourselves covered in Bengay and sitting on the exam table more than most."

Why do Americans report aches and pains in higher numbers than people in other countries? Are we just more expressive about our pain? Are we more sensitive? Are we less willing to "tough" out pain than people in other places? Were we always this way or is this a problem we are more aware of today than in earlier generations? Did our ancestors just live with more pain? Are there environmental factors that drive greater levels of pain?

One explanation for Reid's experience is a lack of physician training on the risks. Another is that our system of fee-for-service healthcare reimbursement has encouraged doctors to be aggressive. After all, if a patient has the money or health insurance coverage to pay for it, then doctors are financially incentivized to join patients in having a low threshold to operate. US healthcare is distinctive in the extent to which private financial incentives can affect care decisions. The influence of pharmaceutical manufacturers on physician decision-making should not be discounted.

Another explanation is that the higher reported incidences of pain in America correspond to America's higher rate of obesity. We are fatter than people in other countries, the theory goes, so we experience more inflammation, joint stress, and interrupted sleep—translating to more pain. Yet another explanation is that our greater willingness to prescribe and take medications also drives a heightened awareness of pain; a person taking pain medication may be more aware of his or her pain than is a person doing nothing and pushing through it.

My suspicion is that all of these things are true. Our healthcare system rewards providers for taking action. And American culture does not encourage stoicism, in which we simply deal with pain as part of life and learn to overcome it with our personal reserves. To the contrary, the national culture of consumerism and instant gratification leaves us looking for quick fixes. We are eager to find pills as a solution. We may very well be experiencing pain precisely because we are unhealthy *and* because we are so focused on dealing with our pain. We are a people who wear our pain "on our sleeve." We search for quick answers and easy solutions. We do not take "deal with it" as an answer when we experience pain. To quote Atul Gawande, "We have to teach people that the goal is not zero pain—the goal is that you have enough pain that there will be an ache but you can do the things you want to do. You can sleep, you can eat, you can go shopping. Third, tell people: 'These are addictive,' and weighing that against your choices."[19]

Dr. Gawande's answer—that part of the solution may lie within us and our choices—is not one that Americans are eager to hear. It is difficult to envision public health campaigns built around developing greater levels of personal resilience, finding solutions within ourselves, feeling grateful for what we have, and turning challenges into positive lessons. All the same, these values may serve as useful guiding principles in thinking about how to steer clear of the American tendency to overtreatment.

PAYERS' SHARE OF RESPONSIBILITY FOR THE PROBLEM

Until now, we've been focused on physicians and healthcare facilities. But what about insurance companies and health plans (including government programs) that are the payers for American healthcare? Are they victim or a villain in the opioid crisis? Did they unwittingly pay for dangerous treatment promoted by greedy drug companies and prescribed by careless doctors? Or were they actually responsible for patients having no choice but to turn to drugs?

One question underlying the opioid crisis is how painkillers came to play such a prominent role in our healthcare system, when there were safe options to address pain. This, in turn, raises the broader question of why our health system seems to prefer pills and prescriptions to solutions that are more labor-intensive for providers and patients. For example, some kinds of pain may benefit from physical therapy. Other types of pain might be better addressed by teaching patients new skills, such as meditation. In some cases (as addressed below in this chapter), there are complex mental health issues that may benefit from extended counseling or psychotherapy.

> One question underlying the opioid crisis is how painkillers came to play such a prominent role in our healthcare system, when there were safer options to address pain.

There has long been a dichotomy within our healthcare system between these two approaches to pain: the simple, straightforward, low-cost option of prescribing a medication, versus the complicated, expensive option of an interdisciplinary team exploring the etiology (cause) of pain and alternative ways to address it.

Our system, as it stands, votes in favor of the ease and simplicity of pills. A pill demands nothing of patients. It demands relatively little of providers beyond diagnosing and examining the patient, and choosing a dosing and duration. Pills are almost certainly payers' favored method of care delivery. Insurance companies, health plans, and government payers prefer medication-driven solutions because they tend to cost less than personnel-intensive, service-driven solutions like physical therapy, counseling, or patient education.

As the funders of the majority of healthcare products and services in America, third-party payers always prefer the lowest cost solution. What could be cheaper and easier than prescribing a pill? By definition, alternatives to prescribing are almost inevitably more expensive because they involve forms of care involving longer-term human interaction addressing pain management by helping patients develop personal skills to manage pain (such as meditation or coping skills) versus quick doctor visits for prescriptions. With their singular focus of cost containment (as well as their own profit) and their outsized power over patients and providers, health insurers have played a disproportionate role in preferring painkilling medication over outpatient therapies or more expensive alternatives.

By contrast, the multidisciplinary model of pain management had briefly been embraced by the medical community in the 1980s and early 1990s, but failed largely due to challenges with reimbursement. When I think about the question of how payers' shifting reimbursement policies affect patients, I frequently return to one of the first Medicare payment dispute matters I handled after coming to California. Medicare had demanded that a doctor I worked with repay more than $1 million of claims paid for patients to receive infusion therapy for a condition known as CIDP (chronic inflammatory demyelinating polyneuropathy). The basis was Medicare's claim that there was no medical necessity for the infusion therapy, intravenous immunoglobulin (IVIG).

I ended up meeting several dozen patients who spanned all ages and ethnicities, men and women. Their stories varied. Some had an autoimmune disorder, such as Lupus or HIV, prior to developing CIDP. Others had been otherwise healthy until the CIDP developed. The condition consisted of terrible shooting pain and burning sensation in their extremities (hands, arms, legs, and feet). Some could walk, but others were in wheelchairs as a result. They all told a similar story: when they received IVIG, it gave them four to five weeks when the pain receded and they could function normally. But before they had received IVIG and when the Medicare denial of coverage prevented them from receiving it, they were in horrific pain that required massive doses of opioids, which left them drugged and unable to get out of bed for more than a few hours each day.

None of them wanted to be on opioids because their side effects were so debilitating, but Medicare left no other options when it would not pay for IVIG. I can tell you from spending time with these people, taking video depositions of those who were too immobilized to be at the hearing, and putting many of them on as witnesses, that CIDP was a very real diagnosis. In this case, we not only persuaded the Medicare administrative law judge to pay for the treatment, but literally had her in tears watching the suffering these people were experiencing based on Medicare's reimbursement policy. While this victory helped a small group of patients, Medicare policy continued to make it increasingly difficult for patients to get the same needed treatment.

I share this story because chronic pain can be hard to respond to unless you've experienced it or known anyone who has experienced it well. We hear diagnoses like fibromyalgia or CIDP for pain syndromes that we don't fully understand. Payers are reluctant to pay for treatments that are expensive, and so we end up with doctors back in the "more is better, take some" approach to pain management that Gawande described at the beginning of this chapter.

In the case of opioids, beyond pressuring for less expensive medication to save money, insurers also bear responsibility for policies that mandated opioids as a first-line treatment option, despite the risks. Methadone, for example, was a factor in roughly one-third of patient deaths from prescribed opioids from 1999 through 2010.[20]

Payers have turned a blind eye to patient safety issues in establishing coverage policies for treatment of pain. It is fair to ask whether insurers bear part of the blame for continuing to pay for excessive medications and turning a blind eye towards the negative health consequences of their policies. Focusing on managing their bottom lines, payers continued to reimburse prescription opioids for years even in the face of mounting evidence year after year that patients were becoming addicted, overdosing, and dropping dead. In the process, they effectively enabled the prescription opioid crisis and share some of the blame for the situation we face today.

THE FDA

Finally, in looking for places where our system failed, it is impossible to ignore the Food and Drug Administration (FDA). The FDA approved these drugs and oversaw the data concerning the risks of their misuse, abuse, addiction, and overdose. The failure of our ultimate national authority to protect public health with respect to opioids calls for soul searching about what went wrong. Behind the unfolding of the opioid crisis was an agency that lacked the funding and resources to manage the unfolding safety issues and identify marketing abuses.

As the guardian of public safety, the FDA provided inadequate regulatory oversight. Even in the face of surging numbers of overdose deaths and insufficient evidence that opioids could be used safely for chronic pain, the FDA readily accepted claims that newly formulated opioids were nonaddictive. The FDA also failed to address risks around misuse of opioids, accepting the patently false claims of drug makers that opioid addiction was a rarity or that the delayed absorption of OxyContin reduced the abuse liability of the drug.[21] One legacy of the opioid crisis should be to ensure that the FDA is able to fulfill its responsibilities in the future to protect the public from pharmaceutical company abuses in the oversight of drug manufacturing and marketing.

THE PATH FORWARD

In August 2016, Surgeon General Vivek Murthy, MD, MBA, wrote an open letter to US physicians asking them to share in responsibility for a new path forward:

> It is important to recognize that we arrived at this place on a path paved with good intentions. Nearly two decades ago, we were encouraged to be more aggressive about treating pain, often without enough training and support to do so safely. This coincided with heavy marketing of opioids to doctors. Many of us were even taught—incorrectly—that opioids are not addictive when prescribed for legitimate pain.... Since 1999, opioid overdose deaths have quadrupled and opioid prescriptions have increased markedly—almost enough for every adult in America to have a bottle of pills. Yet the amount of pain reported by Americans has not changed. Now, nearly two million people in America have a prescription opioid use disorder.[22]

Dr. Murthy's words laid out a roadmap for a shift in US health policy: a new focus on training physicians to treat pain differently, on applying evidence-based standards in treating opioid use disorders (OUDs), and approaching addiction as a chronic illness. As we will explore in Chapter 7, these shifts would bring significant challenges to addiction treatment.

KEY TAKEAWAYS | CHAPTER 5

• •

- The single biggest challenge for physicians in treating pain has been a lack of training and education, both on how to utilize opioids and in utilizing other treatments for pain. A significant part of the problem has been a lack of understanding of the risks of physical dependency associated with opioids, which are reflected in the percentages of people who receive short-term prescriptions and are still continuing to take opioids at the twelve-month mark. Another issue has been the lack of training on constantly evolving alternatives to treat pain and the unique effectiveness and euphoria associated with opioids.

- There are many nonpharmacologic options for treating pain, but few doctors are trained to utilize them and many insurance companies will not pay for them. Even for doctors aware of the benefits of options other than medications, it is much faster and easier to give patients medications than to explain why a doctor is not providing more pills. The only way that regulators have pressured doctors not to prescribe is by raising the documentation and compliance standards to a level where they hesitate to prescribe for patients based on fear of regulatory action against prescribing doctors.

- Physicians and the US health system went through a pendulum swing from the law enforcement crackdown of the 1920s on opioid overprescribing to mounting pressure by the 1990s to focus more on patient pain. Throughout this time, the link between opioids and addiction was not well understood until the overdose death rate associated with OxyContin in the early 2000s called attention to the problem.

- Beyond physicians, there were numerous points of health system failure that led to the opioid crisis, including the Joint Commission's campaign to treat pain as a "fifth vital sign," putting pressure on hospitals to survey patients and keep them happy. Regulators, including the DEA at a federal level and state medical boards, contributed to the crisis by driving patients away from physicians to illegal sources of opioids, including heroin and fentanyl traffickers. Insurance companies demonstrated a strong preference for low-cost pills, and covered them in excessive amounts, while declining more expensive, less addictive forms of treatment. The FDA failed to police abusive pharmaceutical company marketing.

- Part of the explanation for why the US consumes a disproportionate share of the world's opioids has to do with deeper problems in American culture, including a higher rate of obesity and a culture that favors instant gratification and is less stoic than other countries.

CHAPTER 6

DEEPER ROOTS OF THE OPIOID CRISIS

"Beating heroin is child's play compared to beating your childhood."

STEPHEN KING, *THE WASTE LANDS*

WHILE IT IS EASY TO POINT FINGERS at drug makers and distributors, healthcare providers, and payers—insurance companies—for the opioid crisis, a set of deeper questions pervade the issue: What else is going on that led to this pandemic? Why is this dangerous medicine so in demand?

For all of the "bad actors" who contributed in one way or another to the crisis—from Big Pharma's drive for profits to sloppy prescribing practices—the question remains: What exactly made America so ripe for this crisis?

The image that comes to mind for me is of the fires across California: It may take someone lighting a fire to spark a brush fire, but the fire only catches, builds, and wreaks havoc because of the dangerously dry conditions—perfectly primed for a conflagration. For me, the hardest question involved in the opioid crisis is similar: is there a deeper set of underlying issues that fueled the fire and catalyzed the crisis?

Without addressing these root causes, we can expend plenty of effort without really changing things. That's not to say that we shouldn't be pushing for nonaddictive pain management therapies; more careful, evidence-based prescribing practices; or healthcare coverage for more than just medication. We need all of these things. But we also need to look deeper for big problems if we are going to find long-term solutions. Otherwise, the same issues will resurface in a different form. Instead of opioids, we will face (as some would say we already do) a benzodiazepine crisis. Or an alcohol, marijuana, or other substance-use crisis.

A 2018 study from the University of Pittsburgh underscores that opioids are only part of a broader trend in which abuse of multiple drugs form a "single, tight exponential curve" of a rising drug overdose rate that shows no signs of slowing, with subepidemics of different drugs over time.[1] The implication is that the solution must be found in the deeper roots of the crisis.

THE DEEPER UNDERLYING CRISIS

The real questions we need to examine are these: Is there is a deeper source of suffering that is driving the opioid crisis? And, if so, can we as a society do anything about it?

I believe that our attention should first be focused on a host of intersecting trends that point to suffering in America—parallel crises that include suicidality, anxiety, depression, and pain. The connections between opioids and each of these issues are apparent.

There is also a deeper underlying issue. We are living at a time of extreme stress in American life. There are profound transformations occurring that are causing the stress and fueling an insatiable need for instant gratification and quick solutions. To get to real long-term change, we need to look at the inexorable structural transformations in technology, the economy, and the broader world—and think about how we come to terms with them in ways that support health.

> To get to real long-term change, we need to look at the inexorable structural transformations in technology, the economy, and the broader world—and think about how we come to terms with them in ways that support health.

Before considering the connections, let's examine the parallel problems that hint at a deeper crisis within American life and, more broadly, modern life: suicidality, anxiety and depression, and stress.

Suicidality

In examining opioid-related deaths, the ever-present question is whether the person overdosing knowingly took his or her own life, or died accidentally. There is an ambiguity inherent in many overdoses. The musician Prince, for example, had reached out to an addiction medicine doctor shortly before he overdosed on fentanyl. Was he giving up when he overdosed? Or did help just come too late?

There is little question that suicidality has risen alongside opioid use disorders. In the same period when the opioid crisis manifested (1999–2018), suicide rates surged to levels unprecedented—an estimated increase of 25 percent from 10 to more than 13 people per 100,000.[2] The suicide rate was significantly higher in particular parts of the country and among particular demographic groups.[3] While the increase is not as striking as the opioid-related death rate, the parallel trend line compels us to take a closer look.

Suicidality has been receiving greater attention in recent years. In 2018, for example, the shocking suicides by celebrities including fashion designer Kate Spade and chef, author, and TV personality Anthony Bourdain called attention to the problem. With disturbing increases in suicide rates in girls as young as ten, teen suicide also is receiving growing attention. The 2017 Netflix television series *13 Reasons Why* called attention to the issue, dramatizing a 2007 novel about a teenage girl who takes her own life under pressure from gossip, destructive culture, and lack of support from her friends and school. While the school shooting epidemic has led to a focus on the issue of access to guns for people with mental health issues, most of these incidents amount to murder-suicides, another strand of the suicide crisis.

The rise in suicide rates in the United States has been noteworthy for increases across all age groups and for both men and women. Historically, men have killed themselves at more than triple the rate of women and still represent a significant majority of all suicides. Recent data, however, suggests a disproportionate surge in the rate of female suicidality (more than a 60 percent increase in the past two decades for middle-aged women and over 200 percent for girls ages ten to fourteen, according to a CDC study).[4]

According to the American Foundation for Suicide Prevention (AFSP), the suicide rate is roughly 13.4 per 100,000 individuals, which translates to 45,000 suicides annually, roughly 123 per day.[5] And for each "successful" suicide, there are 25 "failed" attempts, making suicide the tenth leading cause of death in America, according to the AFSP.

A recent study suggests that, in some cases, there is a link between chronic pain and suicide. In other words, while one response to physicians declining to prescribe opioids has been a shift to illegal sources, another response to inadequate treatment of pain has been the decision to bring life to an end.[6] Even if the majority suicides are not linked specifically to pain, the question remains what the connection is between these two trends.

Anxiety and Depression

Alongside the rise in suicidality, another observable recent trend has been the sharply rising reported levels of anxiety and depression, particularly among teenagers and young adults.[7] A 2016 study reported by the American Academy of Pediatrics observed a 37 percent rise in the rate of major depressive episodes in adolescents from 2005 to 2014, with a particularly pronounced rise among teenage girls.[8] The rise in anxiety is even more pronounced, with talk of an emerging crisis. An estimated 25 percent of thirteen- to eighteen-year-olds reportedly suffer from mild to moderate anxiety, with eleven as the median onset age.[9] In the eighteen- to twenty-two-year-old demographic, the American College Health Association reported that, in 2016, 62 percent of undergraduates reported overwhelming anxiety.[10] Most distressing of all, the number of hospital admissions for suicidal teenagers has doubled in the past decade.[11]

Theories to explain the increase have included the rise of social media and social patterns that lead to more isolation in an era of digital communication, where younger people communicate more and more by text and other means, in lieu of face-to-face exchanges. I watch this trend with my own kids: they are constantly texting with their friends, often instead of actually spending time with them. Their high school classmates participate in a grade "group chat" and smaller subgroups for their friends. They regale us with the drama of the group chat. The net result is plenty of time reading each other's messages, deciphering the online absurdities and offenses, and less time actually talking to each other.

The economist Seth Stephens-Davidowitz points to a telling contrast in the world of social media. While we put a positive spin on our lives to impress "friends" on Facebook, we are more honest in our Google searches when no one is watching what we input.[12] On Facebook, we post pictures of our vacations and blast out message after message about how wonderful our spouses are and how smart our kids are. When I type "my wife" into Facebook, it suggests as related searches: "My wife is my best friend" and "My wife is my life." On Google, when I type the phrase in the same two words, "my wife," three of the top options that the "auto-fill" function offers to finish my query with the most popular options are: "My wife is having an affair," "My wife hates me," and "My wife is lazy."

Google search trends show that we search for answers to problems with our spouses and kids. Facebook is where we show off; Google reveals what's really on our minds. Stephens-Davidowitz suggests that we spend less time making ourselves miserable with unfavorable comparisons of our lives to those of peers on Facebook, and more time consoling ourselves by searching on Google and realizing we are far from alone in the problems we are struggling with.

Although the rise in anxiety and depression seems to be worst among the young, the trend seems to be evidenced across all ages and demographic groups. While some researchers have questioned whether there is an actual increase in the rate of depression, as opposed to an

> It is impossible to ignore the pervasive anxiety about our national political dysfunction, extremism, and the deepening divide between Americans of different beliefs and values.

increase in detection and diagnosis,[13] Americans are reporting more stress over issues ranging from healthcare, safety, financial security, and relationships. It is impossible to ignore the pervasive anxiety about our national political dysfunction, extremism, and the deepening divide between Americans of different beliefs and values. No matter where you stand politically, we live in an era of a heightened degree of fear on all sides—anxiety about terrorism and gun violence and about government taking away access to guns, anxiety about secure borders and about preserving America as a beacon for immigrants seeking a better life, anxiety about climate change and about government over-regulation. The list goes on and on.

While our awareness of mental health issues has unquestionably improved, there is evidence to support an overall rise in unhappiness. Specifically, according to a 2017 study by David Blanchflower and Andrew Oswald for the National Bureau of Economic Research, Americans have been getting progressively less happy since the 1970s.[14] The trend is correlated with lower levels of education, meaning less-educated people report being less happy. But the trend extends across all socioeconomic levels. Something (perhaps many things) is making us more anxious and depressed.

Trauma and Chronic Stress

I frequently get questions about how I manage stress. I run one business with over fifty employees and chair the boards of multiple other organizations. Ask anyone who knows me and they will tell you that I am compulsive "plate spinner," jumping from one problem to another and taking on too much. My answer to questions about stress management is that I maintain a positive state of mind and keep a smile on my face, and those two things make it possible to process bad news and move with surprising speed through negative emotions (such as anger, frustration, and despair) toward solving problems. I am a diehard believer that maintaining a positive frame of mind is the only way I can possibly manage stress.

I particularly notice the way my state of mind affects my sense of well-being. When I stay positive, I feel strong: I eat better, sleep better, exercise regularly, connect with friends, and stay healthy. Similarly, from time to time, I get thrown off my game and stuck in a bad mood, distracted and frustrated. When I hit these periods of negativity, I find myself becoming vulnerable to injuries, colds, and sinus infections. My energy level is lower, which creates openings for worse problems. I keep reevaluating what else needs to be in the mix of wellness activities. This past year, I committed to set aside time for daily prayer and to begin the day with time to meditate and reflect.

I don't pretend to be a scientist, but I believe that we all develop neural connections from our brains to our central nervous system that respond to the situations in which we find ourselves. Sometimes we take on positive adaptations, creating new neural pathways that support good behaviors, like managing to let the stress of a bad encounter go. And we are also at risk of developing negative neural connections, when the adaptations cause us to get stuck in a negative emotional state, such as anxiety or depression. Think of times when you have had a tense conflict with someone and felt a lingering headache or tension in your back afterward.

One theory about our pain crisis that I subscribe to is the role of trauma, stress, and post-traumatic stress disorder in it. Many of us go through life carrying pain from past experiences. Sometimes it is physical or mental abuse or violence. In other cases, family tragedies, like losing a parent or growing up in extreme poverty, are a source of trauma. There have been numerous studies drawing links between traumatic experiences in childhood and negative effects that manifest in adulthood, including chronic physical and mental illness, and pain.[15] Sometimes it is not a major trauma but chronic stress that negatively affects our health.

In this view, pain and stress are experiences that our brains create through our neural pathways. This doesn't mean the pain isn't real in the form that it manifests. There may be a reinforcing quality where the negative experience actually changes how our brains and nervous system process inputs. We end up in a vicious cycle where negative experiences (such as stressful encounters) lead to negative emotions (such as fear and anxiety), which leads us to manifest pain in our nervous system; the sensation of pain, in turn, leads us to move less and to perceive ourselves as able to stretch and exercise less, holding our physicality in a negative state. In short, trauma and stress lead to greater potential for pain.

In several best-selling books describing the "mind-body connection," John Sarno, MD, argues that chronic pain has psychological origins as negative emotions produce tension that manifests physically as chronic pain—including back pain, gastrointestinal disorders, headaches, and fibromyalgia.[16] This theory does not deny that biochemical processes lead to a physical reality of pain, only that the roots of pain in many cases emanate from a mind-body connection.

While Dr. Sarno's theories are controversial based on a lack of peer-reviewed research to support his claims, a growing number of studies have backed up his findings, including the theory that simply reading educational materials and journaling about emotions can reduce pain significantly.[17]

DEEPER STRUCTURAL FORCES

In our book *From ObamaCare to TrumpCare,* Rob Fuller and I examined the extent to which the most powerful forces transforming healthcare were not policy choices, but structural economic and technological changes.[18] These changes have much broader ramifications beyond our healthcare system: they are redefining the way we live. And I believe their footprint is unmistakable on the underlying forces driving our stress and unhappiness.

The Creep of Consumerism

We are living in a time when consumers have incredible power. Technology and the marketplace have offered us an ever-growing list of choices. No matter where you turn, we have an unlimited number of choices as consumers—innumerable channels of content to choose from. Choices about how to order our coffee or tea. What type of nondairy milk to buy. We can find a smartphone app to change the channels on our televisions, to read what we want, and to watch what we want, when we want.

While these trends are in many ways positive, there is a dark side to our expectation that we can buy a ready-made solution to whatever problem ails us. With the ability to find immediate relief and instant gratification, we become more passive and lose our ability to solve our own problems.

The convenience of constant communication, for example,

has created an expectation that we never have to wait for anyone or anything. My teenage children look at me with amazement when I tell them about the days before email existed. They cannot imagine how businesses functioned before we could transmit information instantaneously by email and text and had to route paper copies for physical delivery. The problem is that the expectations of convenience constantly ratchet up: why bother to call a taxi when Uber lets me press a button on my smartphone and have a car there in minutes without talking to anyone? Why should I look at a map to navigate when Waze offers me real-time traffic-optimized directions that tell me exactly when I will arrive?

These are just small examples of the way that a consumerist expectation of convenience has made us worse at problem-solving. We are impatient and expect someone else to solve our problems for us. The problem is that, when it comes to addiction and the other crises of suffering, the solution requires us to shift out of passivity in experiencing what is happening and taking ownership and control. We need to *not* expect a doctor or a pill or anyone or anything to provide the answer. This is not to say we need to solve our problems ourselves, but we need to shift out of the often paralyzing mindset of consumerism.

Decaying Social Networks

Beginning in a 1995 essay, "Bowling Alone: America's Declining Social Capital," the political scientist Robert Putnam described the problematic trend of decayed social networks that once used to animate American life.[19] Pointing to the decline of volunteerism and participation in both religious and secular communal organizations, Putnam observed that diminished social interaction and civic discussion, resulting in political disengagement, poses a long-term threat to our democratic political norms.

Putnam's observation is striking because it predates the rise of technology and social media—the opposite of a social network—as a force leading to dramatically less social interaction. The first iPhone and Android smartphones were not even released until 2007–08, twelve years after Putnam first articulated his theory of social decay. Walking through almost every public space today and seeing people glued to their screens, it is easy to see that smartphones and other forms of technology have moved most Americans to engage less with people around them.

Similarly, the years since the publication of "Bowling Alone" have seen other indicators of diminished social interaction. The Pew Research Center has documented continuing declines in participation in religious life across America.[20] Likewise, census data has tracked the declining rate of Americans who are married (which has fallen below 50 percent) and the rising number of single-parent families.[21]

While Putnam focused attention on the implications of our growing "silo-ization" in our politics (witness the rise of media channels where people can read and hear viewpoints they already agree with), the trend has significant implications with respect to addiction, suicidality, anxiety and depression, and even pain. It is no accident that these problems have worsened in an era of diminished social interaction. Social support and mutual engagement hold enormous power to help us heal and manage. A critical element of the solution to the opioid crisis is supporting reengagement and development of supportive communities of friends, family, and social and religious organizations.

Social support and mutual engagement hold enormous power to help us heal and manage.

Automation and a Future with Less Work

In his 2016 book, *The Rise of Robots: Technology and the Threat of a Jobless Future*, futurist Martin Ford describes the way in which technology—automation, artificial intelligence, and robotics—is making workers obsolete.[22] He projects a rise in the rate of structural unemployment that follows these trends, as our national and global economies have less need for human productivity.*

Many people have theorized that the communities hardest hit by the opioid crisis—the "hot zones" where overdose rates and death rates are the highest—correspond to places experiencing worker obsolescence through lost jobs in recent decades, higher rates of unemployment, and communities with fewer options. In addition to areas where industrial jobs have disappeared (such as New England and Ohio, two opioid hot zones), we also see opioid hot zones in rural areas where work opportunities are fewer and residents live far from the cities where the jobs increasingly are.

Regardless of how closely the scarcity of jobs in a community is correlated with opioid overdose deaths, there's no question that economic and technology changes have much to do with the uncertainty, anxiety, and suffering in American life today. I grew up in suburban Detroit, a city that lost more than 60 percent of its population as the American auto industry faded from its glory days—providing hundreds of thousands of jobs to more than a million people, and billions of dollars in manufacturing wages. My childhood memories were of a city contracting, as friends' families and cousins moved out of state to where the jobs were. The decline manifested in many ways: more people living in poverty, more crime, and more

---

* While the 2016 election focused on blaming China and other culprits for the loss of high-paying US industrial jobs, there was no discussion of the real issue: jobs are disappearing faster than moving overseas as the result of technology.

unemployment. It is no mystery that economic decline also manifests psychologically, contributing to higher rates of depression and suicide.

While some parts of the country have been harder hit by the loss of what used to be higher-wage industrial jobs, the broader picture is more profound. Automation and machine learning are eliminating jobs throughout our society, from agriculture to retail to middle management. Technology, together with the trend of globalization that shifts work all over the world (think of the customer service call centers located all over Asia) has reduced jobs in America. It's little surprise that, for the vast majority of Americans, wages are flat or trending downward.[23]

While we used to think of this job disappearance as a problem for factory workers and the industrial sector, technology and globalization are also negatively affecting white collar sectors. Lawyers, middle management, and other professionals are also seeing a shrinking pool of jobs and flat to lower compensation. As a lawyer for the past twenty-five years, I've noticed that the striking trends in my career have been the rise of technology-driven solutions that handle work that used to keep lawyers busy and cost much more (think LegalZoom), along with the rise of law firms relying on attorneys earning less in lower-cost cities.

If you doubt this is a real trend, just ask a recent college graduate. The number of graduates finding decent-paying jobs has been in steady decline, leaving more and more graduates with low-wage options.[24] The picture is even worse for people without college degrees, with steadily shrinking wages.[25] More and more people are employed in low-wage service sector jobs. Short of a global Luddite revolution to destroy all computer technology, governments and political leaders have no answers. The good jobs that politicians promise to bring back are never coming back. They represent a bygone era.

This trend is unlikely to slow down. Driverless cars and delivery robotic drones (which Amazon has reportedly been testing) may still be a few years away, but think about what they will do to the people who make their livings by driving. We are already en route toward a future with a profoundly higher worldwide "structural" unemployment rate. The implications for many people already include not only unemployment but underemployment (working in jobs below a person's skill level, education, or training), more growth in the divide between haves and have-nots, and an increasing focus on finding meaning outside of work. In place of factory and professional jobs that paid relatively more, the future will be one where more people are serving food, providing nonskilled care for seniors, or working retail sales—all jobs that pay less.

Because employment and productivity are not only a matter of economic survival but a driver of identity and of hope for so many people, we cannot fully address the opioid crisis and the related crises of suffering without considering how to address the impact of technology and automation on employment and the economy.

Dealing with Rising Unemployment and Underemployment

What does this mean for the opioid crisis and the other crises we've been talking about? The trend points to a higher percentage of people displaced and needing support: healthcare, housing, social networks, and retraining for the jobs of the future. There are going to be many more Americans in need of public assistance ahead.

Because employment and productivity are not only a matter of economic survival but a driver of identity and of hope for so many people, we cannot fully address the opioid crisis and the related crises of suffering without considering how to address the impact of technology and automation on employment and the economy. In my view, this requires talking about the problem rather than ignoring it. Acknowledging the reality of how our country (and the world) is changing and how people are being affected is the beginning of addressing the problem.

Once we acknowledge that jobs are not coming back, we can begin to look at other solutions. Once we accept that the problem is structural, we can focus on solutions that extend beyond worker retraining toward creating programs that fill the gaps resulting from unemployment and underemployment. More broadly, the challenge of the future will be how to support the building of vibrant communities and meaningful lives that are not oriented around work. As we develop a deeper understanding of what it will take to keep people healthy and to restore people struggling to overcome addiction to good health, many of the answers may turn out to be social determinants of health, including stable housing, employment, education, and other forms of social support.

A Lost Sense of Purpose, Safety, and Belonging

Beyond the practical isolation and loneliness caused by the decay of social networks is an existential crisis. Underlying the opioid crisis and related crises of suicidality, anxiety, depression, and pain is a lost sense of purpose. Americans are more than ever detached not only from each other, but also from any sense of meaning.

In his 2002 book, *The Purpose Driven Life,* Pastor Rick Warren offered a prescription for living with profound implications.[26] "It's not about you," Warren begins. Instead, he articulates a vision of personal fulfillment, happiness, and purpose in service to others. The solution to not feeling a part of anything is to be a part of something that moves you.

Warren's ideas and his call for a purpose-driven life have capti-vated me since I first encountered them. While his book resonates with me as a religious person (I am a son and grandson of rabbis), I believe Warren's message has equal force for people irrespective of their religiosity or lack thereof. As we will explore in Chapter 7, I believe that an essential part of sustaining recovery from addiction is having a spiritual path and being part of a spiritual community. This can take different forms for different people. For some, it may mean participation in an organized religious community; for others, it may mean finding a non-faith-based community oriented around values such as compassion that inspire its members to do what is right and good for themselves and for other people.

As human beings, we have a dual drive for both survival and for purpose. In Abraham Maslow's hierarchy of needs, our most basic needs from childhood are not merely physical survival, but much deeper.[27] Think for a moment about what makes you feel most secure. Chances are that most people feel the same way. There may be variations on the themes, but our most fundamental needs distill into three things:

- We need to feel *safe.*

- We need to feel *loved.*

- We long to feel that *we belong*—on this earth, in our country, within society, and within our family.

The opioid crisis, like the parallel crises of suicidality, anxiety, depression, and pain, reflects a deeper underlying reality: we are living in a time with multiple forces converging to undermine our sense of safety, of belonging, and of purpose. When our needs are not met, we are stressed and at risk of self-medicating as a solution.

We cannot move beyond the opioid crisis without addressing these root problems. We must find healthy outlets to manage stress, including physical exercise, connection to others, and community. We need to eat and sleep in healthy quantities. And we must discover and cultivate ways to process and cope with the myriad of challenges we face. Without safety and security, love and healthy human and societal connections, we'll always be searching for pain relief—which can all too easily lead down a path to substance abuse and addiction.

The other fundamental challenge that we need to address is removing the shame that people feel around these underlying issues, so that we can talk about them openly and find a way to share what worries us and brings us down, so that people do not feel they are alone in any of these challenges. We will not solve these deeper social issues in one fell swoop, but they need to be part of our conversations and our consciousness. As we find ways to support each other, we step forward on the road to establishing a foundation for an America that can overcome the opioid crisis.

In our final chapters, we'll look at three different aspects of the path forward. In Chapter 7, we'll look at the state of addiction treatment and see how it needs to move forward to address opioid addiction. (Chapter 8 diverges slightly, exploring the role of cannabis in society and in relation to the opioid crisis.) In Chapter 9, we'll examine the proposed solutions put forward to address the crisis. In Chapter 10, we'll return to the question of how to make progress on the deeper issues underlying the crisis, and consider where we go from here.

KEY TAKEAWAYS | CHAPTER 6

- Beyond the health-system failures that led to the opioid crisis, there is a deeper and broader crisis in American life reflected in a rising rate of depression and anxiety, suicide (in some cases, caused by undertreatment of pain), and reports of pain. We cannot fully address the opioid crisis without seeking to understand this broader crisis of human suffering—the byproduct of a culture of chronic stress, trauma, and increasing isolation as a result of technology and the erosion of social support in our communities.

- There are underlying societal transformations driving stress, anxiety, and a lost sense of purpose, including economic and technology changes that have taken away meaningful work from many communities, leaving many people suffering and uncertain about the future.

- The antidote to these crises is a focus on the social determinants of health, including the role of employment, housing, education, and other forms of social support. At the same time, we need to rebuild vibrant, supportive social and spiritual communities that help us restore our lost sense of purpose.

FIXING ADDICTION TREATMENT

"People ask why I do [medication-assisted treatment for opioids]. I tell them I don't want to go to another funeral."

CHARLES NOPLIS, MD[1]

BEYOND THE HEADLINE-GRABBING TRAGEDY of the staggering death toll, the deeper and broader challenge for doctors and our healthcare system is dealing with patients living with an opioid use disorder (OUD)—both treating patients and preventing relapse. In other words, the opioid crisis demands of our health system not just resources to reduce the body count of the dead, but also access to care for those living with OUDs.

How big a problem are we talking about?* Roughly twenty to twenty-four million Americans—one in sixteen people in this country or one in ten adults—are estimated to have a substance use disorder (SUD), with roughly 55 to 60 percent of them, about twelve million, having an opioid use disorder (OUD).[2] This includes nearly a million heroin users in the US, with 170,000 first-time users coming on board annually. As many as sixty to eighty million Americans are believed to be at risk for an SUD.

> Roughly twenty to twenty-four million Americans— one in sixteen people in this country or one in ten adults—are estimated to have a substance use disorder, with roughly 55 to 60 percent of them, about twelve million, having an opioid use disorder.

The economic cost associated with OUDs has been documented as more than $504 billion.[3] Some estimates put the number at more than $1 trillion. Given the magnitude of the problem of addiction, the story of how limited access to addiction treatment has been, how

---

* Given the prominent role of Medicare in setting direction for our health system, it is interesting to note that one in ten Medicare beneficiaries nationwide received opioids on a regular basis via Part D (Medicare prescription drug coverage). In 2016, this included more than 5 million beneficiaries who received opioids for three months or more, an indication of heightened risk for continued dependence. Of these 5 million beneficiaries, 3.6 million received opioids for six or more months and nearly 610,000 received opioids for the entire year. Source: Centers for Disease Control, "CDC Guideline for Prescribing Opioids for Chronic Pain—United States, 2016," *Morbidity and Mortality Weekly Report (MMWR)* 65, no. 1 (March 18, 2016): 1-49.

undeveloped it is relative to the rest of the healthcare system, and how differently we have treated addiction in comparison to other health issues is particularly astounding.

THE NORMALIZATION OF ADDICTION TREATMENT AS PART OF HEALTHCARE

As reflected in the history of opium, addictive substances have represented a problem throughout human history. In the American context, until the very recent past, addiction has been seen more as a sin or moral failing than a healthcare issue.

The evolution in perspective that led us to see addiction as both a public health crisis and a biological, rather than a moral, condition occurred gradually throughout the twentieth century and into the early twenty-first century. If we look at addiction treatment in the late 1800s or early 1900s, our system amounted largely to spa-style retreats for people with the money to pay from them out of pocket, with minimal resources devoted to those who could not afford to pay for treatment themselves. The proliferation of treatment programs that today dot the Southern California and Florida coasts are, in many ways, a legacy of that history. Similarly, decisions made in the 1960s to limit Medicaid funding for residential addiction treatment were a legacy of fear that a "bottomless pit" of poor people with addiction would require the devotion of too much publicly funded resources. Addiction was seen as a personal failing rather than an essential healthcare problem.

While the shift from a moral to a medical view of addiction began decades ago, it was not until the 2000s that the law actually mandated that change. In many ways, the culmination of the legal recognition that addiction treatment is an integral part of healthcare came through two laws that focused on insurance coverage.

First, in 2008, the national mental health parity law declared an end to discrimination against addiction treatment relative to medical care. Entitled the Mental Health Parity and Addiction Equity Act (MHPAEA), the law prohibits the imposition of more restrictive financial requirements and treatment limitations on both mental health and SUD benefits in group health plans, in comparison to the handling of medical and surgical benefits. The law represented a sea change, putting pressure on insurers to abandon the argument that addiction treatment was something other than healthcare and could be subjected to a double standard. At the same time, it did not force all health plans to cover addiction treatment.

That shift came in the second significant law: The Affordable Care Act (ACA) of 2010, which mandated the inclusion of mental health and substance use disorder (SUD) treatment services as part of the minimum essential coverage. While the Mental Health Parity Act ordered an end to discriminatory practices, the ACA went much further by imposing an affirmative mandate that took effect in 2012. The ACA articulated a list of ten essential health benefits that every health plan needed to cover, including SUDs on the list. Insurance companies scrambled to respond to this mandatory expansion of coverage and an explosion of claims for addiction treatment from across the country.

Before we discuss how the transition to addiction treatment as a healthcare benefit is proceeding, it is important to understand the legacy how differently we have treated addiction historically in comparison to other health issues. This history offers insight into how undeveloped addiction treatment is relative to the rest of healthcare, and the challenges ahead in closing that gap.

ADDICTION TREATMENT THROUGH THE EARLY TWENTIETH CENTURY

Beyond the challenge of being treated as a moral rather than a health condition, addiction has also been poorly understood practical terms. In the 1800s and even into the early 1900s, the primary issue was seen as how to help people avoid the uncomfortable experience of withdrawal. As a result, the primary form of treatment utilized by doctors was maintenance to people with addictions by keeping them supplied with the addictive substance, accompanied by an exhortation to exercise personal willpower. At the time of the original American opioid crisis of the early 1900s, the crackdown and imprisonment of physicians stemmed from their prescribing heroin and other opioids for maintenance purposes. The only other prevalent model to maintenance was replacing one addictive substance with another, such as substituting cocaine for opiates.

There were bright spots. Benjamin Rush (1745–1813), a signer of the Declaration of Independence, is often credited with pioneering the first therapeutic approach to alcoholism and addiction in the United States, treating it as a medical condition. Rush developed what may have been the first sober living residences in America. In 1858, the State of New York opened the Inebriate Asylum in Binghamton, a facility to treat opioid addiction (opium and morphine) along with alcoholism and cocaine addiction.[4]

But there was no shortage of quackery. By the 1880s, America had its first national brand in addiction treatment: a series of over 120 "Keeley Institute" spa-style franchises modeled after the approach of Leslie Keeley, MD (1836–1900). The "Keeley Cure" consisted of four weeks of four daily injections every two hours of bichloride of gold (yes, the metal), along with other tonics. Dr. Keeley would not disclose his secret cures, which led to theorizing about other mystery ingredients.[5]

Alongside bad medicine offered at spa-style private sanitaria for wealthier people with addictions, the 1900s saw the emergence of the "drunk tank" as the site of addiction "treatment" for the poor. In the 1920s, police-run public health clinics were established to provide morphine maintenance for the poor, but these were closed under federal pressure from the Department of Treasury, which viewed maintenance of addicted individuals as part of the problem.

The Twelve Steps

The year 1935 marked an important development in addiction treatment history: the beginning, in Akron, Ohio, of Alcoholics Anonymous (AA) by Bill Wilson, known as Bill W., and Robert Holbrook Smith, MD, or Dr. Bob. They introduced what has come to be known as the Twelve Steps. Twelve Step recovery became extremely popular in the 1940s and remains so today; Narcotics Anonymous (NA), a program that addresses opioid addiction, emerged in the 1950s, utilizing the Twelve Steps.

It is impossible to understand the development of addiction treatment without understanding the role of Twelve Step recovery. Over the past eighty years, no philosophy of recovery has come close to having the same dominant impact as the Twelve Steps. They began as religious principles but have been adapted into a recovery process to be followed irrespective of a person's faith, completed in the following order:

> It is impossible to understand the development of addiction treatment without understanding the role of Twelve Step recovery.

1. **Honesty**: admitting powerlessness over the drug and inability to control its use

2. **Faith**: believing that a higher, external power could restore sanity

3. **Surrender**: deciding to turn your life and will toward the higher power

4. **Self-searching**: doing a "fearless moral inventory"

5. **Transparency**: admitting the particulars of wrongdoing

6. **Readiness**: being prepared for removal of defects of character

7. **Humility**: asking with humility for removal of your shortcomings

8. **Accounting**: preparing a list of people harmed to ask for forgiveness

9. **Amends**: seeking forgiveness from these people

10. **Maintenance**: continuously taking stock

11. **Spiritual contact**: prayer and meditation to improve contact with a higher power

12. **Service to others**: using the steps for the benefit of others who are addicted

From the outset, AA has been an abstinence and sobriety model. The challenge with respect to opioids, as articulated by Surgeon General Murthy in Chapter 6, is that, for the majority of people, addiction may be a chronic condition, with relapse expected. The National Institutes of Health (NIH) has moved to a chronic disease model of treatment, under which relapse does not signify that treatment failed, but rather that addiction treatment is a long-term process with continual evaluation and modification as needed, similar to the approach taken for other chronic diseases. As an alternative to abstinence models, for example, the health policy community espouses a harm-reduction approach, which focuses on managing the negative behavior, such as by encouraging a heavy drinker to drink less, or by providing sterile syringes to reduce the spread of infections from drug users sharing needles.

In contrast to AA's harder line on abstinence as the only option for participants, NA has taken a more nuanced position. While abstinence remains the goal, NA literature acknowledges the reality that relapse happens, that people who relapse to drug usage should continue to participate in group meetings, and that they should use relapse as a source of awakening, to renew and rededicate themselves to the steps needed to sustain recovery.

PRESSURE FOR EVIDENCE-BASED APPROACHES

For the addiction community, the shift to integrate addiction treatment into American healthcare brought tremendous promise, including the availability of unprecedented funding to dramatically increase the number of people who would have access to care. At the same time, it brought challenges, including a demand for evidence-based proof of effectiveness. This gave rise to a conflict, most visibly between payers (insurers) and addiction treatment providers, that has highlighted the confusion and lack of clarity over standards in addiction treatment, from legal compliance to clinical.

The reality is that addiction treatment remains in fundamental ways underdeveloped in comparison to other parts of our healthcare system. At the most fundamental level, we are still trying to agree on a definition of what constitutes effective addiction treatment and the metric by which we decide how successful a particular approach to drug treatment is. What is the goal: complete abstinence and sobriety or harm reduction? In an abstinence model, having to take medication, such as methadone, to remain sober is not viewed as success. Similarly, in an abstinence model, relapses where a person begins using opioids again are viewed as failures and setbacks. In a harm-reduction model, by contrast, the goal is different—to restore a person to functional work and personal relationships. If addiction is treated as a chronic condition, then relapse is expected, along with prescription of medications having no end point.

Much of the pressure for clarity and standards has come from payers. Through the lack of insurance funding for most of the last fifty years (since the Medicare and Medicaid programs launched), addiction treatment developed without the same pressure for compliance or evidence-based models that has predominated in the rest of healthcare, where government programs and insurance companies drove standards. Instead, addiction treatment developed in a siloed model, where many providers operated on a small scale, doing things their own way, depending more on cash payments than health plans, and not integrating into larger health systems.

One byproduct of this practice has been a high degree of variation in the ways states have licensed addiction treatment. When I look at hospital licensing and operational regulations, there are only slight differences from state to state. By contrast, state licensing and operational rules governing addiction treatment vary wildly. In the early 2000s, when several physician clients introduced me to the treatment programs they were working with, I was shocked to discover how few rules there were relative to hospitals, nursing homes, pharmacies, and other settings where I had worked.

As one example, the state of California requires no license, offering only a voluntary certification, to operate an outpatient addiction treatment program. In other words, in California, anybody who wants to open an outpatient treatment program

The state of California requires no license, offering only a voluntary certification, to operate an outpatient addiction treatment program.

and promote it to the public can do so, without concern for meeting licensing standards. By contrast, most states require anyone seeking to provide outpatient addiction treatment services to have a valid program license. Insurance companies have tried to fill the void in California by demanding that programs obtain the voluntary certification or an accreditation, but ultimately, there is no basis for them to insist on such steps. Similarly, addiction treatment counseling remains a certificated, but not a licensed, profession, limiting the enforcement of standards. While there has been a move towards consolidation, there remain multiple different professional certification options with distinct standards.

We will know that addiction treatment has "arrived" in terms of its integration into healthcare when we have relatively uniform professional and program licensure requirements from state to state—something seemingly decades away.

DIFFERENTIATING BETWEEN TREATMENT AND RECOVERY

In addition to the need to standardize licensure of programs and professionals, addiction treatment has also been under pressure to standardize its methods and outcomes reporting, so that we can understand what is and is not effective. One recurrent issue has been questions concerning the effectiveness of various social model recovery programs.

Programs that utilize the Twelve Steps are often referred to as social model programs because they focus on peer support in regular group meetings, self-help, and experiential learning, as distinguished from mental health or medical models of treatment. Other social model programs include SMART Recovery* and Narconon,** a non-medical model that dates back to the 1960s.

As payers have pushed for more evidence-based approaches, one challenge for some social model programs has been either limited data to support their effectiveness or data of limited value. Many programs establish their effectiveness based on contact with alumni who return or maintain contact, creating a data pool concentrated with success stories rather than people who relapsed. Programs that integrate AA and NA can be constrained by these programs' commitment to anonymity, which limits the collection of data needed to establish support for an evidence-based models of recovery. In April 2015, journalist Gabrielle Glazer, writing in *The Atlantic*, asserted that the success rate of Twelve Steps may be as low as 5 to 10 percent, and that its enduring popularity is mostly because the subset of attendees for whom the program works are the only ones who stick around to talk about their success (their current run of sobriety)—the so-called survivorship and recency bias.[6]

At the same time, studies criticizing Twelve Step's effectiveness suffered from multiple flaws, including ambiguity as to the time period of analysis, an inadequate sample size, and lack of follow-up contact. More than sixty thousand NA groups meet weekly around the world, alongside a much larger number of AA meetings, translating to several million people who are active participants. The power of the Twelve Step model is that it offers an established, inclusive

---

* SMART Recovery is a non-faith-based alternative with its own techniques based on a cognitive behavioral therapy (CBT) model that examines relationships between thoughts, feelings, and behaviors to improve coping and better understand and modify patterns of thinking that lead to self-destructive actions.

**Narconon is based on the works of L. Ron Hubbard, founder of Scientology, and it treats drugs—from illegal street drugs to psychotropic medications—as a source of human misery and enslavement. The program utilizes an approach involving nutrition, therapeutic drills and exercises, and an educational curriculum focused on rebuilding lives in a community-focused way.

framework for social and spiritual support to sustain recovery.

One important distinction that often gets lost is between treatment—addressing withdrawal symptoms, cravings, and the immediate issues to discontinue opioid or other drug use—and recovery, meaning ongoing peer support and other psychosocial and spiritual support to minimize the risk of relapse and prevent a return to an opioid or other substance use disorder. However much NA, AA, and other Twelve Step programs may contribute to the process of treatment, their contribution to recovery as the predominant form of peer group support is inarguable and an essential component of the recovery landscape.

EMERGENCE OF MEDICAL MODELS OF ADDICTION TREATMENT

Long before the enactment of the Mental Health Parity Act and the Affordable Care Act, healthcare payers pressed for clinician-led "medical models" of treatment in place of the predominant peer-supported, self-help-oriented "social models." This issue emerged in the 1960s as some health insurance plans began to cover alcoholism treatment. For those health plans offering coverage, the basis for doing so had been the reframing of addiction as early as the 1940s (by the National Committee for Education on Alcoholism (NCEA)) as a disease rather than a moral condition—on an individual level and as a public health crisis on a macro level. But it was not until 1967 that the American Medical Association (AMA) characterized alcoholism as a disease. The NCEA (today known as the National Council on Alcoholism and Drug Dependence (NCADD)) advocated for detoxification in hospital settings, provision of local alcohol information centers to promote education, clinics to diagnose and treat alcoholism, and establishment of "rest centers" for the long-term care of alcoholics. In

1972, the Joint Commission, which we talked about in the context of pain surveys asking patients to rate their pain, began to accredit addiction treatment programs for the first time.

Progress towards expanded addiction treatment coverage was not linear. In the 1980s, for example, the rise of managed care led to a reduction in insurance coverage for inpatient and residential addiction treatment, leading to growth in outpatient models of addiction treatment and also the growth of sober-living recovery residences. In 1988, the Fair Housing Act was amended to include recovery from addiction as a protected class of disability. Recovery from addiction was also identified as a category of disability protection in the 1990 Americans with Disabilities Act. While not advancing access to care, this federal recognition extended housing rights and represented a significant part of the gradual rethinking of the nature of addiction in America.

> In 1988, the Fair Housing Act was amended to include recovery from addiction as a protected class of disability. Recovery from addiction was also identified as a category of disability protection in the 1990 Americans with Disabilities Act.

By the early 1990s, the need for better addiction treatment was on the national agenda. In 1992, two agencies, the Substance Abuse and Mental Health Services Administration (SAMHSA) and the Center for Substance Abuse Treatment (CSAT), were formed within the US Department of Health and Human Services (HHS) to increase the availability of effective treatment and recovery services. In 1998, the first funds went via block grants to states and community-based groups for these services. While the Clinton health reform bill (known as HillaryCare) failed to pass in 1993, it was noteworthy for its inclusion of a proposal for a national benefit that covered substance use disorders.

Medication-Assisted Treatment

In recent years, medication-assisted treatment (MAT) has gained attention as a component of medical models, which historically have been driven by psychiatric and psychological approaches. The first form of MAT in its modern iteration dates back to 1972, when the FDA approved methadone as a maintenance medication for people addicted to heroin. For historical context, this same year marked the beginning of the Nixon Administration's launch of a declared national "war on drugs" and drug abuse, which each of the eight subsequent American presidents has continued.

Following the approval of methadone as a form of MAT for heroin addiction, in 1995 the FDA approved naltrexone, an opioid antagonist, to treat alcoholism. In 2002 the FDA approved buprenorphine, the third major form of MAT; other forms include disulfiram (Antabuse) and acamprosate (Campral).

Methadone: Although methadone is the oldest form of MAT, it remains the most structured and limited in its method of distribution. Methadone's predominant method of distribution (other than hospital pharmacies) has been in closed-system Narcotic Treatment Program clinics. These clinics are subject to significant recordkeeping requirements (along with special physician DEA and FDA registration requirements) because of concerns of potential diversion as a drug of abuse. The distribution in clinics where addicted people would congregate for a daily dose gave rise to a stigma associated with methadone, exemplified by a scene in the 1977 movie *Annie Hall,* when Woody Allen reminisces about classmates. A boy of about ten looks straight into the camera and says: "I used to be a heroin addict. Now I'm a methadone addict." This line encapsulates the fear that MAT merely moves people from one addiction to another.

Buprenorphine: In contrast to methadone, the 2000 Drug Addiction Treatment Act (DATA) created an option for qualified physicians to utilize buprenorphine in their offices, subject to issuance of a waiver from the DEA. Buprenorphine is best known as the brands Subutex (pure buprenorphine), Suboxone (a combination of buprenorphine and naltrexone), and the most recent, Sublocade (a subcutaneous injection that dissolves slowly over four weeks). The ability to obtain buprenorphine in a private office setting or to administer it in hospitals, health departments, and prisons enhanced the appeal of this easily accessible MAT.

The rise of buprenorphine has revealed a tension between medical and nonmedical perspectives of addiction treatment and recovery community and the clinical community. In the recovery community, buprenorphine, like methadone, is viewed by many with suspicion, in part because it is yet another profit center for the pharmaceutical industry and because some percentage of people for whom it is prescribed are likely to stay on it indefinitely. Doctors I consulted while writing this book acknowledged that it can be difficult to wean some patients off of the drug, and that a percentage of people who take it (perhaps 20 to 25 percent) may have long-term dependency indefinitely. Many younger patients want to get off of Suboxone because it can interfere with intimacy (suppressing testosterone) and can create a challenge in pregnancy, requiring newborns to be weaned off of opioids at birth.

Another negative facet of methadone and buprenorphine is that, by addressing the opioid addiction with an alternative, they relieve the pressure to focus on deeper issues that gave rise to the addiction. A person addicted to OxyContin may find his or her needs met by switching to a dependency on buprenorphine, without any interest in pursuing the work needed to develop a better self-understanding or seek to become medication-free.

As a result, for many in the abstinence community, being on buprenorphine is not the equivalent of being "clean." While weaker than methadone, buprenorphine still operates chemically as an opioid. The difference is that buprenorphine only partially activates one of the primary opioid receptors, muting the pain relief, euphoria, and respiratory depression. As a result, within the recovery community, many people regard buprenorphine, like methadone, as a substitute that produces milder versions of the effect of the opioids they are replacing.

In contrast to the abstinence community's ambivalence or resistance, the clinical community utilizing a harm-reduction model is much more enthusiastic about buprenorphine. In its view, the focus on abstinence is a moral approach, while treating addiction as a chronic condition means that some portion of people may very well be on methadone or buprenorphine for life, in the same way that a person with diabetes or heart disease is prescribed certain medications for life. They point to data such as a Massachusetts study from 2012 to 2014 finding that, for those receiving medication-assisted treatment, opioid overdose deaths decreased significantly—by 59 percent for those receiving methadone and by 38 percent for those receiving buprenorphine.[7]

Naltrexone: The other alternative form of MAT that has attracted growing interest is naltrexone. Most well-known by the brand Vivitrol, naltrexone differs from methadone and buprenorphine in that it *forces* sobriety in recovery. Naltrexone is an opioid antagonist, meaning that it occupies the receptors in the brain such that opioids have no effect and therefore have no allure. While naltrexone has been available for many years in an oral tablet, it has gained attention in recent years for a monthly intramuscular suspended solution, as well as a slow-release subdermal implant that lasts for eight weeks. (Naltrexone has also been illegally imported into the United States in a pellet form used elsewhere in the world, but not approved by the FDA.)

Leaving aside low-dose naltrexone as a pain therapy (another use), naltrexone is also needed for shorter period of time. Typically, naltrexone therapy advocates recommend a twelve-month course so that, even after the cravings for drugs subside, the person can develop stability in personal relationships and his or her environment to sustain recovery.

On the front lines of the opioid crisis, such as in hospital emergency room settings, naltrexone is of less interest because naltrexone therapy cannot commence until a person has completed detoxification. A person still going through withdrawal with drugs in their system may become sicker as a result of naltrexone. As a result, it can only be used at a later point in the process by a smaller population who have already gotten through detoxification. In contrast, buprenorphine can still be administered during the early stages of withdrawal, as soon as twelve to twenty-four hours after the person last took opioids, making the transition easier.

The competition between Suboxone, Subutex, Sublocade, and other forms of buprenorphine on one side, and naltrexone on the other, parallels a deep and long-standing divide in addiction treatment. For the recovery community, naltrexone is much easier to embrace because it prevents opioid effects and decreases any craving for opioids, supporting a person in recovery maintain sobriety. Buprenorphine, by contrast, has encountered resistance as a partial opioid agonist, meaning that a person taking it may feel the same sense of euphoria that opioids provide, albeit in more muted fashion.

UNDERLYING TENSIONS: SOBRIETY OR PAIN-FREE EXISTENCE?

The tensions over buprenorphine echo a deeper, long-standing divide within the addiction treatment community. For many decades, when it comes to people whose addiction is linked to underlying pain, the peer-supported recovery model primarily oriented itself around abstinence and no use of medication. On the other side, the psychopharmacology community focused on addressing physiological and often mental health issues, tending to make medication an inevitable part of the process.

I first encountered these battle lines in the context of a battle between doctors at the Betty Ford Center. In 1978, fresh out of the White House, the former First Lady's family staged an intervention. They forced Ford to admit that her addiction to alcohol and opioid painkillers—prescribed for a pinched nerve a decade earlier—was a problem. "I loved pills," she wrote in her memoir. "They took away my tension and my pain."[8] She went into treatment for substance abuse. Following a Twelve Step program, she gave up pills and became drug-free. In 1982, she established the Betty Ford Clinic in Rancho Mirage for treatment of chemical addiction, which she ran until 2005.

In 2006, I got called into a fight between two camps within the treatment program. The abstinence advocates had been in the leadership, but were increasingly being challenged by psychopharmacologists advocating a medication-centered treatment model. I got a crash course in a tense standoff that had been ongoing for decades. The psychopharmacologists argued that abstinence didn't work for many patients. The abstinence people argued that the psychopharmacologists were pushing drugs that created an obstacle to true recovery.

The distrust across this issue highlights a deeper problem: a lack of consensus on the ultimate goal. Is it spiritual restoration—getting people back to their true selves? Or is it functional—getting people get back to work?

Perhaps the biggest challenge in addiction treatment is the complexity of addiction itself. Addiction goes far beyond physical health challenges. There is no cure for addiction in the way that there is for high blood pressure. Addiction may be a byproduct of trauma, dysfunctional relationships, stress, spiritual crisis, or a wide range of mental health issues. Often, drug use is only a symptom of deeper underlying issues. Far from being uniform, the root causes of addiction are multifaceted and different for many people. As a consequence, treating addiction is more than merely weaning a person off physical dependence or learning how to use nonharmful coping mechanisms to respond to trauma, stress, or crisis. Treatment without support to sustain recovery leaves people vulnerable to relapse and repetition.

> **Perhaps the biggest challenge in addiction treatment is the complexity of addiction itself. Addiction goes far beyond physical health challenges. There is no cure for addiction in the way that there is for high blood pressure.**

CONTINUED PRESSURE FOR EVIDENCE-BASED STANDARDS

As addiction treatment moves forward, perhaps the most pressing question facing all programs is what will be required to demonstrate that they are clinically effective and evidence-based. Over the past forty years, the federal government and each state have established numerous agencies that are dedicated to providing guidelines for effective treatment of drug and alcohol abuse as part of the essential regulation of substance abuse, including the National Institutes of Health (NIH), the National Institute on Drug Abuse (NIDA), the Substance Abuse and Mental Health Services Administration (SAMHSA), and the National Institute of Alcohol Abuse and Alcoholism (NIAAA), just to name a few. With a multiplicity of federal agencies leading academic research into the process of treatment and recovery from drug and alcohol abuse, it would be reasonable to expect definitive treatment models and therapy protocols for effective rehabilitation.

Unfortunately, nothing close to that has occurred. In many respects, the consequence of addiction having been treated as something other than a health condition is that, in comparison to other health conditions, relatively little in-depth research has been done on effective addiction prevention and treatment. Awareness of the lack of a basis in evidence for prevailing recovery models in the US has spurred extensive academic analysis of both how to measure "success" in drug rehabilitation, as well as how to identify data markers that indicate a primary therapy model.

In 2003, for example, Stanford University professor J. W. Finney, PhD, surveyed the studies that had been done on the subject and identified more than 150 academic papers. His conclusions are sobering to anyone trying to unlock the secret of what makes rehabilitation programs effective:

> Overall, many of the measures reviewed have only minimal psychometric data available and have been used in only a limited number of studies (in some cases, only one). Additional research is needed to more accurately gauge their reliability and validity....
>
> New measures of treatment and treatment processes also should be developed. Better conceptualization of treatment processes should be a precursor to the development of those

instruments, so that variables of the greatest relevance are focused upon....

Additional efforts to improve the assessment of alcohol treatment and treatment processes would be well placed. They can help improve the provision and monitoring of patient care, as well as enhance the ability of research to identify more effective forms of treatment, how they work, and for whom particular types of treatment are indicated.[9]

Like almost everything else studied in the area of drug and alcohol rehabilitation, for many decades, there was not even a consensus about how to measure efficacy. Early efforts attempted to "code" taped therapy sessions or interviews, scoring a patient's self-reported relapse rates, outlook on life, ability to demonstrate retention of therapy training, and a myriad of other data points that the interviewer would try to elicit.

Eventually, researchers began to develop surveys for addiction treatment program participants, which were used with varying success. One of the now more commonly accepted survey formats is derived from the 135-item Center for Substance Abuse Treatment (CSAT) National Outcomes Measures. This tool has achieved widespread acceptance as part of most program grant funding applications for NIDA and NIAAA, as well as a licensing document for many state agencies. Although considered a benchmark, use of this study has proved problematic in the field due to its length and time required by both interviewer and interviewee to complete.

Today, surveys of participants post-treatment are the norm, even though many surveys continue to be criticized for lack of rigor. In the words of one public policy forum, "Drug surveys vary widely from one to another and have been criticized for their inability to obtain a full and accurate understanding of the population they are sampling. Limitations [also] include the degree of confidence subjects have in the confidentiality of their responses."[10] At least for now, survey results, even with all of the "noise" included in the data, are the best tool at the disposal of researchers. There is a reasonable degree of confidence that they can measure efficacy of treatment, at least during the short-term period after program completion.

Even as we have made progress on the issue of how to measure efficacy, the difficulty of staying in contact with alumni of treatment programs has meant that the vast majority of these studies have only tracked graduates of treatment programs for as little as one to three years, offering a very limited window into effectiveness.

Despite these limitations, it is possible to articulate a consensus view on effective treatment models from the research describing evidence-based therapy programs for drug and alcohol rehabilitation. The key elements seem to be

- a decisive intervention;

- psycho-social skill therapy and cognitive-behavioral therapy (CBT); and

- longer-term assimilation of new coping skills and/or ongoing maintenance of skills to confront urges to relapse.[11]

In the literature, CBT is considered to be a research-validated technique insofar as it helps the addicted person recognize the prompt that triggers drug use and to learn to how to redirect thoughts and reactions away from it. At the same time, external factors, socioeconomic forces, developmental history, and basic acceptance of life condition all seem to play a role in relapse, regardless of the therapeutic program.

This consensus may be of limited value, as the "decisive" intervention may well be simply the patient seeking treatment. In other words, the decision to seek treatment for addiction by the patient may be statistically as "effective" as the treatment itself.[12]

Critically, longer-term treatments (beyond the typical thirty-day rehab) are cited as the best evidence-based programs. In the words of Mark Willenbring, MD, a former director of treatment and recovery research at the National Institute for Alcohol Abuse and Alcoholism, "You don't treat a chronic illness for four weeks and then send the patient to a support group. People with a chronic form of addiction need multimodal treatment that is individualized and offered continuously or intermittently for as long as they need it."[13]

So while hard and fast rules are not yet definitive, as noted above, there is an emerging general model of rehabilitation: intervention, followed by effective cognitive-behavioral recognition of the triggers of addictive behavior, followed by training in coping skills, and a very long-term program or access to program support.[14] Beyond the components and time of effective treatment programs, the National Institute on Drug Abuse notes that effective treatment needs to address not only the person's drug abuse, but also "any associated medical, psychological, social, vocational, and legal problems."[15]

This may be the most distinctive part of addiction treatment relative to other healthcare issues. Throughout healthcare, we are seeing increasing attention in recent years on the "social determinants of health," meaning the economic and social conditions that influence differences in health status: education, environment, housing, income, and social connection. In addiction treatment, these factors take on an even bigger role. Challenges like not having a stable place to live, a social network of support, and employment can easily become active impediments to a person's ability to sustain recovery.

THE FRAUD AND ABUSE PROBLEM
IN ADDICTION TREATMENT

The availability of insurance to cover treatment since 2012 has driven explosive investment in development of more addiction resources. Many existing programs leaped at the opportunity to grow and provide more services with insurance reimbursement available. New programs opened across the country, with particular concentrations in Florida and Southern California, both homes to the so-called "Rehab Riviera," centered around Delray Beach in Florida and from Newport Beach to Malibu in California.

As has happened time and again in US healthcare, the availability of insurance coverage reimbursement started out with promise but eventually devolved into an ugly mess. As a healthcare lawyer, I have seen this scene play out at least a dozen times: insurance plans or government programs begin to reimburse a new diagnostic test, procedure, or durable medical equipment (DME) item. Early on, a group of healthcare providers start utilizing a new or newly discovered billing code for a particular test, procedure, or product. Doctors are pleased to discover that the new test has clinical value, and also is a source of good reimbursement. The enthusiasm of early adopters over a clinically and financially beneficial billing opportunity gives way to more and more providers and marketers pursuing the opportunity, some inevitably driven cynically by profit opportunity rather than by clinical value.

As the volume of claims grow, the insurance companies respond with their own playbook: to tamp down on claims growth, they audit for overutilization, lack of medical necessity, and excessive testing. The payers use their special investigation units (SIUs) to investigate and examine pervasive problems of kickbacks and fraudulent marketing inducements. In addition to the heightened scrutiny of claims, providers also find that payers are dropping the reimbursement as the volume of billing expands. There is inevitably a particularly greedy subset of providers or marketers trying to grow their claim volume even more aggressively, trying to cash in on a profit opportunity that they perceive to be time-limited. Overaggressive billing practices, in turn, drive more aggressive investigations, higher standards for coverage, and lower reimbursement.

As a healthcare lawyer dealing with reimbursement disputes over the past two decades, I could rattle off dozens of examples of this phenomenon, from power wheelchairs to a never-ending series of diagnostic tests, including nerve conduction studies, electromyography, and genetic testing. In the early days of any new diagnostic test or code, we see a group of clients who are trying to understand the landscape and operate in compliance with laws and regulations. Many of these providers have learned from the past that new billing opportunities need to be pursued with caution, that profits will be illusory if the government or insurers have the right to demand repayment because codes are not billed correctly or medical necessity is not well documented.

Later, we inevitably see a different stream of clients, late arrivals to the same opportunity who didn't ask questions on the front end, moved aggressively towards a healthcare revenue opportunity without worrying about the details, and then need legal representation when they start running into problems originating from noncompliance or accusations of fraud and abuse. Something triggers a visit to the lawyer: the insurance companies stop paying or launch an audit and demand for repayment, or, in the worst cases, transmit their files to law enforcement for criminal investigation.

The story in this cycle within healthcare usually culminates the same way: whistleblowers emerge seeking a portion of the recovery for blowing the whistle on bad behavior. The government and insurance companies pursue and recoup large financial settlements. The worst actors are charged criminally. Over the past several years, and for years to come, we have been and will be watching prosecutions for criminal conduct and demands for repayment of the latest inappropriately billed products and services.

> The story in this cycle within healthcare usually culminates the same way: whistleblowers emerge seeking a portion of the recovery for blowing the whistle on bad behavior.

Urine Drug Screening

In addiction treatment, this cycle first began with urine drug screening (UDS). UDS in response to the opioid crisis first gained popularity in workers' compensation, based on concerns that a growing number of patients were engaging in drug-seeking behavior based on addiction and also diverting drugs by selling them on the street for their cash value. As the standard of care shifted towards UDS as a best practice, insurers started covering the test. Doctors treating injured workers with pain medications were happy to add it to their practices; it protected them by confirming that their patients were actually taking the drugs they prescribed and not also taking other drugs from other sources.

Laboratories and the marketers working for them were even more excited than doctors about UDS. After all, a newly covered test was a new reimbursement opportunity. More testing translated to more revenue. Nationwide, marketing representatives encouraged doctors to "make it rain" (an unfortunate internal communication from one lab), meaning to order as many UDS screens as possible. Marketers encouraged doctors to start screening Medicare beneficiaries, even though there was little evidence of drug-seeking or drug diversion by seniors. In some cases, marketers paid out cash to doctors per test. In other cases, the schemes were more intricate, offering doctors investment opportunities in new labs where the return on investment was proportionate with the volume of UDS referrals.

The results of this marketing effort were staggering. In 2000, Medicare paid nationwide for approximately 101 point-of-care urine tests, in which the color of a urine sample changes color based on an immunoassay strip at the bottom of the cup.* By 2009, the number of similar tests paid for by Medicare had grown to more than three million. The volume of tests paid for by private insurers was even higher, with much higher amounts, often thousands of dollars, paid for so-called "quantitative" tests, performed in labs for more data and to confirm the point-of-care results.

In this environment, the Affordable Care Act opened up insurance reimbursement to addiction treatment, and the infrastructure that had developed to monetize UDS in other settings went to work. While high-volume laboratories and marketers had already been cashing in with injured workers and Medicare beneficiaries, the ability to test addiction treatment patients in large numbers led to even more explosive claim volume. By 2012, insurance reimbursement turned urine into a billion-dollar business.

Addiction treatment providers embraced urine toxicology screening, in many cases oblivious to the illegality of being paid by marketers for referring tests to their labs in higher volumes and using the more expensive quantitative lab testing as much as possible. In some cases, providers billed for daily UDS, even though federal SAMHSA

---

* Point-of-care testing cups are known as CLIA-waived qualitative tests because they can be done onsite in physician offices or wherever the patient gives the sample and provide a quick positive or negative result, as opposed to quantitative testing in a laboratory, which provides numerical results of any substances in the sample.

standards warned against false positives with overly frequent testing because of the slow rate at which drugs metabolized. UDS had an obvious appeal in addiction treatment because it offered a deterrent effect of keeping people in treatment from trying to use substances surreptitiously. The question, from a healthcare perspective, is when a UDS was ordered by a physician and medically necessary.

By the time UDS began to grow explosively in addiction treatment, federal prosecutors had already begun cracking down on UDS fraud and abuse in the Medicare Program. (In healthcare, fraud and abuse does not simply refer narrowly to deliberate deception, but also to all kinds of practices that do not conform to standards in submitting a claim for payment, including payments to referral sources.) Typically, the FBI and other federal law enforcement focus on fighting fraud and abuse against federal health programs, like Medicare and Medicaid, while leaving state law enforcement to take on fraud and abuse against other insurers. In this case, the FBI made an exception, launching a nationwide task force to stop lab-marketing fraud in the addiction treatment context. The impetus seems to have been a perception that the scale of fraud occurring in UDS billing was unprecedented, and was unlikely to get timely attention without federal intervention.

In tandem with law enforcement response, insurance companies did their best to clamp down on UDS fraud. They reduced the amounts paid for UDS testing. They tightened their coverage criteria to limit the frequency of testing and the circumstances in which a quantitative lab test (as opposed to a point-of-care cup) would be paid. They launched medical necessity audits, changed their billing, coding, and documentation requirements, and demanded repayment of claims. The ensuing conflict between insurers and the addiction treatment community has continued to expand to a growing set of practices.

Other Fraudulent Acts

Insurers complained that addiction treatment providers were committing fraud in a variety of ways beyond UDS kickbacks, including procuring insurance or housing of patients in need. They made the same allegation with respect to patient financial responsibility, when providers waived deductibles, copays, and coinsurance for people with limited financial resources. This was also a confusing area where addiction didn't fit squarely into traditional categories. Insurance companies throughout healthcare complain that discounts and waivers offered to patients for their part of the bill amount to fraudulent inducement, luring patients to one program over another. They claim that, by not collecting the amounts required under the terms of a particular policy or by charging discounted cash prices, providers misstate their usual and reasonable fees. Health plans impose multi-thousand dollar deductibles and require patients to pay amounts often in the range of 20 percent or more of the bill as a utilization control to ensure that patients have "skin in the game" when seeking care, and they argue that ignoring these requirements interferes with the terms of coverage.

Meanwhile, addiction treatment providers protest that these requirements amount to a barrier that would deny access to most incoming patients, who are in no condition to afford the high cost under many insurance plans. Among the ways in which addiction is different from heart disease or diabetes or other health conditions is that it often undermines people's ability to work and their relationships with family. Overcoming an addiction is often the first step in rebuilding. As a consequence, a significant number of patients newly in addiction treatment lack the wherewithal to pay the high cost of health plan deductibles or coinsurance, even if they are lucky enough to have insurance. They often lack stable housing. As a consequence of the frequency of relapses and repeated stints in detox and treatment, even supportive families are financially exhausted and have no money left to pay any share of cost. In this environment, treatment centers are adamant that providing scholarships and waiving patient financial responsibility is essential to getting people the help they need are acting out of compassion.

The result has been continuing conflict, as health insurance companies use allegations of noncompliance as grounds not to pay or to demand repayment from providers. It is an unequal playing field in which insurance companies have the power simply to turn off the spigot of reimbursement, leaving treatment providers without a diversified payer mix (that is, patients with different insurance carriers) exposed. In many cases, addiction treatment programs that have been delivering good care have found themselves vulnerable for even smaller deficiencies, like inadvertently insufficient documentation to meet insurer expectations. The result has been that, over the last several years, despite an overall need for more access to care, high-quality addiction treatment programs have been shut down—a loss for operators, devoted staff, and patients desperately in need of care.

ROGUE REHABS

Beyond the ongoing conflict between addiction treatment providers and payers over reimbursement, the opioid crisis has driven a unique set of problems around patient safety. While most of my work has revolved around responding to more mundane compliance issues, by the late 2000s, I began seeing a rising trend of patients dying in addiction treatment from overdoses, suicides, and medical conditions that required a higher level of care. The problem was that addiction treatment programs were taking care of people in fragile condition, and patients were dying at an alarming rate. The situation that made everyone sit up and take notice was A Better Tomorrow, a program in Temecula, California, run by a publicly traded company, American Addiction Centers, which had at least five patient deaths in five years:

Roberta McMinn, a sixty-eight-year-old woman with a history of asthma, hypertension, and multiple strokes died three days after she was admitted in 2008. She had been unable to walk into the residence under her own power when she arrived. She was found pale and vomiting in her bed, and a staff member helped her change her shirt. A second worker arrived and, while assisting Roberta in cleaning up, noticed that her skin was turning blue and white. They called 911 but no one on staff performed CPR, and she was dead before paramedics arrived. A Better Tomorrow staff had given her anti-depressants that were contraindicated based on other medications she was taking, without any prescription from a doctor.

James Sisk, who weighed 300 pounds and had a history of diabetes, hypertension, and obstructive sleep apnea, died at the facility in 2009. A Better Tomorrow staff gave Sisk medications, including Ativan, a benzodiazepine, without his seeing a doctor. He had seizures and died just hours after his admission.

Arizona resident Gary Benefield, who was approaching his fifty-third birthday in 2010, came to A Better Tomorrow to address his alcoholism. Concerned about his emphysema (shortness of breath) and chronic obstructive pulmonary disease (COPD), as well as a recent hospitalization for pneumonia, his wife confirmed in advance that the facility was equipped to deal with his need for constant oxygen. Benefield missed his flight and hitchhiked to the facility, showing up with an empty oxygen tank. The staff gave him antidepressant and anti-anxiety medications from their "extra supply" left by other patients, without Benefield ever being examined by a doctor. The staff on site, having fallen asleep, failed to check on him throughout the night. He was found dead the next morning.

Gregory Thomas came to the facility in 2010 just after being released from a hospital where he had been on a seventy-two-hour 5150 involuntary psychiatric hold.* On the way to the facility, he warned the driver that he was suicidal. Thomas, who was addicted to bath salts, was able to leave the facility without being followed. He committed suicide by hanging himself from a bridge just four hundred yards away from the facility.

Shawn Reyna, admitted to the facility in 2013 in the midst of severe withdrawal symptoms that included delirium tremens, was unable to sleep. Concerned about his paranoia, anxiety, and hallucinations, a staff member suggested an immediate psychiatric evaluation in an emergency room (ER). The suggestion was rejected, with the recommendation instead that Reyna not be disturbed while he slept off his symptoms. He was found dead, having slit his own wrist and throat with a razor.

While this particular facility attracted statewide and even national attention for the number of patient harm incidents, it reflected an industry-wide problem as the opioid crisis was worsening. As a healthcare lawyer, I was used to giving advice on issues of fraud and abuse avoidance and compliance with licensing and operational requirements. The most I would typically delve into clinical issues would be drafting an informed consent document or developing guidelines for documenting medical necessity. And yet the calls started to come in from around the country about serious patient-harm incidents. The themes were consistent: residents smuggling in drugs and overdosing; addiction treatment facilities giving out medications before newly admitted clients were seen by the doctor; residents leaving the facility

---

* 5150 is the number of the section of the California Welfare and Institutions Code, which allows a person with a mental illness to be involuntarily detained for a 72-hour psychiatric hospitalization.

and overdosing; patients committing suicide on site; and patients with complex health issues dying before 911 arrived.

In response to the Temecula incidents and other similar incidents in Southern California, in 2012, the California Senate Office of Oversight and Outcomes published a report analyzing the issue. The report, entitled *Rogue Rehabs: State Failed to Police Drug and Alcohol Homes, with Deadly Results*, offered an indictment of the regulatory oversight of the industry, noting a "long-term legacy of overlooking dangerous problems" in residential treatment, and a widespread disregard for the state's prohibition against facilities providing medical care.[16]

In reality, the nature of treatment had changed with the opioid crisis. Many more patients, many of them with complex medical needs, were flowing through a system that has been designed for nonmedical programs, and which had no allowance for medical care to be provided. That changed in 2015, with the passage of the Stone Act, which created a new exception to the corporate practice of medicine ban. The Stone Act enabled doctors to provide certain care on site at residential treatment facilities that had applied for and been granted an optional Incidental Medical Services (IMS) certification. IMS-certified facilities would be permitted to obtain patient medical histories, assess patients' health status, manage medications, and monitor patient health condition. The law did not go as far as requiring that all facilities adopt a medical model, and did not address what was supposed to happen in outpatient settings, but it nonetheless addressed a major safety gap in addiction treatment. In many respects, the legal changes created an avenue to address the desperate need for medical oversight in addiction treatment, without acknowledging that, in the age of the opioid crisis, all addiction treatment may require medical oversight.

Patient Brokering and Human Trafficking

While the patient deaths in Temecula were an extreme example of the problems fueled by the rapid growth of and lack of clear standards in addiction treatment, the other rogue practice that has vexed the industry has been patient brokering. The introduction of insurance coverage for addiction treatment over the past decade spawned an unprecedented series of marketing practices that crossed into the arena of human trafficking. Street marketers, call centers, and digital lead-generation centers cropped up around the country selling referrals for thousands of dollars per patient. Marketers simply needed to find people with an addiction wherever they could, even in NA or other peer support groups, and sell them as leads to

> Street marketers, call centers, and digital lead-generation centers cropped up around the country selling referrals for thousands of dollars per patient.

treatment programs. In short order, marketers were paying people cash to refer patients and even paying patients themselves to go drug rehab. In the worst cases, patients could get paid repeatedly, simply by reusing drugs and giving a positive urine drug screening. Some marketers would send people into a drug treatment program as moles, posing as patients in order to recruit and steal away other patients.

If these shocking practices had been attempted in a hospital or medical clinic setting, the facility operators would have run in the other direction, knowing full well that practices like these would lead to serious government intervention, either through criminal investigation or whistleblower cases. In addiction treatment, however, programs happily took these patients, in many cases unaware of the illegality. Likewise, families that unwittingly contacted patient brokers, thinking they were talking to treatment centers, and often without any clue that the programs being recommended were simply the highest bidders for their children.

The regulatory challenge that allowed this situation to develop included outdated and confusing laws and regulations, along with regulators overwhelmed by the explosion of licensing applications and not able to police marketing practices effectively. As just one sign of how overwhelmed state and local law enforcement have been, in the fall of 2018, bipartisan congressional support led to the enactment of Section 8122 of the SUPPORT for Patients and Communities Act, a new federal law making it illegal to give or receive kickbacks for referring a patient to sober housing, an addiction treatment facility, or for UDS screening.

The problems of human trafficking and patient brokering were so disturbing that, in 2017, the organization I chair, the Behavioral Health Association of Providers (BHAP) took the initiative to develop the first-of-its-kind e-learning and workshop training certificate standard for addiction treatment marketing, the C-ATM. I felt strongly that it was essential to create standards where none existed and to create ways to help differentiate good and bad actors in the marketplace.

Having examined the multifaceted state of addiction treatment, we next explore the role of cannabis in society and in relation to the opioid crisis in Chapter 8, then examine the proposed solutions put forward to address the opioid crisis in Chapter 9. In Chapter 10, we'll return to the question of how to make progress on the deeper issues underlying the crisis, and consider where we go from here.

KEY TAKEAWAYS | CHAPTER 7

• •

- The inclusion of addiction treatment as a covered healthcare service in the United States came about through the 2008 Mental Health Parity Act, which called for an end to discrimination between coverage of medical care and behavioral health, and the 2012 Affordable Care Act, which required insurers to cover substance use disorder treatment as a minimum essential health benefit.

- The transition of addiction into healthcare is ongoing, and has involved significant adaptation in the clinical model and licensing rules, with new pressure for evidence-based standards and a more medical focus, exposing tensions between the recovery community's focus on social model programs emphasizing abstinence and sobriety and the medical community's focus on harm reduction, including the role of medication in treatment and recovery.

- The adaptation of addiction to insurance standards has also led to conflict, in some cases as a result of profiteering by marketers and in other cases by a lack of understanding of compliance issues. These initially came to a head over urine drug screening (UDS) but are continuing on a host of issues, including paying for referrals and discounting or waiving deductibles and coinsurance.

CHAPTER 8

CAN CANNABIS AND OTHER ALTERNATIVE THERAPIES HELP FIGHT OPIOID ADDICTION?

"The evidence is overwhelming that marijuana can relieve certain types of pain, nausea, vomiting, and other symptoms caused by such illnesses as multiple sclerosis, cancer, and AIDS—or by the harsh drugs sometimes used to treat them. And it can do so with remarkable safety. Indeed, marijuana is less toxic than many of the drugs that physicians prescribe every day."

JOYCELYN ELDERS, MD, FORMER SURGEON GENERAL OF THE UNITED STATES[1]

IN THE SPRING OF 2009, Attorney General Eric Holder announced that the DEA would no longer be raiding cannabis collectives. This declaration represented the first significant shift in federal policy: not a change in the law, but a radical change in *enforcement* of the law.

Almost immediately, my phone started ringing off the hook. Entrepreneurs needed advice about cannabis compliance in making products, opening dispensaries, and cultivating. As a result of my expertise on general DEA compliance, people assumed I understood federal and state policy in this very specific area. At first I declined, saying that cannabis compliance wasn't my area of expertise—that they would be better served by someone more knowledgeable about the subject. I told the callers that I would find out who the experts were and share their names.

The problem, I quickly discovered, was that there *were* no legal experts on cannabis; at the time, there was no such thing as a cannabis compliance lawyer, only criminal defense lawyers and political activists. After some soul searching and conferring with many colleagues about the ethical risks, I became the first regulatory attorney in California to start advising on cannabis as a regulatory healthcare and life sciences subject. (Some of these colleagues offered to defend me if we got into trouble for advising on subjects that were illegal under federal law, which thankfully never happened.)

Why did I decide to branch into this area of law? Essentially, I decided that cannabis was simply too important of a topic within healthcare and life sciences to ignore. For me, one of the overriding arguments—apart from the vast, unexplored terrain of healing properties within the world of cannabinoids—was that, while opioids were killing people, cannabis was not. In fact, I discovered, research studies in states that have decriminalized or legalized cannabis have seen reduced rates of opioid prescribing and abuse, and fewer overdose deaths.[2]

Today, in the early years of the twenty-first century, there is no cannabis crisis to parallel the opioid crisis for a simple reason: cannabis isn't deadly. There is no dose at which people overdose on cannabis and stop breathing. Cannabis doesn't kill people by poisoning them. Most of the examples of cannabis dangers have to do with bad decision-making by people who are high, such as getting behind the wheel of car under the influence ("drugged driving") and causing traffic accidents or other dangerous conduct.*

Saying that cannabis is less dangerous than opioids does not mean that we should ignore the problems with it, including the danger that people may self-medicate or use cannabis in unhealthy ways. But as the state-by-state trend toward greater legalization has proceeded, nearly 55 million adults describe themselves as current users—roughly the same number that smoke tobacco cigarettes.[3] Even as increased access to cannabis may reduce reliance on opioids and opioid-related overdose deaths, we need to acknowledge and address negative impacts of increased access to cannabis.

THE COMPASSIONATE USE ACT

In 2009, when I began receiving phone calls for cannabis compliance advice, it had been thirteen years since California voters had passed the 1996 ballot initiative known as Compassionate Use Act, making California the first state in the country to decriminalize medicinal use of cannabis. The law created a profound dissonance between

---

* Two recent studies examining the effects of marijuana legalization on car accidents came to differing conclusions. The Insurance Institute for Highway Safety concluded that legalization in Colorado, Washington, and Oregon caused a small increase in the number of car accidents, while the *American Journal of Public Health* found no increases in fatalities following legalization in Colorado and Washington.

state and federal law. Under the Controlled Substances Act (CSA), cannabis remained a Schedule I controlled substance, meaning it had no possible medicinal use as far as federal law was concerned. The Clinton Administration took the position that the change in California law was meaningless, insofar as federal law continued to criminalize

The law created a profound dissonance between state and federal law. Under the Controlled Substances Act, cannabis remained a Schedule I controlled substance, meaning it had no possible medicinal use as far as federal law was concerned.

marijuana possession, cultivation, and distribution. The federal government threatened to ignore California law and continue raids and criminal prosecutions against physicians.

In January 1997, a group of physicians and seriously ill patients filed suit in federal court, claiming that the federal government violated their constitutional rights by threatening to sanction—even criminally prosecute—physicians for exercising their free speech right to recommend that patients use medical marijuana. In 2002, the Ninth Circuit federal court of appeals unanimously agreed, ruling that doctors had a free speech right to "recommend" cannabis, which they technically could not "prescribe" as a result of its Schedule I status.[4] Writing for the court, Judge Mary Schroeder observed that the federal government's policy of prosecuting doctors for recommending cannabis "leaves…no security for free discussion." In a concurring opinion, Judge Alex Kozinski noted the prevailing evidence on the medical utility of marijuana.

At the same time, the court found that state law did not prevent the federal government from criminally prosecuting anyone who cultivated, dispensed, or otherwise handled cannabis. Irrespective of the recognition of doctors' free speech, pressure from the DEA forced the cannabis community into the shadows for well over a decade after passage of the Compassionate Use Act.

In the interim, more states joined California in decriminalizing cannabis for medical use: Alaska, Oregon, and Washington in 1998; Maine in 1999; and Colorado, Hawaii, and Nevada in 2000. Over the next eighteen years, the number would keep climbing, leaving a shrinking minority of states as holdouts from permitting the use of cannabis for medical purposes. In 2012, Colorado and Washington became the first states to allow adult use for nonmedical (recreational) purposes, a trend that California and five other states have since joined as of this writing.

The backstory of the Eric Holder announcement was that, during the 2008 presidential election, then-candidate Barack Obama had signaled his intention to respect state laws on medicinal use of cannabis. Nonetheless, the DEA, under pre-Obama leadership, continued to raid marijuana collectives. To put a stop these raids, on March 18, 2009, US Attorney General Holder declared a new policy under which the DEA and the federal government were to leave people complying with state law alone, and limit their efforts to stopping people who were trying to misuse the state liberalization for infractions such as interstate trafficking or other criminal activity.

As the Holder announcement underscored, the convoluted, complicated history of cannabis laws in the United States reflects the divergent views its citizens have about marijuana. Against the backdrop of the opioid crisis, the potential efficacy of cannabis as a solution rather than a gateway to addiction is worth exploring.

PART OF THE PROBLEM OR PART OF THE SOLUTION?

Assessing alternative forms of treatment for pain should be at or near the top of the list of things to do to get control of the opioid crisis. In this chapter, we'll explore important questions about where exactly cannabis-based compounds fit into the opioid crisis and what other alternatives may help mitigate the problem, including the following:

- As more states decriminalize cannabis use, are cannabis-based drugs a promising avenue for a therapeutic alternative to opioids for managing pain and aiding sleep? Or is cannabis worsening the problem of addiction and portending even more problems ahead?

- What about possible alternative therapeutics like ibogaine and other plant-based psychedelics, viewed by some as an alternative way to overcome addiction?

- Should the United State remove legal obstacles, including the Schedule I controlled substance status, in order to facilitate clinical research of these naturally occurring psychoactive substances as potential pathways for overcoming addiction?

THE PROMISE OF CANNABIS AND CANNABINOIDS

While most of the activity occurring within the states that have decriminalized cannabis has consisted of cultivation, dispensing, and product manufacturing, a handful of cannabis therapeutics research ventures have pursued significant work in recent decades, seeking to explore the potential benefits of the various compounds within cannabis.

Raphael Mechoulam, PhD, an Israeli scientist, is credited with the scientific discovery isolating several hundred of distinct cannabinoid compounds, including THC, in 1964. In 1988, a team of scientists led by Allyn Howlett, PhD, and William Devane, PhD, discovered an internal endocannabinoid receptor in a rat brain. By 1990, researcher Miles Herkenham, PhD, had established locations of endogenous human cannabinoid receptors.

In other words, these scientists found that just as our bodies have receptors that make opioids so powerful, humans are also hardwired internally with a separate system of cannabinoid receptors in every organ. These receptors interact with the cannabinoid compounds. Many researchers believe that the endocannabinoid system has a significant role to play in human health, and can be positively affected through interactions with cannabinoid compounds. The fact that we are wired this way has important potential for scientific and therapeutic discoveries.

These scientific advances changed the landscape, driving interest in cannabis as an alternative medication for chronic pain. Unfortunately, much of this research has happened outside of the United States, because the Schedule I controlled substance status continues to obstruct domestic research. The DEA and FDA continue to impede the development of cannabis products in the US, requiring DEA licensure of the research site and sourcing of cannabis only from the National Institute on Drug Abuse. This has driven a number of our clients outside the country, to more welcoming, less restrictive research environments such as in Europe and Israel—the latter of which already is a popular multi-national clinical trial site for American biotech companies.

Will cannabis-based pain-relieving compounds be discovered that will displace and reduce the need for opioids? Researchers are still in the early days of exploring the power of various cannabinoid compounds on the human body. The FDA has approved a handful of cannabinoid-based medications (Marinol, Cesamet, and Epidiolex) for conditions *other* than pain relief, such as nausea and vomiting associated with cancer chemotherapy, weight loss in patients with AIDS, and seizures. A handful of other countries (including Canada and the United Kingdom) have approved a cannabinoid medication, Sativex, a THC-CBD combination medication, for particular kinds of pain relief, such as to alleviate cancer pain and for symptomatic relief of neuro-pathic pain related to multiple sclerosis and other conditions.

The broader picture on cannabis and pain relief is mixed.[5] While research has supported the claim that can-nabinoids may reduce inflam-mation and resulting pain,[6] it also suggests that cannabinoids may not directly reduce pain.[7] Instead, THC and other can-nabinoids may simply make it easier for people to regulate the emotional dimension of pain and associated sensations.[8] Even if this conclusion is more firmly established in the future, it still marks a meaningful alternative option to opioids.

> While research has supported the claim that cannabinoids may reduce inflammation and resulting pain, it also suggests that cannabinoids may not directly reduce pain. Instead, THC and other cannabinoids may simply make it easier for people to regulate the emotional dimension of pain and associated sensations.

In the end, the most that can be said about cannabinoids in terms of an alternative solution to opioids for pain is that they hold out promise that requires further exploration, as reflected by the fact that only a handful of cannabinoid-based medicines have earned FDA approval, while many more remain in the research pipeline.

There are four primary cannabinoid compounds on which research is focusing:

- **THC** (delta-9-tetrahydrocannabinol): Beyond THC's psychoactive properties, it is believed to help fight glaucoma[9] by reducing intraocular pressure.[10] THC is also reported to alleviate nausea and insomnia. Some studies also show potential benefits easing post-traumatic stress disorder (PTSD) and anxiety.[11] These findings have led to FDA approval of several drugs, including Marinol and Syndros (dronabinol), a synthetic tetrahydrocannabi-nol (THC). These drugs are indicated for alleviating loss of appetite associated with weight loss due to AIDS, and to ease nausea and vomiting associated with cancer chemotherapy in patients who have failed to respond adequately to conventional treatments. The FDA has also approved Cesamet (nabilone), a synthetic similar to THC that inhibits chemotherapy-induced nausea and vomiting.

- **CBD** (Cannabidiol):
CBD has garnered enormous public interest as a cure-all "wonder drug." Some of the interest in CBD relates to the fact that it can be harvested not only from cannabis, but from newly legalized industrial hemp cultivation. Although hemp cultivation was prohibited beginning in the 1930s under the theory that hemp extracts were legally indistinguishable from cannabis, in 2013, President Obama signed into law the Farm Bill, which enabled states to begin authorizing industrial hemp cultivation. As more and more states established hemp programs, state laws defined hemp-sourced CBD (and other cannabinoid extracts) as being completely legal and distinct from cannabis. Meanwhile, the DEA has continued to treat CBD as a Schedule I controlled substance even when it is hemp-sourced. The DEA also harbors suspicions that the claims of industrial hemp sourcing are being exaggerated to cover up actual sourcing from cannabis.

Another source of appeal of CBD may be that, in contrast to THC, it is not euphoric. While many people mistakenly claim that CBD is not psychoactive (which would preclude the possibility of its benefit in treating conditions like anxiety), the more precise distinction is that it is not *psychotropic*, meaning that there is no "high" associated with CBD use. As a result, CBD has seen widespread experimentation in drinks, food, topical compounds, and medications without worry about users getting "stoned."

Much of the CBD product craze is highly questionable, particularly considering the minute quantities of CBD contained in many products and the much more substantial amounts at which physical effects have been documented in research. Nonetheless, CBD is increasingly featured as a component of beauty and wellness. A growing number of Los Angeles-area coffee places will infuse CBD into your beverage for a small upcharge; CBD cosmetic products have proliferated, thanks to its perceived positive effects on psoriasis, acne, and other skin conditions.[12]

Ironically, much of the current appeal of so many CBD may be in reaction to distrust or dislike of pharmaceutical industry products, even as the lack of FDA oversight over the burgeoning CBD product marketplace leaves much to be desired in verifying product ingredients, dosing, and marketing claims. As CBD offerings continue to expand without federal oversight, it is difficult to differentiate the inevitable hype and fakery from legitimate uses.

Meanwhile, the most promising potential for CBD is on therapeutic uses. Multiple studies going back over twenty-five years indicate that CBD relieves anxiety, making it a promising alternative to benzodiazepine anti-anxiety medications like alprazolam (Xanax) and diazepam (Valium).[13] Given the dangers of these benzos and other drugs, which show up frequently with opioids in interactions leading to overdose deaths and are often harder to taper patients off than opioids, the prospect of CBD as a natural solution to anxiety demands attention.

Beyond anxiety, at least one study suggests that CBD may be effective as a therapeutic intervention to reduce the risk of relapse in opioid addiction.[14] The possibility that CBD may play a role in preventing opioid relapses[15] is beyond exciting, and worthy of more attention and study.

Finally, in 2018, the FDA approved the first CBD-based drug, Epidiolex, an anti-seizure medication for children with epilepsy. How far will CBD continue to show promise as a therapeutic agent? According to the NIH research database, roughly 150 different studies of CBD's effect on various health conditions are currently underway. CBD is being studied for its ability to relieve pain by reducing inflammation and to lower high blood pressure; it has been or is being studied for possibly alleviating insomnia,[16] as well as for treating neurological disorders and degeneration.[17] CBD may prove effective in the future as an antipsychotic, a diabetes preventative, and even as an inhibitor of cancer growth.

While the slow FDA process of drug approval is likely to mean that more CBD-based drugs are years away, it is reasonable to expect that Epidiolex is just the first of many CBD-based medications. The big question is how long the current open marketplace will be allowed to flourish within particular states before the FDA begins to impose federal regulatory oversight, creating pressure to move more products towards the drug approval process. The future is bright for CBD products—but only time will tell whether its full promise will come to fruition.

- **CBN** (Cannabinol):

   CBN is a mildly psychoactive cannabinoid compound believed to act as a sedative, inducing sleep.[18] Among these other applications, CBN is being studied for other health benefits, including appetite and bone-growth stimulation and the regulation of skin cell production (potentially useful in treating psoriasis or burns). Further research will be valuable to validate these claims.

- **CBG** (Cannabigerol):

   CBG is appears to share many similar effects with the other compounds, including functioning as a sleep-inducing sedative;[19] reducing pain, inflammation,[20] and seizures; stimulating appetite; functioning as an anti-bacterial; and inhibiting cancer cell (tumor) growth.[21] CBG is believed to block metabolic action and to stimulate brain cell growth, reduce inflammatory bowel disease (IBD),[22] and ease symptoms of glaucoma. CBG may also influence the "fight or flight" response to stress and anxiety by suppressing the release of norepinephrine (noradrenaline) and other physiological reactions, including blood flow.[23] There are also suggestions that CBG facilitates cognition.

In addition to these "Big Four" cannabinoids—THC, CBD, CBN, and CBG—there are at least a hundred other cannabis compounds just beginning to undergo research. For example, terpenes—including essential oils such as myrcene, limonene, humulene, and terpinolene, which provide flavor to cannabis—are also believed to work with cannabinoids to regulate the human endocannabinoid system and amplify certain cannabinoid-driven biological effects.

Unfortunately, clinical research on THC and these other cannabinoids in the US has been stifled and delayed by federal policy. The DEA's ongoing regulation of cannabis and all of its chemical compounds (the cannabinoids) as Schedule I controlled substances prevents many American researchers (such as those at many federally funded research centers still wary about federal criminalization) from fully exploring the full potential of cannabinoids.

Nonetheless, cannabinoids have shown significant promise that should not be understated. While their biochemical mechanics are substantially different than opioids, different cannabinoids appear to reduce inflammation, resulting in diminished pain. This makes it easier for patients to emotionally regulate themselves while in pain, and to sleep despite pain. These and other indirect benefits hold out significant promise for alternative forms of treatment to reduce the use of opioids.

> While their biochemical mechanics are substantially different than opioids, different cannabinoids appear to reduce inflammation, resulting in diminished pain. This makes it easier for patients to emotionally regulate themselves while in pain, and to sleep despite pain.

IS CANNABIS A BIGGER PROBLEM THAN A SOLUTION?

As access to cannabis has expanded across much of America, it has also brought a host of challenges. For all of its therapeutic potential, many people whom I respect in both the addiction treatment community and in health policy regard cannabis as a much bigger problem than any solution it may hold. I have struggled personally with this issue, and have come to see cannabis simultaneously as a problem and a solution.

The claim that cannabis is a "gateway drug" to more dangerous drugs, including opioids, is controversial. Many people are skeptical about negative health claims pertaining to cannabis after many decades in which the government propagandized ideologically against "Reefer Madness." On the other side, despite the lack of physical dependence, cannabis is psychologically addictive and can present a risk of impairing people's work and social relationships when abused.

In the course of preparing this book, I informally interviewed roughly three dozen people who had experienced opioid addiction either personally or vicariously through their children. In one story after another, cannabis featured as a starting point of substance use or followed closely after alcohol. The theme that came out of these conversations is that, in many if not most cases, substance abuse begins as a kind of self-medication, leading to addictive behavior. The most common pattern of childhood substance use dependencies (SUDs) that I heard repeatedly started with alcohol stolen from parents' liquor cabinets or at parties, when adults got up to dance or go to the restroom, leaving behind a drink for the opportunistic pre-adolescent or early teenager. Cannabis was a common next step. This trajectory explains why, in my many conversations with addiction treatment providers on the subject, the vast majority fear that the growing (so to speak) availability of cannabis for adult recreational use will greatly increase the prevalence of addiction.

Beyond the general concern about cannabis as a pathway to opioids and other drugs, a separate concern is the neurotoxicity of THC, the primary psychotropic/euphoric cannabinoid compound that makes people feel high. There are serious questions about the impact of THC on brain development, including whether it impairs memory, learning, or neurocognitive performance, or affects emotional regulation.[24] In children, teenagers, and young adults, for example, research studies have raised concerns that cannabis can negatively affect brain development, causing a loss of IQ, increased impulsivity, and diminished attention spans.[25] We need better research to understand the long-term effect of cannabis (and, in particular, THC) on adolescent brain development.

In spite of these serious problems, the movement to decriminalize cannabinoids and accompanying attitudes have shifted so far that it is difficult to see any direction other than further decriminalization. The shift toward allowing adult recreational use seems increasingly to reflect a perspective parallel to alcohol, a substance to which adult access is unlimited despite significant danger, addictive risk, and negative public health effects.

In weighing the problematic aspects of cannabis and the promise of cannabinoids in addressing opioid abuse and addiction, the irony is the absence of national food and drug safety infrastructure. The continued federal ban has meant that CBD and other cannabinoid products are developing in many states without any FDA oversight (except for the handful of approved drugs noted above). As a consequence, the overriding challenge is the uncertainty of what consumers are actually getting from particular manufacturers, and the veracity of the claims being made about particular products. For the time being, the absence of FDA review leaves consumers in a "buyer beware" mode for many promising claims and products, topicals, and medications coming onto the market. It's hard to know the quality, purity, dosing, or response that different people may have to different products. While not ignoring the potential for products that will help people, we must be mindful that we are living in the early days of cannabinoid refinement, where the array of unproven products expands on a weekly basis. As a result, despite the potential to address health issues, consumers need to be cautious about both the claims and contents of cannabis products.

IS THERE A PLACE FOR PSYCHEDELICS IN ADDICTION TREATMENT?

While the public health community is abuzz these days about the promise of medication-assisted treatment (MAT) involving buprenorphine, the addiction recovery community is reluctant to embrace a pharmaceutical solution.[26] Many people regard buprenorphine itself as a problem drug, disguised as a solution.[27]

Ibogaine

One of the most interesting series of conversations I had in my research for this book was with people in recovery from opioid addiction who advocate ibogaine, a plant-based psychedelic derived from *Tabernanthe iboga*, a shrub found in West African rainforests, touted as a more effective way to overcome addiction. By contrast, when I asked public health researchers, they had not even heard of ibogaine.

Advocates argue that ibogaine, which induces hallucinogenic effects, eliminates the withdrawal symptoms that an opioid-dependent person would ordinarily experience, dramatically reducing cravings for weeks or even months.[28] The idea is that ibogaine shocks the system, affecting brain chemistry so that people do not experience weeks of the agonizing withdrawal symptoms. The ability to avoid that unpleasantness, coupled with a significant decrease in cravings to return to opioid use, has driven interest in ibogaine as a natural alternative to MAT.

I also asked many addiction treatment doctors about ibogaine, and heard over and over again that ibogaine is not evidence-based, and how the success stories that have led to all of the attention are anecdotal. However, a number of physicians acknowledged that ibogaine appears to have helped people overcome addiction and requires more exploration.

The problem is that, as with cannabis research, research into ibogaine has been stifled by its Schedule I controlled substance status, meaning it is illegal to import, prescribe, or possess the drug. Before the federal government defunded research on ibogaine, in the mid-1990s there was a limited amount of research.[29] In one of the few reported studies, throughout three decades, 75 percent of people with heroin addictions treated with ibogaine (twenty-five of thirty-three people) reported that their withdrawal symptoms resolved within twenty-four to seventy-two hours. Health concerns about ibogaine raised in the study indicate that the drug is inadvisable for those with heart conditions, may interact negatively with other drugs, and can cause excessive sleeplessness.

Those who want to try ibogaine often travel to clinics outside the United States since ibogaine is a legal form of addiction treatment in many countries, including Canada, Mexico, Costa Rica, Brazil, and several European countries.[30] I have also heard about illegal underground purveyors domestically—and this raises the issue of drug purity in the absence of any oversight. The addiction medicine doctors I interviewed strongly recommended that anyone interested in ibogaine travel to a country where clinics operate lawfully and therefore more safely.

Ayahuasca

Ibogaine may be the most talked-about psychoactive plant with potential to help people overcome opioid addiction, but others have received interest as well. As with ibogaine, ayahuasca—derived from the *Banisteriopsis caapi* vine in South America, and often associated with Peru—appears to have been "discovered" from local usage as a drink for ritual and healing purposes attracting international interest from people seeking psychedelic spiritual and psychological experiences. This interest, in turn, has led to experimentation as a treatment for opioid addiction and dependency.

Where ibogaine is reported to be intensely stimulating to the point of leaving people unable to sleep, people I interviewed describe ayahuasca as a much gentler, more mellow, shorter-lasting psychedelic experience—more of a warm buzz and dream state than the intense, awake, multiday experience of ibogaine. They essentially viewed ayahuasca as a distant second to ibogaine for effectiveness in overcoming addiction. And while ayahuasca may not induce a rapid heart rate, it can pose other dangers, particularly in its interactions with other medications. People who have taken ayahuasca reported vomiting and diarrhea—which has also been reported with ibogaine.

As with ibogaine, ayahuasca is a Schedule I controlled substance in the US. Until more research is permitted, the challenge remains a lack of clear clinical evidence about the efficacy of this and any similar substance, leaving providers and consumers to make difficult choices about which addiction treatment options to pursue.

ALTERNATIVE THERAPIES

One of the most striking features of addiction treatment is a steady stream of emergent therapies, each with physicians and patients who swear that a particular therapy is a panacea—and also a corresponding group rejecting it as ineffective. The reality is that there is no one-size-fits-all solution, just as there is no substitute for good clinical research. At the same time, many consumers and healthcare providers may conclude that the urgent need

> One of the most striking features of addiction treatment is a steady stream of emergent therapies, each with physicians and patients who swear that a particular therapy is a panacea—and also a corresponding group rejecting it as ineffective.

to find solutions for patients suffering from opioid addiction or chronic pain does not afford time to wait. It is interesting to examine two currently popular alternative therapies, nicotinamide adenine dinucleotide (NAD) infusion and the ultra-rapid detox.

NAD Infusion

NAD infusion therapy as a means to detoxify from opioid addiction has garnered some interest. A coenzyme of the vitamin niacin, NAD—infused intravenously for several hours per day for lengths of time typically ranging from ten days to two or three weeks—is believed to ease withdrawal symptoms and diminish cravings.[31] In many cases, people use NAD in conjunction with some other initial course of MAT and follow the infusions with other drugs.

There have been relatively few clinical studies addressing the effectiveness of NAD infusions—or other alternatives—for addiction treatment. As a consequence, the jury is still out on whether anecdotal reports of its efficacy will ultimately be scientifically supportable.

Ultra-Rapid Detox

Ultra-rapid opiate detox (UROD) or anesthesia-assisted rapid opioid detox (AAROD) refer to another treatment methodology intended to accelerate and overcome the worst symptoms of withdrawal. Andre Waismann, MD, credited with pioneering these methods, refers to them as "Accelerated Neuroregulation," or ANR. In this expedited form of detoxification, patients are sedated with anesthetics and receive large doses of naltrexone to "cleanse" them much more quickly, avoiding the worst symptoms of withdrawal.

As with other therapies, ultra-rapid detox has supporters who view it as an unrivaled breakthrough in addiction treatment and skeptics see it as unproven, experimental, and excessive in some of its marketing claims of being painless and enabling opioid detox to be completed in hours rather than days or weeks.

How do you know what—and whom—to believe when it comes to innovations in pain management or addiction treatment? Eventually, clinical research will either bear out or disprove claims as to any therapeutic innovations.

Whatever the answers to the questions about how new cannabis-based therapeutic agents or other approaches may relieve pain that leads people into opioid dependency or enable people struggling with addiction to break the dependency in the short term, cannabis and other alternative addiction therapies cannot take the place of addiction recovery services. Ultimately, as many studies have shown, addiction recovery must encompass a behavioral approach that provides spiritual support, social connection, and tools for handling stress, environmental triggers, or other underlying issues.

KEY TAKEAWAYS | CHAPTER 8

- While cannabis may not result in iatrogenic physical dependency—unlike prescribed narcotics introduced by physicians through medical treatment or diagnostic procedures—it can be psychologically addictive and impair life function (such as work and social relationships) like any abused drug. However, it simply cannot be compared with the horror show of opioids.

- Studies show a significant reduction in opioid addiction as reliance on prescribed opioids diminishes, and fewer people die of overdoses in "cannabis friendly" states.

- In the search for opioid addiction treatment, it is possible to find a variety of therapies that have not been well researched but make promising claims. The best approach may be to approach these alternatives with a degree of openness to the possibilities, balanced by a healthy skepticism.

········ **CHAPTER 9** ········

THE ROADMAP FOR HEALING
A BROKEN SYSTEM

"We always hope for the easy fix: the one simple change that will erase a problem in a stroke. But few things in life work this way. Instead, success requires making a hundred small steps go right— one after the other, no slip-ups, no goofs, everyone pitching in."

ATUL GAWANDE, MD[1]

MOST OF THIS BOOK HAS FOCUSED ON what went wrong in our health system to allow the opioid crisis to happen, and how our government and health systems have responded so far over the past two decades. Two words sum up that response: stopgap measures. From cracking down on doctors to distributing the overdose drug naloxone, until now, we have been strictly in the mode of damage control. So it should not be a surprise that the opioid crisis continues to worsen, leading to more despair and suffering.

So *do* we have a national plan—a prescription for tackling the opioid crisis? There are a multitude of proposals on the table from various government agencies and other institutions for how to address these various strands of the opioid crisis. Some are beginning to happen, while others are still on the drawing board or are small experiments that need to be done on a larger scale.

The key to truly solving the opioid crisis lies in not only drastically reducing overdose deaths, but in addressing two fundamental problems that got us here: poor management of ongoing issues for Americans living in chronic pain and systemic inadequacies in addiction treatment. We need to make effective addiction treatment and recovery support more widely accessible. There are twelve million people living with an OUD, and they need to be able to access to safe and effective addiction treatment and continuing support to maintain their recovery. And we must realistically address the need to provide pain relief to those who need it most.

CARA AND SUPPORT FOR PATIENTS AND COMMUNITIES

Many policies that make up the federal response have already earned official support, if not needed funding, in the two major federal laws addressing the opioid crisis: the Comprehensive Addiction and Recovery Support Act of 2016 (CARA) and the Substance Use-Disorder Prevention that Promotes Opioid Recovery and Treatment (SUPPORT) for Patients and Communities Act of 2018. CARA and SUPPORT for Patients and Communities were both bipartisan, sweeping legislative efforts that combined numerous smaller bills, providing a useful picture of how the response to the opioid crisis is unfolding.

CARA, the 2016 law, sought to expand services across the care continuum, from prevention efforts to support for addiction treatment. It funded and authorized easier access to naloxone for overdose reversal, as well as significant funds for criminal justice to stop the spread of illegal opioids. CARA sought to expand access to MAT, in particular buprenorphine, by, among other things, authorizing physician assistants and nurse practitioners to prescribe and dispense the drug for the first time. CARA provided funding for more addiction treatment and recovery resources, including training programs.

In October 2018, the SUPPORT for Patients and Communities Act demonstrated renewed support for all of CARA's priorities, as well as an expanded set of concerns, including expanding the use of telemedicine for addiction treatment and taking aim at the practice of patient brokering. While many of the law's provisions are addressed in greater detail below, several noteworthy aspects included a new law taking aim at marketing kickbacks in addiction treatment, requiring electronic prescribing (e-prescribing) and electronic prior authorization approvals for controlled substances covered by Medicare Part D.

The big problem for these and all other proposals is that it takes a

> **The big problem for these and all other proposals is that it takes a massive investment of funds, personnel, and effort to disseminate information and implement solutions on a national scale.**

massive investment of funds, personnel, and effort to disseminate information and implement solutions on a national scale. Even after we articulate how to fix the problem, the challenge on the ground will be to find the means to make it happen.

SEVEN NATIONAL PRIORITIES: REDEFINING "O-P-I-O-I-D-S"

To understand the pieces of the puzzle, I've organized the various public health priorities into seven pillars:

- Public health **outreach** and education to improve prevention and early intervention

- Improving **physician** practices

- **Innovation** to improve therapeutics and care

- **Overdose** interventions

- Expanding **interdiction** efforts to stop illegal sources of opioids

- Using **data** analytics to address health risks

- **Strengthening** access to addiction treatment and recovery support

To help remember them, I've organized them below into the acronym **OPIOIDS**: **O**utreach-**P**hysicians-**I**nnovation-**O**verdoses-**I**nterdiction-**D**ata-**S**trengthening Access. These priorities reflect the conventional wisdom that policymakers, legislators, and leading academics have rallied around as the solution to the opioid crisis. While Chapter 10 explains where I think the prescription needs to go further, it is first critical to understand the best thinking out there on how we take the crisis on.

O for Outreach: Public Health Education for Awareness, Prevention, and Early Intervention

One critical pillar of addressing the opioid crisis is to invest resources in **outreach** to improve public awareness of the risks, as well as developing effective prevention and intervention strategies along a continuum of care. At one end of the spectrum, we employ strategies to *promote* behavioral health and wellness, meaning to provide positive support for people to be and stay healthy. Then we can move to outreach strategies trying to *prevent* known risks, such as SUDs and OUDs.

Some prevention activities, including education, awareness, and engagement campaigns, are universal strategies addressed to the entire population. Other prevention strategies are selective to particular at-risk populations targeting specific needs, such as students with poor academic performance or people living in an area with high crime rates. Particular behavior may justify intervention if it is an identifiable problem in the group—for example, high school students who show early signs that they are using illegal drugs and having related problems, like failing grades and skipping school.

Intervention occurs when prevention has not been enough: a person has begun to misuse opioids, so the focus shifts to intervening in the behavior by encouraging the person to seek treatment. If and when that person completes treatment successfully, the focus again shifts to long-term compliance, and, ultimately, to aftercare.

Public Awareness Campaigns

In the course of writing this book, I've had conversations about opioids with hundreds of people. The striking takeaway for me is how much confusion and misinformation is out there about opioids. People have told me how glad they were that their doctor had prescribed a non-opioid medication, only to then share the name of an opioid (such as hydrocodone), which they simply hadn't recognized. People have asked me whether the problem was caused by physician greed. (It wasn't.) People are quick to recite that it all began with drug company marketing. (OxyContin may have been the match that lit the fire, but it took multiple points of system failure for it to spread as it did.)

These examples highlight a massive need for a universal educational media campaign to address the danger of opioids, reduce the stigma associated with seeking help for OUDs, and increase awareness of what is going wrong and resources available for those in need of help. Many people have no idea whether the medication prescribed to them is an opioid, let alone what that means or what the risks are. At the same time, many patients who could legitimately benefit from the relief afforded by opioid pain medications are too concerned about addiction and stigma to even consider opioids as a sometimes-merited option.

In the face of messaging throughout our culture that drug use is normal (particularly with the spread of cannabis decriminalization doing away with the taboo around a longtime illegal drug), it is important to develop credible, coherent messages about drugs.

We have yet to see a campaign about opioids that comes anywhere close to the force and ubiquity of the famous television campaign from 1987, fourteen simple words and fourteen seconds long: "Okay, last time. This is drugs. This is your brain on drugs. Any questions?" The simple force of the image of a greasy, sizzling skillet ("drugs") and an egg dropped and frying ("your brain on drugs") had so much power that, thirty years later, it comes back to mind immediately. The messaging around opioids today is neither as loud or as clear. We live in a time when fragmented media channels make it harder to disseminate the message, making outreach to spread the message much more challenging.

We need to find a way through the noise and the new media landscape to be heard. Younger Americans are "digital natives" who need to be reached with social media outreach that incorporates voices of people to whom they listen. My kids watch videos on YouTube much more than they ever tune in to the type of regularly scheduled television shows where my friends and I saw the "Your Brain on Drugs" campaign.

The other challenge is that, for all the reasons explained at the beginning of the chapter, opioids are a more complicated problem—not just a menace, but also a source of pain relief. We need multiple campaigns here. The messages must be well-grounded in behavioral science and highlight the dangers, including the death toll from opioid misuse and the distinct risks around illegal opioids and the misuse of prescription drugs.

Beyond a universal campaign, we also need campaigns focused on particular at-risk populations. There is a critical need to provide parents, caretakers, and seniors with information about avoiding the risks of opioid addiction, and how to seek treatment.

The dangers and risks of opioids relative to other drugs warrant particular attention, including a focus on fentanyl being mislabeled, killing unwitting drug takers. Alerting people to the realities of the opioid threat may be the best preventive measure; encouraging people to seek help without fear or shame is a powerful interventional strategy available.

Of course, the stories that resonate most for people are when their loved ones are affected. This may have less power in communities where opioid abuse is rampant, but in those where it's often flying under the radar, sharing real stories can be very powerful. I've noticed a trend of a small but growing number of "authentic" obituaries, in which families share information about the addiction that killed the deceased, rather than offering glowing words about the deceased that gloss over it. Honest stories are heart-wrenching and extremely powerful.

Kate O'Neill, sister of Madelyn Linsenmeir—who died in October 2018 of a drug overdose—wrote a frank description of addiction in her sister's obituary and later said in an NPR interview, "It never really occurred to me not to share Maddie's addiction and that part of her life. It was so central to who she was as an adult. Her addiction didn't define her, but it defined the way she lived. And so to not include that would not have been an accurate honoring of who she was."[2]

Expanded Use of SBIRT in Schools and Healthcare Settings

Screening, Brief Intervention and Referral to Treatment (SBIRT) is an interventional approach to identify people who are at risk and need treatment. SBIRT emerged as a healthcare tool for doctors in talking to patients, an efficient way to address a health problem and to motivate people at risk to change their behavior. Typically, the SBIRT brief interventions are five- to thirty-minute sessions that can follow a variety of different models for people who are at risk, as opposed to already dealing with a full-blown addiction or overdose emergency. The goal is to refer and get the person, if willing, into treatment as soon as possible, ideally within twenty-four to forty-eight hours.

One big question is when we are going to start applying the SBIRT model for all of the people who are being turned away from prescription opioids. Instead of simply declining to treat people who are coming to doctors because they are red-flagged for drug use, we need to apply the SBIRT model and find them resources. Our current model leaves these people to find the medicines they seek on the illegal market, letting them

Our current model leaves these people to find the medicines they seek on the illegal market, letting them hit bottom before we provide treatment resources, if they are still alive.

hit bottom before we provide treatment resources, if they are still alive.

The 2018 federal law, SUPPORT for Patients and Communities, reflects the focus on SBIRT, for example, by calling for new SUD screening in the initial examination for new Medicare beneficiaries. While use of SBIRT is an important skill that health professionals need to develop for patients of all ages, perhaps the biggest opportunity identified by policymakers to address the crisis in the years ahead will be its expanded use in schools. In Chapter 10, I make the case that SBIRT, which can be used effectively by trained non-health professionals, is something that more of us need to learn and that we should use in our workplaces and communal organizations.

In school settings, including middle school, high school, and college, SBIRT has potential to be particularly powerful in addressing the risk to younger people. One of the most shocking aspects of the opioid crisis is the age at which overdose and addiction risks manifest. This is not a crisis only at the high school and college level and older, but one that affects middle schoolers ages ten to twelve.[3] Many kids are subject to environmental pressures and individual circumstances that heighten their risk level, including traumatic experiences, foster care, developmental disabilities, and other childhood risk factors. Sadly, one of the most at-risk group of children are those whose parents have OUDs, raising both potential issues for newborns exposed to opioids, and challenges for keeping families together while parents are struggling with their own recovery from OUDs.

P for Physicians

The opioid crisis shined a light on the extent to which **physicians** and other health professionals, including physician assistants, nurses, and nurse practitioners, have not been trained to address treating pain and addiction. Another pillar of the response to the crisis is a focus on physician and health professional education around opioids and developing uniform resources for health professional training, prescribing, and informed consent.

Physician Education on Pain Management and Opioid Prescribing

The problem of inconsistent guidelines and physician training around pain management and opioids prescribing is a massive issue. The vast majority of doctors are not current on best practices with regard to treating pain or prescribing opioids. Other doctors avoid prescribing opioids altogether to bypass the risks, effectively leaving the patient's issue unresolved.

One of the most frustrating things for me as an attorney offering guidance to physicians has been the inconsistency between the Centers for Disease Control (CDC) 2016 and Medical Board of California (MBC) 2014 Guidelines for Prescribing Controlled Substances for Pain. While the CDC guidelines may be the authoritative resource on recommended prescribing practices, physicians in California need to be mindful of significant differences in the approach taken by the MBC.* For example, while the MBC emphasizes the need for primary care physicians (who prescribe half of all opioids) to refer patients to pain specialists, the CDC guidelines emphasize that PCPs should work with their patients to manage pain.** Which is it? The MBC recommends forty-five-day initial opioid trials, and cautions doctors on the risk to patients after ninety days. The CDC Guideline advises that risk is present with a seven-day prescription. The CDC recommends caution over 50 morphine milligram equivalents (MMEs) and

---

* An overview of the CDC Guideline can be found at www.cdc.gov/drugoverdose/pre-scribing/guideline.html. The Guideline itself can be found at https://www.cdc.gov/mmwr/volumes/65/rr/rr6501e1.htm?CDC_AA_refVal=https%3A%2F%2Fwww.cdc.gov%2Fmmwr%2Fvolumes%2F65%2Frr%2Frr6501e1er.htm.
** The Medical Board of California Guidelines can be found at www.mbc.ca.gov/Licensees/Prescribing/Pain_Guidelines.pdf.

avoidance of exceeding 90. The MBC advises caution over 80 MMEs.

This kind of inconsistency is maddening. If we are going to improve physician prescribing practices, we must develop a uniform national curriculum and standard of care for opioid prescribers, as well as an approach for SBIRT and DEA training around controlled substances. There is a need for condition-specific guidelines and training, so that doctors and health professionals have access to better resources to identify the distinct issues around pain management and opioids in different healthcare contexts.

The American Society of Addiction Medicine (ASAM) has recommended that, as a condition of DEA registration to prescribe controlled substances, physicians must complete a course to demonstrate competency in safe prescribing, pain management, and substance use identification. A number of states have adopted continuing medical education (CME) requirements for opioid prescribers, something that is likely to expand further as we develop better resources. These initiatives are positive from a safety and risk management perspective, but they are far from the resources needed to meet the needs of people living in pain (without opioids or with fewer opioids to the extent possible) and to bring physicians up to speed with safe and effective prescribing of opioids when they are necessary.

In my work with physicians in private practice, inside large managed groups and at academic medical centers, the vast majority of physicians think they understand prescribing guidelines, but my sense is that only a fraction actually do. A big part of the problem is that none of us recognize what we don't know, and in the area of prescribing, our knowledge of the risks has changed dramatically. As a result, I constantly find myself alerting doctors to how little they actually know about the current guidelines.

According to the National Opioid Commission Report, only

20 percent of physician prescribers have received training on safe prescribing.[4] For anyone who thinks that physician greed or profit motives are the problem, these issues are a drop in the bucket compared to the lack of physician education. Most physicians could use detailed and specific training on how to analyze and address clinical problems around pain, drug choices, dosing, quantities, and—critically—tapering off these medicines. They also need compliance training on how to document appropriately the grounds for their prescribing decisions. They need training on how to help people in pain who have been flagged as risky, and turned away by the system. The decision to reject patients amounts to making their issues someone else's problem, increasing the likelihood that they turn to illegal sources.

Incorporating and Standardizing Pain Treatment and Addiction Curricula in Medical and Dental Schools

The question about what training would make an impact is different for people who are still in medical school or training as physicians and dentists. There is a valuable opportunity to revise the curriculum and training requirements for future generations of doctors around prevention, intervention, and appropriate treatment of pain, without waiting for them to encounter the issues in practice. New doctors should be well-versed on opioid prescribing and SBIRT. The National Opioid Commission report recommended that the CDC and FDA work with the Accreditation Council for Continuing Medical Education (ACCME), a national certifying organization to develop national training standards that would begin in medical schools and continue through residency programs and into private practice.

Informed Consent

Informed consent refers to the process of disclosing the risks, benefits, and alternatives to a particular therapeutic approach. Over the years,

I've tried to stress to doctors that informed consent is not merely a document that patients sign acknowledging that they understand the risks and alternative options, but also the conversation that takes place around the issues. With respect to opioids, there has not been a standard process of obtaining informed consent, let alone any uniformity in the disclosure itself.

Since the early 2000s, I have been an advocate of informed consents for opioids and benzodiazepines, even if

> Informed consent is not merely a document that patients sign acknowledging that they understand the risks and alternative options, but also the conversation that takes place around the issues.

doctors are not accustomed to offering them for other medications, because they call patient attention to the seriousness of the choice to begin taking these medications. In the wake of all of the data showing risks to patients, conversations to ensure patients understand the risks and the practical instructions around opioids and pain medications are essential. In 2017, New Jersey became the first state in the country to require doctors to have conversations with patients before a new opioid prescription, to discuss risks and alternatives. There is a profound need for better information for patients who are being prescribed opioids and for their families explaining the risks of overdose and addiction. Patients have little idea about the risks that accompany even short-term prescriptions, as well as the temptation to find emotional relief in opioids.

Doing Away with Pain Surveys

As noted earlier, the use of pain survey questions in the US created incentives that fed the growth of the opioid crisis. As late as 2011, the Joint Commission was still pushing pain as "the fifth vital sign" in its publications.[5] In 2016, the Joint Commission finally withdrew the requirement that hospitals survey patients on pain as a standard for accreditation.[6] Despite this, many providers and facilities have continued to utilize these surveys. Doing away with this legacy should be a priority, given the problem of patient overreporting of pain and incentivization for providers to prescribe opioids to get better scores.

Ensuring Comprehensive Scope of Treatment

CARA and the SUPPORT for Patients and Communities Act both reflected a need to broaden the care continuum for addiction treatment. Citing Shelly Greenfield, MD, MPH, of McLean Hospital in Middleborough, Massachusetts, the National Opioid Commission recommended that all treatment include the following elements:

- Complete evaluation for OUDs and other co-occurring SUDs, psychiatric disorders, and medical disorders

- Consideration of medication assisted treatment (MAT)

- Access to psychosocial treatment in forms such as group, family, or individual therapy in a clinically appropriate inpatient, residential, or outpatient setting

- Treatment of any co-occurring mental health disorders, including post-traumatic stress disorder (PTSD), depression, and anxiety

- Treatment of any co-occurring medical condition, including infectious disease(s), cardiac, dermatologic, or other health issues

My perspective is that comprehensive treatment means going even further beyond the traditional notion of the care continuum to rethink more broadly about the support needed at different stages. Our system should not be built only to support people at points of high severity, hitting the proverbial bottom; given the ubiquitous nature of the risk and the chronic nature of the condition, we need to offer services at varying levels of intensity for people who are early into misuse of opioids or living with more moderate OUDs, as well as options that focus on unique cohorts (such as age-based groups and people with particular physical conditions) with their own distinctive issues.

I for Innovation: More Research and Development to Develop Safer Pain Therapeutics and Care

The deeper we examine the opioid crisis, the more it becomes clear that we desperately need **innovation** to come up with missing pieces of the puzzle to meet the needs of people in pain—without the side effects of physical dependency and addiction that come with opioids. Until we find another drug or device able to replace opioids for so many kinds of pain, we are basically stuck with opioids for certain kinds of pain. One pillar of the national response to the opioid crisis is innovation in the form of new medications and medical devices, as well as a better understanding of the way our brains and bodies work with respect to pain and addiction.

Nonaddictive Pain Medications

One top national innovation priority needs to be for academic medical centers and pharmaceutical companies to develop nonaddictive therapeutics (such as drugs that cure or manage a condition) for pain. We are already seeing promising drugs becoming available, albeit often without insurance coverage, limiting access for all but the wealthiest Americans.

One example of a nonaddictive therapeutic is Exparel (bupivavaine liposome), a long-acting injectable suspension that is used for post-surgical pain for a growing number of procedures. As a longer-acting anesthesia, Exparel enables patients to avoid or reduce opioid usage. Lack of insurance coverage has limited access to the drug, as has the need for professional training to expand its utilization.

Promising areas include new opioid antagonists that reverse overdose, new drugs for detoxification, and opioid vaccines. In fact, the development of the Narcan nasal delivery system grew out of a partnership between the National Institute on Drug Abuse (NIDA) and a drug maker. New therapeutics are also likely to emerge as we develop a deeper understanding of the biology of pain. It is extremely challenging for patients, doctors, and others to understand the full range of new non-opioid treatments available, and we would benefit from more systematic information sharing as new options become available and are assessed to identify the most effective options.

Diagnostic and Digital Advances

There are also many other opportunities around the opioid crisis. We are living in a time of significant scientific advances in research into genomics, neuroscience, and brain function, which can help us develop not only pharmacotherapy, but also diagnostics (such as tests and devices to measure and find conditions) that help us better understand pain syndromes and addiction, and to use biomarkers to help people better understand their risk status for opioid addiction. We may also come to discover effective digital interventions, such as use of smartphone applications that can help support or sustain recovery.

Recent examples of diagnostic advances:

- Smartphone and smartwatch apps that provide behavioral feedback, monitoring, and coaching through reminders to sustain recovery

- Biosensor technologies that can detect substance use in real-time, avoiding the need for the intrusion, delay, and cost associated with urine drug testing

- Wearable devices that and can alert the user, a loved one, or a first responder of respiratory depression and low blood oxygen levels, requiring an injection of naloxone

- Apps on electronic devices (phones, watches) that can function as behavioral coaches and reminders

- Telemonitoring technologies that transmit vital signs

Perhaps most exciting of all is the prospect of medical devices that can provide pain relief by modulating nerves that cause pain sensations.[7] Medical device manufacturers have identified a massive opportunity in offering wearable or implantable devices to take the place of drugs, and we are likely to see a wave of device innovation addressing the opportunity in coming years.

O for Overdoses: Prevention and Intervention

While the long-term solutions to the opioid crisis revolve around **outreach** to expand awareness and prevention efforts, **physician** and health professional training, and research to drive **innovation** towards more drug and device alternatives, the immediate issue that screams out for attention is reducing the number of **overdose** deaths by efforts such as more targeted and effective distribution of naloxone.

Naloxone

As we saw in Chapter 1, if one item of the response to the opioid crisis has garnered overriding national consensus, it is the value of putting Narcan and other forms of naloxone into the hands of every first responder and law enforcement officer in the United States, every hospital and urgent care clinic where people experiencing overdoses show up, and every patient taking home opioids at a dose that puts them at risk for overdose. CARA included funding for healthcare providers to coprescribe naloxone along with buprenorphine and for states to develop "standing order" programs for pharmacists to make naloxone available without doctor prescriptions. In some states, naloxone is available over the counter, while in others it remains a prescription drug.

While everyone agrees we need to naloxone more available, questions abound about the best ways to do so, about how to distribute it, how much to train people on its use, and how to bring its price down. These are real issues. When naloxone is distributed under various grants or by organizations and then goes undispensed for too long, it passes the expiration date, leading to unnecessary waste. In general, naloxone has an active shelf life of eighteen to twenty-four months, but is supposed to have twelve months prior to expiration from the time it is prescribed and dispensed.[8]

Supervised Injection and Needle Exchange

One proposal that remains controversial is supervised consumption sites, also known as "safe injection sites." A related policy proposal has been for needle exchange programs, in which drug users can swap contaminated syringes for sterile ones. The argument in favor of these programs is that they prevent the spread of HIV, Hepatitis B, and Hepatitis C. These infectious diseases accompanied the heroin wave of the opioid crisis, thanks to sharing dirty needles used for an injectable form of heroin.

Seattle, Philadelphia, and several Canadian cities (including Vancouver, Toronto, and Montreal) have adopted variations on supervised injection, and many states have adopted needle sharing programs. The idea behind supervised injection is to establish a location at which people who are addicted can use injectable heroin or other opioids or other illegal drugs with staff on hand to oversee the provision of clean needles, respond to overdoses, and attempt to refer patients to detox and treatment. Opponents argue that safe injection sites essentially facilitate illegal activity in the interest of preventing people from dying of overdoses or infectious diseases transmitted by dirty needles or needle sharing.

Supporters, arguing for a harm-reduction model, assert that the public health advantages of reducing infectious diseases and preventing more deaths override the issue of facilitating illegality.

> The idea behind supervised injection is to establish a location at which people who are addicted can use inject-able heroin or other opioids or other illegal drugs with staff on hand to oversee the provision of clean needles, respond to overdoses, and attempt to refer patients to detox and treatment.

According to this view, these sites offer an opportunity for outreach to the addicted population, and potentially an opportunity to persuade people with addictions who show up and encouraging them to consider treatment as an alternative to continued use.

At present, there is no allowance under federal law for super-vised injection sites, meaning that participants could theoretically be charged with aiding and abetting the use of illegal drugs. That risk has not come to pass in Seattle or Philadelphia, and many more American cities are likely to consider the model in the future.

I for Interdiction: Shutting Down Illegal Sources of Opioid Supply

In light of the extent to which the death toll has been driven in recent years by illegally imported heroin and fentanyl, it is critical that we do whatever we can to limit the supply of illegal opioids entering the country. **Interdiction** of illegal opioids, including fentanyl, its precursor chemicals, and heroin is a key pillar of federal policy.

Interdiction of Importation of Illegal Opioids

While the importation of heroin has been a longtime problem, the issue of fentanyl smuggling is a relatively new phenomenon. Fentanyl is flowing into the United States in massive amounts by mail, as well as over the borders. The low cost of fentanyl due to its lab-based manufacture allows for massive profits. According to the DEA, a few thousand dollars for a kilogram of fentanyl powder can produce hundreds of thousands of pills, translating to millions of dollars. With profits like these, it's little wonder that criminal organizations that were losing marijuana profits as they were squeezed out by state cannabis decriminalization focused intently on the fentanyl opportunity.

As I described in Chapter 1, China has been a major source of illegal fentanyl, with websites offering the option to have fentanyl mailed directly into the country. The Mexican drug cartels are also reputed to have embraced fentanyl. Although the death toll indicates that the flood of illegal fentanyl into the country began in 2013, it appears to have taken three to four years for US Customs and Border Protection (CBP) to adapt and train drug dogs to recognize the scent of fentanyl, which is a challenge given its synthetic origins. The lack of scent-based detection also may have encouraged illegal fentanyl importers to expand trafficking by mail, made easier by a potency that allows the use of ordinary letters and small sizes. This may explain why the first few years of the fentanyl wave of drug overdoses have been so explosive.

For more effective interdiction, CBP needs to develop the capacity to screen inbound international mail effectively before release to the US Postal Service and private carriers for domestic delivery. The need for more trained dogs capable of detecting fentanyl remains a significant limitation; beyond drug dogs, CBP is attempting to utilize Advanced Electronic Data (AED) to identify potential drug shipments using analysis of senders, recipients, and other data. A major leap forward would be algorithmic analysis of the same type that credit card companies use to identify suspicious transactions.

It is interesting to note that what is being emphasized about shutting down illegal opioid trafficking has not been accompanied by calls to ramp up criminal penalties against addicted people caught up in low-level opioid possession. We have a legacy of prisons across America full of people arrested for drug-related crimes. The opioid crisis has brought growing awareness, if not consensus (yet), that the solution does not lie in punishing people who are addicted through our criminal justice system. Many proposals have called to expand a drug court system to route people with addictions into treatment, in lieu of prison. Many policy advocates have called for further decriminalization, using the model of countries like Portugal. Under Portuguese law, people who deal drugs are charged criminally, but people whose only crime is possession of a personal (ten-day or less) supply of any drug, including opioids, is referred to local resources, including medical, legal, and social work options, to learn about treatment and available health services. My sense is that these policies are gaining traction and will continue to do so in coming years as the opioid crisis progresses.

Disrupting Precursor Labs

In addition to stanching the flow of heroin and fentanyl into the country, another key focus for the DEA needs to be disrupting the laboratories and traffickers around the world that are producing the precursor chemicals, NPP and ANPP. These are the starting materials needed to manufacture fentanyl. In one DEA report, six kilograms of pure fentanyl made with these precursor chemicals was enough to make 46 million fentanyl doses.

Take-Back Days

While some of the "supply-side" problem of opioids is coming from criminal organizations, a more basic problem is the enormous amounts of unused, often expired prescription opioids laying around people's homes, which provide a source of drugs for children, adolescents, and other people at risk. Over the past fifteen years, the DEA has organized national "Take-Back Days" to encourage people to turn in their drugs on collection days to eliminate the risk associated with undisposed medications. The National Opioid Commission also recommended encouraging more pharmacies, hospitals, and clinics to become year-round authorized collectors of unused medications.

FDA Oversight

While we generally think of drug manufacturers as the suppliers of legal, prescription opioids, the story of the opioid crisis reflects that, in fact, greed drove pharmaceutical companies into illegal conduct. More than a few people are concerned that FDA decision-makers have a history of being prone to being bought off by the pharmaceutical industry.[9] To prevent future recurrences of the FDA being rendered ineffectual, it is critical that the FDA undertake more aggressive post-market research and surveillance programs to address overdose deaths and other patient harm quickly and aggressively. We need the FDA to expand its oversight into dosing, duration of prescribing for particular indications, and risk issues associated with opioids. The FDA has, in recent years, begun to implement policies to clamp down on abusive practices, but greater attention is needed on issues of misuse, tampering, and diversion, as well as post-market surveillance of addiction and other long-term consequences of drug use.

Validating Patient Use

One persistent concern has been patient diversion, meaning that a subset of people are posing as patients in need to acquire and then sell opioids for their high street value. The National Opioid Commission proposed several mechanisms to prevent diversion, including limitations on mailing prescriptions and also requiring patients receiving prescription fentanyl to provide proof of use, such as empty transdermal patch envelopes, as a condition of getting refills.

D for Data: Using Analytics to Identify Opioid Issues and Intervene Promptly

Along with a focus on outreach, physicians, innovation, overdoses, and interdiction, attention to opportunities to utilize **data** analytics is a key part of national opioid strategy.

PDMPs

As we saw in Chapter 1, prescription drug monitoring programs (PDMPs) predated the opioid crisis, but they have become significant due to their ability track the "last mile" of controlled substances flow—from physician and pharmacy to patient. Key goals include

> Prescription drug monitoring programs predated the opioid crisis, but they have become significant due to their ability track the "last mile" of controlled substances flow—from physician and pharmacy to patient.

- ensuring that prescribing and dispensing data across state lines is integrated into an interoperable national system to provide complete information in clinical decision-making, and also for law enforcement efforts to detect diversion and prescription forgery;

- integrating PDMPs into electronic health records for improved physician and health professional utilization in prescribing pain medicine and treating addiction; and

- providing hospital emergency rooms with diagnostic information on the relevant medication leading to overdose quickly for compliance with the Emergency Medical Treatment and Labor Act (EMTALA), which requires hospitals to screen and stabilize people without regard to their ability to pay.

PDMPs can also play a valuable role in ensuring that naloxone and other overdose drugs are deployed optimally to respond to overdoses. The big challenges ahead for PDMPs will be creating robust but uniform data to support decision-making by health professionals and pharmacies, as well as enforcement efforts to address potential problems.

Limits on Privacy

At the same time that data privacy and security compliance are a growing source of concern throughout our society, the opioid crisis has called into question whether they have gone too far in addiction treatment. In Chapter 1, we looked at the questions raised by the opioid crisis about whether we might be better off with less respect for privacy in the interest of empowering healthcare providers to access information and make informed healthcare decisions for people with SUDs.

The Health Insurance Portability and Accountability Act (HIPAA) establishes a baseline of privacy and data security that many people are well accustomed to. In a nutshell, when you go to the doctor or are admitted to a hospital, you receive a Notice of Privacy Practices, which explains how your information will be used. Under HIPAA, the general rule is that, based on this disclosure, your doctor does not need any further authorization for purposes of treating you (even if this means sharing information with other health professionals who are coordinating your care), for the purposes of getting paid, or for operational purposes, like performing quality assurance functions. As long as your doctor lets you know that he or she is communicating with your family, if you do not object, HIPAA permits that communication.

The challenge is that, in addiction treatment, Title 42, Code of

Federal Regulations Part 2 imposes significantly more stringent limitations that disallow all of the above. Driven by concern about people being stigmatized as addicts for having sought treatment for SUDs, these regulations, which predate the digital era, make it exceedingly difficult to share information about addiction treatment. Conflicts between HIPAA and Title 42 requirements have been a source of frustration for many healthcare providers and payers.

In 2017, the government attempted to revise the requirements to facilitate the use of data for payment and healthcare operational functions such as claims management, quality assessment, and patient safety, and to enable healthcare providers to work with subcontractors. From the healthcare community's perspective, the revisions went nowhere near far enough to let information flow smoothly between different health professionals or to facilitate communications with families. The consequence is that, when it comes to addiction treatment, many providers do not even try to address issues with other doctors or with families. Electronic health records (EHR) systems certainly do not make such information readily available.

The result, as in the tragic case of Jessie Grubb that we discussed in Chapter 1, is that we have too little information sharing, often at the expense of patient safety. Parents and doctors who have treated SUDs are often left out of critical conversations, leading to the prescribing of opioids to people who should not be reintroduced to these drugs. We may very well see a law in the future that rolls back privacy to facilitate more communication among providers and also between providers and families to allow them to be involved in a loved one's treatment. In the interim, the best strategy may be to seek permission to have conversations and learn about patient addiction histories before prescribing opioids for pain.

Improving Accuracy and Tracking Effectiveness

With all of the resources flowing into combating the opioid crisis, there is an urgent need for tracking where funds are going to prevent fraud, abuse, and waste, and also to see what's actually working. It only makes sense to continue funding projects that are producing demonstrable results. Having real-time surveillance data of the opioid crisis at all levels will provide invaluable insight into where the problems are, what prevention and interventional measures are working, what treatment modalities (for pain and addiction) are effective, and which ones are not.

One of the biggest data opportunities is understanding the actual count of opioid-related deaths. For such a pressing social problem, we are relying on inexact numbers and a significant delay; most of the data on which we are basing our policy response is from 2016. Currently, the attribution of causes of death is haphazard, as medical examiners apply inconsistent standards nationally. This leads to suspicions of undercounting and unreliability of the data. Is the problem worse than we think? Not as bad? Lack of reliable data is a challenge unto itself. Every time I hear another politician suggest that opioid deaths have crested and that the worst of the crisis is over, I know they must be looking at bad data.

By developing standardized measurement tools, we can better track data on drug overdose deaths and nonfatal overdoses, as well as progress on prevention, treatment, and interdiction efforts. This, in turn, will enable us to develop coordinate risk-reduction strategies tailored locally and regionally to hot spots of the opioid crisis.

S for Strengthening Access: Breaking Down Barriers to Addiction Treatment Access

The final pillar of national opioid policy is **strengthening** access to care. What percentage of people who need treatment for an opioid use disorder actually *get* appropriate treatment? The 2017 National Opioid Commission reported that only 10.6 percent of people with OUDs who are appropriate for treatment actually receive it. The primary explanations for the nearly 90 percent of people not getting access to care are a need for funding, needed changes to remove legal barriers, and enforcement of requirements that impede care.

IMD Exclusion

From the inception of the Medicaid Program in 1965, The Medicaid Institutes for Mental Diseases (IMD) exclusion is a federal law dating back to 1965, when Medicaid was first created. It prohibits states from receiving Medicaid funds for people under the age of sixty-five who are patients in IMDs, which are defined as "hospital[s], nursing facility[ies], or other institution[s] of more than 16 beds" that treat mental health and substance use disorders.

The IMD is a relic of the pre-Medicare, pre-Medicaid era (pre-1965) when states funded inpatient behavioral health services. The purpose of the exclusion was to prevent states from shifting mental health and addiction treatment costs that they were absorbing at the time through state-run psychiatric hospitals (IMDs) to the federal government. The problem was that by the late 1960s, most state-funded behavioral health institutions were closing, leaving a badly underfunded, massive shortage of residential or inpatient beds for people with mental health and SUD needs—without any alternative available.

While the IMD exclusion nonetheless outlasted the enactment of Mental Health Parity and the Affordable Care Act in 2008 and 2010, the opioid crisis finally undermined it (at least temporarily, until a 2023 sunset) in 2018. Specifically, Section 5052 of the SUPPORT for Patients and Communities Act repealed or narrowed the exclusion by enabling states to reimburse for SUD treatment of patients ages twenty-one to sixty-four in facilities with up to forty beds, for up to thirty total days of care during any twelve-month period. The legal change went far beyond the Center for Medicare and Medicaid Services (CMS) current state-by-state approach of negotiating waivers with roughly half the states, increasing funding for desperately needed behavioral health and addiction treatment infrastructure for Medicaid beneficiaries.

Insurance Coverage

Beyond Medicaid beneficiaries, the challenge of strengthening access also requires us to find solutions for everybody else—the uninsured, people who buy their own commercial health insurance, people who obtain insurance through an employer plan, and other government programs. One of the essential issues in strengthening access to care is providing people with acute or chronic pain non-opioid options to manage pain. This includes non-opioid medications, physical therapy, neurofeedback, and meditation. The challenge in many cases is that opioids

> It is critical to push insurers and government programs to cover non-opioid treatment, even if it means spending more to achieve this priority.

are a preferred option for their low cost. It is critical to push insurers and government programs to cover non-opioid treatment, even if it means spending more to achieve this priority.

For people with an OUD, ensuring life-saving access to affordable healthcare benefits is an essential tool in fighting the opioid epidemic. One of the outgrowths of the way that addiction treatment developed in a silo separate from the rest of our health system is that our model of service delivery is expensive. The challenge is not merely to find effective, evidence-based approaches to recovery, but to find value-based solutions that are sufficiently low-cost that we can make them affordable and widespread under insurance plans of all kinds for a much greater percentage of Americans in need of treatment.

Parity

The 2008 enactment of the Mental Health Parity and Addiction Equity Act (MHPAEA) prohibits health insurers from discrimination in coverage for behavioral health conditions relative to traditional medical health. In essence, it constrains insurers from making it harder for patients to access behavioral health benefits and for providers to be paid for mental health and addiction services.

The MHPAEA instilled hope in the addiction treatment provider community that the longstanding limitations on insurance coverage for SUD treatment were no longer permitted. Addiction treatment programs, for example, had grown accustomed to many limitations that medical providers do not face, including these:

- Prior authorization for coverage of new patients at the time of admission by utilization review nurses

- Nontransparent claims denials

- Requiring proof of collection of deductibles or coinsurance

- Medical management standards limiting or excluding benefits based on medical necessity or medical appropriateness

- Limited provider networks, including use of standards to limit provider admission to participate in networks

- Fail-first "step therapy" policies that require the cheapest option to be ineffective before utilizing other options (such as only authorizing outpatient treatment and denying coverage for residential treatment)

- Restrictions based on geographic location, facility type, provider specialty, and other criteria that limit the scope or duration of benefits for services provided under the plan or coverage

Providers expected that health insurance plan denials of coverage and obstacles to payment of billed claims would fade away once the foregoing practices were prohibited. The problem, as with all compliance requirements, is that these requirements are widely ignored unless and until government agencies begin to enforce them in a way that gets the industry's attention. Until government agencies (in this case, the Department of Labor) begins to police insurance companies and penalize them in a meaningful way for parity violations, many in the industry have adopted a wait-and-see attitude while continuing to engage in discriminatory practices that treat addiction treatment differently than medical care.

The optimal solution to getting compliance would be to establish a private right of action that would allow adversely affected individuals and providers to sue employers and insurance companies for continuing to impose obstacles that limit access to care. (The same lack of a private right of action accounts for a similar problem of noncompliance under the HIPAA privacy and data security laws.) In its original and current form, the MHPAEA lacked "teeth" to help addiction treatment providers or patients do anything about it or to impose penalties for noncompliance.

One key to strengthening access to addiction treatment is to increase the risk of liability, penalties, and active enforcement by the Department of Labor and other agencies to go after violators. The National Opioid Commission Report called for both a standardized parity compliance tool by which to assess health plan behavior, as well as an increase in the scale and risk of penalties for violators.

MAT (Medication-Assisted Treatment)

As we described in Chapter 7, MAT has come to be seen as an integral part of addiction treatment based on the data that it reduces overdose deaths, keeps people away from illegal drugs and in continued addiction treatment, and reduces the risk of relapses. The lingering resistance to its spread is reflected in the 2017 National Opioid Commission Report's observation that MAT is only available in roughly 10 percent of US addiction treatment facilities. This seems to be a legacy of the widely-held perception in the recovery community that MAT is not a true form of recovery, and that goal should be abstinence and sobriety.

Under the Drug Addiction Treatment Act of 2000, physicians who complete an eight-hour training course on its use can obtain waivers to use buprenorphine in their office settings. In 2016, CARA provided $80 million in funding for addiction prevention, treatment, and recovery, allowed nurse practitioners (NPs) and physician assistants (PAs) to obtain similar waivers to prescribe buprenorphine, subject to a five-year sunset provision under which the allowance would expire in 2021 unless renewed or made permanent. Section 2005 of the SUPPORT for Patients and Communities Act eliminated the sunset provision, making NP and PA prescribing of MAT permanent. PAs and NPs continue to require a hefty twenty-four hours of training to qualify for the DEA waiver, in contrast to the eight-hour requirement for physicians.

The regulations have also been changed to expand patient limits. Under DATA 2000, in the first year, physicians could prescribe to no more than thirty patients. In subsequent years, doctors could apply to go up to one hundred patients. In 2017, regulations allowed a doctor with a hundred-patient waiver for at least one year to obtain a waiver for up to 275 patients at a time. The SUPPORT Act formalizes this increase in the patient limit for physicians prescribing MATs, and authorized Medicare coverage for MAT at outpatient Opioid Treatment Programs (OTPs), which previously required beneficiaries to pay out-of-pocket for receiving MAT at OPTs. The Act directed that Medicare reimburse OTPs via "bundled payments," rather than as fee-for-service, as a pilot program focused on what the Act considers to be a "holistic" approach to treatment.

Telehealth

Given the need for more specialized expertise in more care settings related to OUDs, as well as an inadequate supply of appropriately trained professionals in many parts of the country, telehealth—the provision of healthcare services remotely by digital means—is an important part of addressing the opioid crisis.

In many cases, state law and health plan coverage criteria specify physician and mental health professional staffing that is often difficult to find locally. The most promising models for providing high levels of care leverage technology to allow remote providers to evaluate, diagnose, develop care plans, and treat patients. Indeed, this policy was reflected in SUPPORT for Patients and Communities Act provisions intended to expand the use of telehealth. Section 3232 of the Act, for example, requires the Attorney General to issue a special registration to healthcare providers to prescribe controlled substances via telemedicine in certain emergency situations, to ensure emergency access to treatment for patients who lack access to an in-person specialist. The Act also directs the Centers for Medicare & Medicaid Services (CMS) to issue guidance to states concerning telehealth services aimed at treating SUDs, and directs CMS to issue a report to Congress detailing best practices for furnishing SUD services to children via telehealth.

Telehealth not only solves problems on the "supply side" of addiction treatment, but also affords patients more privacy, access, and flexibility about the setting of care. For health plans, telehealth also drives the expense of care downward. The ability to leverage experts who are on point, while avoiding the expense of health professional travel for face-to-face treatment sessions, translates to improved quality at reduced costs—the sweet spot of value-based care. Advances in remote monitoring technologies are close to making ongoing, low-cost support services for sustained addiction recovery a reality.

Expanding Physician Extenders and Staffing to Treat SUDs

Expanding the use of physician extenders—nurse practitioners (and other advanced practice registered nurses) as well as physician assistants—is essential to providing care in areas of the country affected by physician shortages. In the words of the National Opioid Commission Report, "There are simply too few physicians and other clinicians with the requisite training to meet the demands of the estimated 19.4 million Americans suffering from untreated SUDs."

As noted above, the 2016 enactment of CARA allows physician extenders to provide MAT, and the 2018 Support Act went further in making the expanded scope of services for PAs and NPs permanent. This is a significant opportunity not only for addiction treatment providers, but also for hospitals. To meet their obligations under EMTALA to staff appropriately for the emergency and post-stabilization needs of people with SUDs, hospitals need not only NPs and PAs, but also recovery coaches and community health workers to provide services.

Funding Historically Unfunded "Social Determinants" of Recovery

In Chapter 7, we touched on the unique role of the social determinants of health in addiction treatment. *Social determinants* refer to the way that nonmedical economic and social conditions and differences in education, environment, housing, income, and social connections can impact health. One of the striking messages of the National

Opioid Commission Report was the importance of providing social support for addiction by connecting people in recovery to and funding housing, services such as job training, transportation, and childcare, as well as peer coaching.

Historically, sober living homes or recovery residences—drug-free housing for people seeking support in recovery—have been an unlicensed category of housing protected from regulation by the Fair Housing Act and Americans with Disabilities Act. As the opioid crisis has expanded, in many parts of the country—most notably Florida and California—there have been complaints from local residents about the proliferating number of recovery residences and bad practices in some facilities. Media coverage has focused attention on examples of badly operated homes that endangered residents or "sold" them to outpatient addiction treatment programs. The resulting negative attention has led to legislative consideration in Washington, DC, and the states are beginning to regulate sober living.

The National Opioid Commission Report identifies a "critical shortage" of recovery residences, noting their value in taking people out of the problematic environment where their addiction developed and providing a community of peer support. The report recognized the important work done by the National Alliance for Recovery Residents (NARR), with whom I am proud to have worked closely. To spend time with NARR members is to meet a group of some of the most dedicated people in the country on the front lines of the opioid crisis, people who are stretching their limited resources to provide beds for people newly in recovery with no place to go.

The report also noted the importance of sober housing on college campuses to support the growing number of students who need access to addiction recovery support while in school. I cannot write about this issue without thinking of Robert Pfeifer, of blessed memory, a friend and visionary who dedicated himself to the challenge for people who never got to college in the first place or were derailed in college by addiction. His model of Sober College deeply inspires me: young people, aged eighteen to twenty-six, going through the challenge of restarting school and recovery in a supportive environment with academic counselors, recovery coaching, and a healthy social environment of fellow students.

In addition to recommending funding for more recovery residences, the Commission advocated federal funding for recovery coaches, particularly in hard-hit areas, and nonclinical recovery support services (RSS) designed to support people in the early stages of recovery with peer-to-peer programs, jobs, and life-skills training. Given the existing lack of federal or state funding for any of these social supports, this recommendation is encouraging. In the words of the report, peer recovery coaches (who are in recovery from an SUD) and other types of community health workers (CHWs), such as health educators, medical assistants, and community health outreach workers, are "uniquely positioned to be trained to provide substance-use screening, brief intervention, referral management, and health and community linkages in primary care and emergency room settings, and to provide outreach and care to substance using homeless populations."

Put simply, no one has credibility with a person considering the hard work of addiction recovery like a peer recovery coach who has done the same work. Peer recovery coaches can offer support for people newly in recovery to connect with recovery community organizations (RCOs), which can be a powerful form of support. RCOs around the country are collaborating with healthcare providers, treatment programs, law

Put simply, no one has credibility with a person considering the hard work of addiction recovery like a peer recovery coach who has done the same work.

enforcement, child welfare systems, and other integral stakeholders in helping people achieve and sustain recovery.

CLARIFYING STANDARDS IN ADDICTION TREATMENT

As we addressed in Chapter 7, addiction treatment is in the midst of addressing a massive gap in standards, both for clinically effective, evidence-based treatment, and for operational compliance around marketing, patient safety, residents' rights, and avoidance of fraud and abuse.

The lack of standards has given the addiction treatment community as a whole a black eye, painting everyone with the same brush as the worst actors. Establishing clear guidelines for how addiction treatment programs are supposed to operate will make it easier to distinguish between programs providing good services and those engaged in illegal practices.

Just as the opioid crisis has involved an unusual level of complexity as a public health crisis, so the solutions are likely to be even more complex.

The seven pillars of the OPIOIDS response and the action items identified above are not just a prospective plan, but in many cases are unfolding on the ground. The problem is that they lack the funding needed to accelerate implementation and move from small-scale beginnings to nationwide operations. Even with the necessary budgeting and raising of significant funding to make this action plan into a full-scale reality, the roll-out will still take years.

The one thing we can count on is that until we *as a society* invest in the needed resources, the crisis will continue to worsen.

KEY TAKEAWAYS | CHAPTER 9

- The government and health-policy community have offered numerous recommendations to address the opioid crisis, which tend to have extensive common elements. Two federal laws, the Comprehensive Addiction and Recovery Support Act of 2016 (CARA) and the Substance Use-Disorder Prevention that Promotes Opioid Recovery and Treatment (SUPPORT) for Patients and Communities Act of 2018 have articulated many of these elements—but funding is woefully insufficient to move this agenda forward.

- The common denominators of the policy elements to address the opioid crisis include reducing overdoses by more targeted distribution of naloxone; more research to innovate how we treat pain and addiction and develop new tools; more timely and better use of data, so that we can understand more accurately what is happening on the ground—what is working and what is not—in addressing the opioid crisis; more focus on improving care through health professional education, guidelines, and evidence-based approaches; and shutting down the porous system that allowed drug traffickers to flood the country with black tar heroin and fentanyl.

- The acronym OPIOIDS summarizes seven overarching pillars of our public health priorities in addressing the opioid crisis:

  - O: public health **outreach** and education to improve prevention and early intervention

- P: improving **physician** and health professional practices in treating pain and using opioids

- I: **innovation** to improve therapeutics and care

- O: improving **overdose** interventions

- I: expanding **interdiction** efforts to stop illegal sources of opioids

- D: using **data** analytics to address the crisis

- S: **strengthening** access to addiction treatment and recovery support

CHAPTER 10

REFLECTIONS: WHERE DO WE GO FROM HERE?

"This commandment that I command you this day is not hidden from you nor is it far off. It is not in the skies, that you should say 'Who will go up on our behalf to heaven and take it for us, that we may hear and do it?' Nor is it across the sea that you should say 'Who will go across the ocean for us over the sea for us, and bring it to us, that we may hear and do it? Because the word is very close to you, in your mouth and in your heart, that you may do it."

DEUTERONOMY 30:11-14

WHEN I THINK ABOUT the government and health system's approach for taking on the opioid crisis (Chapter 9), the thing that strikes me most is how much it feels tactical rather than strategic. The policy agenda is as itemized as a grocery list. Given the complexity of this crisis and the multiple points of system failure that led to it, I understand that there are multiple prongs to our approach. But we need a unifying strategy. The biblical quote above is my favorite reminder that, as tempting as it is to throw up our hands and see the solution as far away—big policy ideas that only government regulators can fund and implement—the truth is that many of the keys are in our hands, if we only look for ways that each of us can make a meaningful difference.

In this chapter, I offer a vision for how we can avoid passivity on an individual level and reactivity on a societal level—how we can both formulate and implement a solution. We can find deeper insights into solving the opioid crisis by thinking more strategically about changes in the way we communicate, live, and work.

SOLVING THREE OVERRIDING CHALLENGES

Many of the policy solutions focus on bringing down the death toll, with fairly vague plans for how we will go about fixing our broken systems of pain management and addiction treatment. Just as we saw at the beginning of this book that the opioid crisis comprises multiple intersecting crises—physician-prescribed opioids, black tar heroin, and illegal fentanyl—we need to address three practical challenges involved in solving these problems:

- Bringing down the number of people being hospitalized and dropping dead from overdoses

- Managing the treatment of pain in a way that doesn't leave people suffering in misery, addicted to opioids, or driven to drug dealers pushing illegal substitutes

- Providing effective treatment and ongoing support for people who have become addicted

These overarching challenges all grow out of the opioid crisis, but they are fundamentally different fronts on the battlefield.

The Death Toll

The most urgent priority is containing and reducing the rapidly rising death toll that has resulted from patients dying of doctor-prescribed opioids and people turning to black tar heroin, fentanyl, and assorted other opioids and drugs on the black market. The loss of human life is a tragedy that touches all of us and calls for immediate action.

The death toll is the component of the opioid crisis that drives headlines and makes a continuation of the status quo intolerable. How many more media stories can we watch and read about this horror show? Researchers point hopefully to the drugs that can cut the death toll, from naloxone to buprenorphine. Regardless of which approach gets us there, we simply must get a handle on the death toll.

The problem is that, if we only focus on reducing fatalities, we will have left the real work of addressing the largest sources of human suffering unfinished. Medications that reverse or prevent overdoses like naloxone and buprenorphine improve the numbers without solving the deeper problems of human suffering—of a nation in pain.

When we consider the broader social impact of addiction to opioids and other drugs, including the devastating human costs to personal and family lives, it's clear there is so much more work to be done. We need solutions that go far beyond the power of pills, to re-instill hope and provide the right tools for people to rebuild lives, families, and communities.

The key to truly solving the opioid crisis lies in not being satisfied with tackling the overdose death issue, but in addressing two of the fundamental problems that got us here: the inadequate management of ongoing issues for Americans living in chronic pain, which overlaps with the second problem of people living with an opioid use disorder (OUD). This breaks down into two separate additional priorities: managing pain, and making effective addiction treatment and recovery support accessible.

Managing Pain

For the twenty million people living in chronic pain, the issue is not only avoiding overdosing but also getting desperately needed safe and effective treatment. The opioid crisis has left many doctors fearful of investigation or prosecution. I know many physicians who are unwilling to prescribe—who simply tell patients that they need to be referred to a pain specialist. In years past, doctors might have been nervous about complaints to medical boards over inadequate treatment of pain. In the current climate, though, many doctors feel a new confidence that they can simply abstain when it comes to managing pain.

Patients face an entirely new challenge with pharmacies unwilling to fill prescriptions. In the past, a prescription meant relief. These days, getting the prescription is just the first step, with a significant hurdle remaining about finding a place that will fill it. For patients with limited pharmacy options, this translates into a denial of access to care, which translates into an existence of misery. Multiple people I spoke with described getting legitimate prescriptions after serious injuries only to be treated by pharmacists as criminals. In March 2018, Florida became the first state to impose a three-day limit on opioid prescriptions for new patients, a measure that the federal government is now considering. Other states have imposed five-day and seven-day limits on the maximum number of days allowed for new opioid prescriptions. These steps amount to roadblocks, temporary ways to slow down the problem. We need to look more broadly at long-term solutions, meaning a system that addresses the needs of people in pain, prevents overdoses and addictive disorders, and also works for doctors and health professionals.

Access to Effective Addiction Treatment and Recovery Support

For the twelve million people living with an OUD, we need to address the need for access to safe and effective addiction treatment, and continuing support to maintain their recovery. Given that it's only been a decade since addiction treatment has been acknowledged as an essential part of healthcare in the US, we still have a significant distance to travel to reach evidence-based and effective approaches. We need to find a far broader range of approaches for people at different stages of struggle, in place of a system that waits for people to bottom out before offering treatment resources.

In the words of one parent who shared her daughter's story of addiction with me, "If I had one piece of advice for parents, it is not to wait. The worst advice in the world is that you need to let your kid bottom out. You need to keep your kid alive." This is true not just of parents and loved ones, but of our treatment systems. We need more options and approaches that meet a spectrum of needs.

RETHINKING THE SCOPE OF OPPORTUNITIES FOR ADDRESSING THE OPIOID CRISIS

In Chapter 9, we saw that one unique aspect of the opioid crisis has been the way it cuts across all demographics, with the risk of OUDs hitting children as young as middle school. One consequence has been growing support to invest in prevention and intervention in resources in middle schools, high schools, and colleges.

While I applaud the recognition that we need to start earlier in life in taking on the risks presented by opioids, if I have one overriding message I hope readers will take away from this book, it is this: *we need to think much more radically about where we are fighting this war.* It is valuable that we have identified our schools as the front lines of the fight against opioids, but really, we must take the fight against opioids not only into schools but also into our workplaces, into our churches, synagogues, and mosques, and into all of our community organizations. These settings are places where we can simultaneously acknowledge the pain around us and also take it on earlier—both preventatively and before use and addiction have reached more severe levels. Building awareness is the first step in this fight, and an opening to recognizing everyone around us who is suffering and in pain, and to providing needed support.

In other words, the front lines of the opioid crisis are not only the places where first responders respond to overdoses armed with naloxone, or where doctors are prescribing for pain, or where customs and borders personnel are searching for inbound fentanyl trafficking. The front lines are all around us. And the opioid crisis compels all of us to see ourselves as active agents with a role to play in the effort of proactive prevention and intervention.

This is not to minimize the essential role that so many health professionals and others play in the work of prevention and intervention, or the value of their training and experience. I am not for a second denying the critical role of health professionals and counselors in screening, intervening, and referring people to treatment. But if there is one thing that we all need to do, it is to begin to see ourselves as having a role and responsibility towards everyone we care about. More broadly, we need to step outside our immediate circles and consider those around us who may be less connected to friends and family, yet may need our support in getting treatment or sustaining recovery.

What does this mean? In Chapter 9, I described the continuum of activity that begins with **promoting wellness** and trying to live healthy lives and support everyone around us doing so. **Prevention** means that we actively educate and engage with the people we care about so that more and more people are mindful of the risks, the triggers, the places to turn for help. There is much that we can do simply to create awareness as a first step. **Intervention** is the hardest part, meaning that opioid use, substance abuse, or other at-risk behavior has begun, and we need to find engagement strategies to encourage the person to seek treatment.

One lesson for me has been the extent to which the opioid crisis is literally all around us. The tell-tale signs of drug use are not hard to spot once people are attuned to the signals. In some cases, behavioral changes are a clue. I once had a doctor client whose office manager became addicted to Demerol after a surgery. She was constantly falling asleep at work (which led her to start abusing Provigil, another controlled substance that helps people stay awake). Signs of excessive fatigue are one of many tipoffs.

Isolation is also a big tell that makes intervention difficult. People who were once social and engaged withdraw and isolate themselves as their abuse escalates, making it harder to reach out to them. Other changes are physical, such as less attention to hygiene, or emotional, such as being in a lethargic state. For high-functioning people, the clues may be excuses for missing appointments, excessive drinking (as a result of loss of self-control), withdrawal symptoms, or other changes, such as lost interest in former passions.

These examples are far from exhaustive. There is work involved to learn the necessary skills and become effective agents for prevention and intervention. But I believe there is nothing more important any of us can do to play a role in unmaking this crisis. Whether we do so as teachers in schools, parents, coworkers, or neighbors, getting trained on these skills has enormous potential to enable us to speak knowledgeably and be effective in prevention—with kids and adults of all ages. And it is much easier to stop people from experimenting with opioids or other drugs in the first place than to intervene after they have started.

PREVENTION AND INTERVENTION SKILLS

One of my overarching goals in writing this book was to create a resource that would not only present the *what* of the opioid crisis, but also explain the *why* in a way that would empower and activate readers to become agents of the solution. In addition to presenting this book as an overall resource, I've included a glossary defining terms, a list of resources with ways to find help or learn more about particular challenges, and graphics and key data points. I also wanted to share some thoughts about things all of us can and should be doing.

Abandoning Shame and Communicating
Openly with Family and Friends

Of all of the unfathomable deaths that the opioid crisis has brought, to me, the most tragic to me are the ones where family and friends didn't even realize that someone close to them had a problem. As I explored in Chapter 6, many people turn to opioids as a form of self-medication, unable to ask for or find the help they need. Shame keeps people silent when they should be asking for help. Shame, in turn, keeps friends and family silent when

Shame keeps people silent when they should be asking for help.

they should be asking questions of the person caught up in substance use and asking for support from professionals and friends.

Shame, in short, is killing people. How do we change this?

Personally, when I hear these days that a person has died at an unnaturally young age, my immediate instinct is to scan the obituary for clues about what happened. On some level, I need to make sense of it. Was it a suicide? Addiction? More often than not, the obituaries don't say all that much. Many families choose privacy and respect for the dead over transparency, and it's easy to understand why. But more people are choosing to be painfully honest when the cause of death was an overdose or a suicide. These losses are a powerful opportunity to use the moment purposefully to spread awareness, reduce shame and hopefully prevent more needless deaths.

Consider Madelyn Linsenmeir's widely shared obituary. "If you yourself are struggling from addiction," wrote her sister, Kate O'Neill, "know that every breath is a fresh start. Know that hundreds of thousands of families who have lost someone to this disease are praying and rooting for you."[1] The obituary continues, "If you are reading this with judgment, educate yourself about this disease…It is not a choice or a weakness. And chances are very good that someone you know is struggling with it, and that person needs and deserves your empathy and support."

I admire the courage of Maddie's family in calling attention to her struggles and the struggles of people who are addicted or in recovery—for the sake of helping other people and families struggling with addiction. The more we know, the more we can help and support each other. We all need to be more honest with each other and with everyone—about the perils of addiction, about those we know who are in pain, about those relapsing, about those who have died. We all need to be more honest about how close to home this crisis hits. We all need to ask ourselves if we are doing enough for those in our communities who are struggling with or have been affected by addiction.

We can use open communication as a tool to show empathy. When I visit with friends who are experiencing terrible pain or have family members doing so, the talking—and especially the listening—itself may not solve the problem, but it is an important moment of empathy, for people to feel heard and know that we care about them. In some cases, we may be able to strengthen each other and instill enough hope to relieve pain. In a world where we communicate digitally more and more, there may be no substitute for taking the time to talk and listen to the people around you.

Modeling: Attitudes and Behaviors around Drugs and Alcohol

The first step in protecting the people we care about is taking responsibility for our function as role models. This means taking a hard look not only at our words, but at our actions. What messages are we sending? How we talk and how we act around alcohol, drugs, and medication sends a powerful message not only to our children, but to everyone in our lives.

The most uncomfortable place for many of us to look may be in the mirror. Am I self-medicating when I enjoy a glass of wine or a shot of whisky? Am I acting responsibly? Living in a time when so many people have been lost to substance abuse and are suffering with addiction calls upon all of us to take a hard look at our own behavior. It also means taking seriously signs of impairment—expressing concern rather than amusement when someone has had too much.

See Something, Say Something

The subject of how and when to express concern, whether to your child, family member, coworker, or friend, is a bigger topic than this book. I've gotten some great insights, in particular, from *Difficult Conversations: How to Discuss What Matters Most*, by Douglas Stone, Bruce Patton, and Sheila Heen, as well as *Crucial Conversations: Tools for Talking When Stakes Are High*, by Kerry Patterson and Joseph Grenny.* These and other books are great resources for skill-building. From them, I have taken away the following insights and key steps for expressing concern about substance abuse, remaining engaged with the person you are worried about, and, when possible, intervening.

"See something, say something" has become a public safety campaign about security threats, but it sums up nicely the work we all have to do in not remaining silent as the people we care about proceed down the path into drug use, addiction, and the harms that follow. When we see the first signs of trouble—unanswered questions, unexplained absences, something that worries us—the best thing to do is to express concerns. There are better and worse ways to have these conversations, but the stakes for waiting too long are too high. While this approach may lead to a situation or two in which you confront someone who doesn't have the problem you feared, it may also save lives when your intervention gets someone to take steps they wouldn't have taken otherwise. Delaying doesn't make these conversations any easier.

How you go about having the conversation is critical, because these are inherently risky and difficult, requiring preparation and care to have the best chance of the effect you want. First, before beginning the conversation, it is critical to think in advance about what your

---

* I owe a debt of gratitude to my friend Sharon Rich, author of *Your Hidden Game: Ten Invisible Agreements That Can Make or Break Your Business,* for introducing me to this model, and coaching me on how to use it effectively.

intention is and what the goal of the conversation is. If the goal is to get the other person to take the issue of substance abuse seriously and to be honest and open, how will you move the conversation there? You're not ready to speak until you've got your intention in mind and you've quieted your own emotional baggage. The goal is to be calm, collected, and specific about what you're seeing and what you're thinking. You're likely to encounter resistance and need to make sure you won't be derailed by your own emotions.

Second, be factual. My experience is that it's critical to initiate the conversation with your own observations, without blame, judgment, or criticism. I make a point of using the language of "What I'm seeing is ... ," deliberately avoiding the subject of what I'm feeling. These conversations need to be about presenting the facts and leaving judgments out. Do your best to be heard out fully, without interruption, and to promise to listen with the same expectations.

Third, hear the person out. Ask them questions that demonstrate that you've heard them, and, more importantly, what they think needs to change in order to reach a solution. Be prepared for them to be defensive and in denial. Be ready to respond patiently, avoiding frustration, blame, judgment, or criticism.

At that point, if your concerns have been heard, the person will be prepared to take some action, whether it is seeing a doctor or considering treatment, and the intervention will have been successful. Alternatively, if the person has heard you out, but denies that there is a problem, the best option may simply be to remain engaged.

If the conversation breaks down, it may be best to take a break and come back to the subject later. The short-term goal should be to maintain your intention, express concern without being judgmental, and to make the person you're concerned about feel safe talking with you. Be clear in communicating that you care about the person and share the goal of his or her wellbeing. The long-term goal may be to get the person to take action that addresses the health risk, but that may take incremental action and follow-up.

Being Patient: Five Stages of Change

In intervening in the behavior of people we care about, it's critical to be not only nonjudgmental and come from a place of concern, but also to be patient and persistent. The real question is how we can support the people we care about in a process of changing their behavior. One popular tool comes from a widely used approach called the transtheoretical model of behavior change and features Prochaska and DiClemente's Five Stages of Change. While the model sometimes gets critiqued for oversimplifying, I find it useful as a framework for thinking about how we remain engaged with and seek to help the people we care about move towards positive change, whether it be stopping drug use early, seeking treatment, or taking steps towards recovery after a relapse:

> In intervening in the behavior of people we care about, it's critical to be not only nonjudgmental and come from a place of concern, but also to be patient and persistent.

1. **Precontemplation**: In this phase, the person does not see his or her behavior as a problem and is not thinking about any change.

2. **Contemplation**: Contemplation is the point at which a person acknowledges that they have a problem, but hasn't yet committed to doing anything about it.

3. **Preparation**: At the preparation stage, people have taken small steps toward changing their behaviors. They are starting the process, but do not yet have a sense of success.

4. **Action**: At the action stage, the person has fully changed his or her behavior, albeit for less than six months—the threshold at which we think of maintenance.

5. **Maintenance**: At this point, the person has sustained the change for at least six months, and he or she is committed to not relapsing.

For each situation, the specific positive change is different and can take different amounts of time at each phase, but these are the basic steps that a person has to move through to effect change. Some people add a sixth stage of relapse, when the person reverts to old behaviors. This progression can be useful as a guidepost for what the realistic goals may be in our conversations with people we care about, as well as for measuring their answers. At the conclusion to this book I've included additional resources, including ongoing resources to utilize this framework, on the website #NotAnotherStat, at http://www.notanotherstat.com.

PREVENTION AT HOME

While the television and newspaper headlines of late have focused on school shootings, if any fear puts a pit in my stomach, it's the risk of my own kids descending into the hell of opioid addiction. As a parent of tweens and teens, the most depressing and urgent insights of the 2017 Opioid Commission Report was the need to focus prevention efforts, including SBIRT, on middle schoolers.[2] The takeaway: kids as young as sixth, seventh, and eighth grade are truly at risk, and we need to be looking younger to help prevent addiction and address the youngest victims.

On one level, it seems hard to fathom. Middle schoolers?! What is going on when thirteen- and fourteen-year-olds in eighth grade are exposed to drugs? Yet this is the environment in which we live.

I've seen too many of the children of my friends experience this cycle. They have kids like Lauren, an upper-middle-class teen who, at thirteen years old, began stealing Vicodin and Percocet (leftover from a medical use) from her parents' medicine chest, and stealing money to buy drugs from kids at school.

Thus began a decade of cycling in and out of rehab—completing five programs—endless relapses, overdoses, and currently, another sober living program.

> As a parent, you don't know what to do. You pull your hair out. Each relapse is worse than the time before and the risk of dying keeps going up. Lauren knows it. We know it.
>
> It's been six months. She's in another sober living, and all I can do is pray. My baby is twenty-four years old and I pray that nothing knocks her off her perch.
>
> I don't know what we would have done without the money to pay for Lauren's treatment. I doubt she'd still be alive. There was a three-day stretch where Lauren was gone when I was fully expecting a call from the morgue. I know parents who have picked out funeral clothes for their kids and cemetery plots, with the grim certainty that they will be burying their kids in their twenties.
>
> It's been ten years since this cycle of hell began. I talk to other parents going through the same thing. You keep praying your child will come to the realization they can live without drugs. But they're so vulnerable. It doesn't matter that you love them, that you don't drink and do drugs, that your home is a safe environment.

Lauren is one of almost a dozen kids addicted to drugs whose parents I count as friends. Among the stories, Lauren's painful story is the benign version of events. I have worked with programs filled with kids who ended up on the streets, who are recovering not merely from opioid use but from having been sex-trafficked. These stories are the starkest reminder that the opioid crisis does not discriminate on the basis of the color of your skin, the size of your bank account, or your zip code. However, there's no denying that when you have money to pay out-of-pocket for treatment, you have more options. For the vast majority of American families who cannot afford the revolving door of treatment programs, the odds of surviving, let alone recovering, are much worse.

So I worry for my own kids, my friends' kids, everyone around me. Who's going to be the next to see the warning signs that their child is addicted or the infinitely worse news that their child is gone? What can any of us do about this?

As we explored in Chapter 6, when I compare my 1970s and 1980s childhood with what my kids are experiencing, it is a different world. They are inundated with so much more data and are so much more sophisticated about how they consume it. Smartphones and social media give them access that we could never have imagined a few decades ago, yet they spend less time than previous generations in face-to-face interaction and learning things like conflict resolution or keeping themselves occupied when they are bored. Don't even get me started about social media and its damaging effect on how we curate our lives and compare ourselves to others. Today's kids are dealing with an inordinate amount of stress, and in turn, they exhibit anxiety at higher levels than ever. Anxiety diagnoses increased 20 percent between 2007 and 2012 for kids six to seventeen, according to an April 2018 study.[3]

Even if you believe that your middle schooler is at a distance from the crisis, the preteen years are a critical period when kids are still talking with relative openness. They may be beginning to assert their independence and testing limits, but not to the extent they will in a few years. This is a foundational period of laying the groundwork for the skills, the internal resources, and the knowledge that will steady them as they get older.

My call to action for parents is to begin talking to their middle-school-age children about examples of how people you know are affected by the crisis at all phases: people getting help, people relapsing, and people overdosing. With people dying all around us from the opioid crisis, at eleven years old, my children are old enough to hear about it. I told my kids how sad I was when two of my favorite musicians (Prince in 2016 and Tom Petty in 2017) died opioid-related deaths. I've shared some stories to make sure they understand this is an equal-opportunity disease, and that it's close to home. I've tried to share that it is an ever-present risk that affects above everyone, sometimes for medical reasons like an accident that leaves someone in pain, and sometimes because of social pressure like anxiety that leads people to self-medicate. Above all, I've tried to express that addiction is something treatable, not a character defect. Tackling the opioid crisis calls on us to express honestly our concerns about drug use, without demonizing users or shaming anyone.

Meanwhile, we should be vigilant in trying to prevent unnecessary exposure to opioids. A few months ago, my older two teenage kids were scheduled to have their wisdom teeth removed, and my wife came home from the doctor with two prescriptions for the painkiller Percocet. My immediate question was, wasn't there another option besides opioids? I've seen too many cases where it took relatively little to get someone hooked. People who are wired for opioid addiction don't know their personal risk until they try them. Doctors prescribe them, without mentioning that parents have to be very careful and sparing in their use. In the course of writing this book, I heard many stories of people who didn't want opioids having doctors prescribing them without talking through the decision. My recommendation is to push back and to ask your doctor or your children's doctors for other options. If your doctor insists there is no other option, it's probably time to look for a new doctor.

In my kids' case, after I expressed my concern to the doctor, I learned that I was far from alone. More doctors are now using Exparel, a non-opioid injectable analgesic for post-surgical pain. Unsurprisingly, it's not (yet) covered by insurance, so it's an out-of-pocket expense. Anything that helps us avoid unnecessary use of opioids is a step in the right direction, but it's frustrating that limited insurance coverage removes this an option for many.

PREVENTION AND INTERVENTION AT WORK

With nearly half of all Americans (155 million people) getting their healthcare coverage through employer-sponsored health plans,[4] the workplace is one of the most underutilized and essential frontiers to address the opioid crisis. Employers not only bear a significant share of the cost of care of addiction and pain management, but also suffer the consequences when health challenges affect productivity, since a growing number of people show up to work but are out of it and underproductive.

Over the past two decades, I have advised employers on workplace wellness programs, typically on privacy issues and other federal and state compliance issues. This work has left me convinced that the American workplace is truly the single biggest missed opportunity for taking on the opioid crisis. Just as policymakers have identified schools as an essential setting to take on the work of prevention and intervention, it is time to leverage the unique advantages of the workplace in similar ways.

For most employers, workplace wellness programs consist of weight reduction and smoking cessation programs. These choices are often driven by concern with running afoul of sensitive issues of employee confidentiality and the need for programs to be voluntary. Many employers steer clear of anything more sensitive than encouraging employees to lose weight or quit smoking because of HIPAA privacy concerns or compliance with the Americans with Disabilities Act (ADA), the Genetic Information Nondiscrimination Act (GINA), and Equal Employment Opportunity Commission (EEOC) rules. These laws limit employers from accessing or utilizing some health data, forcing resources on employees, or penalizing employees for not participating in wellness and health programs. Employers are entitled to a snapshot of aggregated information across the company, but are not supposed to be able to access, utilize, or share employees' or their family members' sensitive medical information.

Given how pressing the opioid crisis is, along with the broader, related issues around substance abuse, chronic stress, and anxiety, we are long overdue for rethinking workplace wellness and the largely untapped role of employers. In Chapter 6, we talked about deeper root causes, including the changing nature of work. For so many people, work has been a defining element in their lives. The workplace can be a site of prevention and intervention efforts, utilizing screening tools, assessments, education, and additional supports to help people with OUDs; it can also provide an effective place to focus on chronic stress, anxiety, and the other behavioral health issues that are part and parcel of the path to opioids for so many people.

A relatively small handful of employers have adopted employee assistance programs (EAPs) to support some employees who are ready to ask for help, but the vast majority of employees with OUDs or other substance use issues continue to fly below the radar. Employers simply shy away, limiting their wellness focus to safer territory. Those employers currently paying attention to substance use mainly do so by drug testing prospective hires as a screening tool, in support of "zero tolerance" policies. These programs may work well for particular employers or in particular jobs where drug use puts other people at risk (such as airline pilots), but they are not what I am advocating, which is a broader focus on prevention and intervention by employers and coworkers.

Historically, employers have underwritten the costs of care, but left choices about what types of care actually provided in the hands of employees, healthcare providers, and health plan administrators. In the face of stalled-out political reform of US healthcare, some employers have already identified the opportunity to be a proactive force in healthcare, launching initiatives to reduce their expenses while improving access and quality of care for employees and their families.

Consider the symbolic January 2018 announcement by Amazon, J.P. Morgan Chase, and Berkshire Hathaway that they would be working together to improve cost efficiency, health outcomes, and employee satisfaction across their companies. With a combined workforce of over one million people, the three companies hired healthcare writer and surgeon Atul Gawande to reenvision their healthcare services. It is too early to tell what the impact of this venture will be, but the attention it received highlights an important lesson: in an era when political leaders are divided and Medicare and Medicaid face the challenge of budget constraints, employers may be the driving force of positive change in healthcare.

The new, proactive mindset of employers has shown up in many different examples. I have seen, for example, a growing number of large employers identifying gaps in traditional face-to-face care, and turning to telehealth—the provision of healthcare services remotely by digital means—to improve workforce health. Digital health companies, in turn, are utilizing predictive modeling, analytics, and new engagement approaches (complying with privacy laws) to answer who is at risk in the workforce and what kind of intervention can make the difference. In the context of OUDs and other substance use, technology now makes it relatively simple to use data to identify people who are at risk or are addicted (for example, by their visits to emergency rooms or urgent care centers), and recommend interventions.

Many of the people who are living with OUDs both at work and in school are finding coping mechanisms or ways to keep going on living through less severe use disorders. In my interviews for this book, for example, one doctor shared a harrowing trend of people who use heroin to "party" on the weekends, and take buprenorphine during the week so they can stay on schedule and hold down their jobs. This may be an extreme example. The far more common anecdotes that I heard involved people who manage to stay below the radar. The bottom line is that we are a missing piece of the treatment resources we need, in terms of prevention efforts to spread awareness and programs to meet the needs of people who are living and working through use disorders. If you are interested in more information about how to bring your workplace or community organization into this effort, please check out the Fighting for Opioid Relief through Collaborative Effort (FORCE) project described at the end of this book.

Leading the Way at Work

I believe there are particular opportunities for leaders to nurture cultures within organizations of all kinds where people can feel cared about and be vulnerable with each other. Sheryl Sandberg, the COO of Facebook, provided a powerful model when she coauthored *Option B: Facing Adversity, Building Resilience, and Finding Joy* while navigating her grief following husband Dave Goldberg's unexpected death.[5] When Elon Musk of Tesla and SpaceX had a mini-meltdown publicly in the fall of 2018 and shared a little about the stress he lives with, it was a powerful reminder of the universal experience of stress (albeit not a model to emulate when he turned to drugs publicly in the process).[6] In the spring of 2018, I watched admiringly as basketball player Kevin Love opened up publicly about his struggles with anxiety on the court and expressed the critical message, "Everyone is going through something that we can't see."[7] Imagine how powerful it would have been for Steve Jobs to talk about his stress and anxiety over his illness, or for other prominent leaders to do the same. Imagine what a powerful leadership model it could be if CEOs of other closely watched companies modeled vulnerability about the struggles they are dealing with.

I believe it is an important exercise of leadership to be transparent, authentic and do away with the myth that people who experience success or exercise power are not also struggling. I asked Lisa Marie Presley to write the foreword for my book precisely because I knew she shared this perspective. In place of more tragic overdoses of actors or musicians, I pray that more celebrities will be courageous enough to share their struggles and their journeys to recovery.

In my own leadership, I try to work through the personal discomfort that comes with being open about the stress and anxiety I am experiencing to create space for other people to share, and lean on each other. While every single person experiences different challenges differently, a critical first step is to create an environment in which people feel safe to share, offer, and receive support.

Beyond leadership acknowledging the issue and creating an organizational culture with space for people to share, the next step is moving from awareness to active engagement. What does this look like? The process is likely to look different in different settings, but common elements to consider are health assessments, annual examinations, and proactive programs targeting opioid and other substance use—and also the intertwined issues of pain, anxiety, stress, and depression. With these elements in mind, companies can offer support groups, coaching resources, and incentive programs that motivate people to set personal goals (like reducing drug usage) or use online tools. It is valuable to move beyond self-reporting mechanisms (in which people may provide information that is inaccurate) to programs with verifiable data that track actual activity.

Given the pace and scale of opioid addiction and its underlying causes, employers that fail to face the issue are missing a real opportunity to make a positive, cost-effective difference in their workforce. The workplace is uniquely fertile soil to take on the challenge, because employers stand to gain so much from supporting these efforts. For larger organizations that self-insure and fund employee healthcare, the payoff for addressing problems earlier shows up in reduced healthcare costs from addressing problems preventatively. But even for smaller businesses that don't bear risk or have the same resources as large companies for robust wellness programs, the return on investment for these efforts shows up in a healthier workforce with less absenteeism, better productivity and less turnover.

> The workplace is uniquely fertile soil to take on the challenge, because employers stand to gain so much from supporting these efforts.

The same opportunity is there with respect to people living in pain. In Chapter 5, we explored the biases that lead healthcare providers and payers to push pills as the easiest, fastest, most efficient way to deal with pain. Employers' interests should be aligned with patients in pushing for more nonmedication alternatives to pain. Workplace wellness programs emphasizing stretching, tai chi, meditation, relaxation, and comfort therapies offer a powerful opportunity to keep people healthier and less at risk for OUDs.

Finally, even beyond the potential for employers to provide options, I believe the opioid crisis calls upon all of us to take a new proactive approach with our coworkers, as with our friends, loved ones, and neighbors. Many of us spend as much if not more time with coworkers as we do with our families and friends. Just as we need to develop the skills to talk without judgment or shame to the people in our personal lives about whom we are concerned, we need to do the same things with our coworkers.

Whether in the workplace or in other settings like churches and civic organizations, all of us can appropriately support each other and make it safe to talk about stress, anxiety, and the problems of self-medicating. In the process of tackling these sensitive issues, we're likely to see the forming buds of greater honesty, transparency, caring, and trust bloom in all kinds of other ways. In time, this approach may provide a model for a broadening range of community organizations, extending the opportunity to identify and take action for the sake of the health of people around us. For more information about these efforts, take a look at the FORCE project at the end of this book.

TOWARDS REBUILDING RECOVERY CAPITAL, SOCIAL CAPITAL, AND FINDING NEW PURPOSE

How can we move beyond our immediate circles and think about rebuilding our communities? How can we respond to the economic disruption of modern life—the fact that many people have lost hope of anything getting better—as a factor in the opioid crisis? How do we address the anxiety, depression, and hopelessness that have led people into pain, opioids, and addiction?

America's shrinking middle class points to the pressures our society is facing. When you examine education, health, and wealth in America, it becomes eminently clear that the deck is stacked against the poorest of Americans both in our inner cities and in rural areas—and also those in the middle. The middle class is both shrinking in size and incomes, which in turn means less education and poorer health. A growing number of Americans are faring poorly across these three key metrics (wealth, education, and health), leading to rising inequality, greater stress, higher risks of opioid use, and more. Unless we address the social determinants of health, including stable housing, employment, education, and other forms of social support, the current situation is a recipe for a social time bomb.

We as a society have work to do. Beyond the work needed on our healthcare system, which I wrote about in my earlier book,* we need to focus on increasing understanding and awareness of the nature of the problems underlying the opioid crisis. More awareness will help end the culture of shame that continues to pervade the crisis. We need to dispel the loneliness that leads people to turn to opioids, and to create a culture where we strengthen each other and build each other up. We need to move away from simply waiting to treat addiction and health issues, and toward proactively increasing all of our "recovery capital" or, if you prefer, social capital.

Recovery capital is a phrase I learned from David Best, PhD, a Scottish professor of criminology and addiction studies and the coauthor of *Addiction, Behavioral Change, and Social Identity.* I met Best at a National Association of Recovery Residences (NARR) conference,

---

* In *From ObamaCare to TrumpCare: Why You Should Care* (2017), my coauthor Rob Fuller and I examined the shortcomings that have made the American healthcare system the most expensive in the world with some of the worst outcomes, as measured by life expectancy, disease states, access to care, and other measures. We argue that the rising cost pressure of caring for an aging American population, coupled with federal budget constraints, are forcing systemic transformation irrespective of the philosophical differences between American political parties.

where he introduced me to the phrase "GOYA," short for "Get Off Your Arse." (It sounds better with a Scottish accent.) The central idea is that recovery is an active process in which the person recovers and sustains recovery by doing *something*. Central to recovery, he said, is having a sense of positive purpose that flows from getting off of one's "arse" and engaging in a project that fosters a sense of belonging to a community, of purpose, of positive identity, and of hope.

Recovery capital fits within a broader concept of social capital— another form of "getting off your arse" that applies to all of us. As we touched on in Chapter 6, in *Bowling Alone*, Robert Putnam credits L. J. Hanifan (1879–1932) with coining the term *social capital*. Hanifan, an administrator of rural schools in West Virginia, defined social capital more eloquently as the "good will, fellowship, sympathy, and social intercourse among the individuals and families who make up a social unit" that lead to societal cooperation for the benefit of both the community itself and each individual who can take advantage of "the help, the sympathy, and the fellowship of his neighbors."[8]

Put simply, the concept of social capital is that our relationships with the people around us can be a source of strength and support when they are plentiful and strong. Alternatively, the absence of such relationships can be a source of weakness and vulnerability.

Consider when your school-age child is sick and stays home. Do you have someone to call who can watch the kid? Consider a natural disaster that forces you out of your home. Do you have people to take you in? People who have a network of family and friends to turn to for help in a pinch have high social capital. On the other hand, a person who has no one to turn to when a problem arises has low social capital. Beyond our networks, social capital also refers to the norms and trust in our community. A person whose network of Facebook "friends" offer expressions of sympathy but not actual help has less social capital than someone whose circle of friends jump to help, whether it be it as empathetic listeners or providing concrete support.

The answer to addressing the deeper issues and parallel crises around the opioids crisis may revolve around finding other ways to restore communities in which social capital has been depleted.[9] This is a thread that runs through the crisis of pain, OUDs and nearly every other social problem of our era.[10] We need to find ways to lessen the sense of isolation, through more communal engagement. When we get to know our neighbors and those in our broader communities, we are able to support each other, to take on common projects. We create more ties, more interactions, and more connections that foster a sense of purpose.

Sometimes, the projects that restore social capital are forced on us. A natural disaster requires people to check on neighbors and help get children, the disabled, or elderly neighbors to safety. We have to find places to house the displaced, to clean up, and to rebuild our communities. While the slow pace of this particular crisis may not feel like an emergency to everyone, the catastrophic loss of life of the opioid crisis demands that we marshal our efforts and work together.

The opioid crisis has been building steadily over two decades and, as we've seen, is continuing to worsen. The opioid-related death toll shows no signs of slowing. The peak is still ahead and probably will be for years to come. The lack of federal and state funding to implement solutions on the ground more quickly gives us little reason to expect otherwise.

The opioid-related death toll shows no signs of slowing.

Even for a relentless optimist like me, we have to be honest in acknowledging that we are living in a bleak time. The opioid crisis is credited with shortening the average American life span for the first time since the height of the AIDS crisis. The rising opioid-related death rate for people in their twenties and thirties has driven down overall life expectancy.[11]

At the same time that we are facing grave, multifaceted challenges, I still believe there is reason to be hopeful. In other words, we can reframe all of the crises that we face as opportunities. We can view them as a test of our resilience and our resolve.

The early responses haven't solved the problem, but they have helped. The proliferation of the overdose drug, naloxone; the advancement of prescription drug monitoring programs to identify overprescribing, drug seeking, and diversion of controlled substances; the expansion of insurance and Medicaid coverage for addiction treatment; the pressure to improve pain medicine prescribing and addiction treatment; litigation against dishonest pharmaceutical companies; the crackdown on overprescribing doctors and inattentive pharmacies—these have all been steps in the right direction.

But they are also drops in the bucket.

The policy priorities outlined in Chapter 9 will move us forward, but in many cases they will take time—potentially decades—before we will see their impacts. They also don't get at some of the underlying root causes, meaning that the same pressures that fueled the opioid crisis may simply be redirected toward other self-destructive activities.

AN OPPORTUNITY TO MOVE BEYOND BEING A BYSTANDER

We have the option to worry only about those closest to us, and simply to be bystanders with respect to the broader societal problem of addiction. We are bystanders when we see the warning signs but mind our own business—when we keep our concerns to ourselves, even when we see or sense that something is wrong. We are bystanders when we think to ourselves, "This is not my problem," or "This is none of my business." We are bystanders when we rationalize our decision not to act, when we tell ourselves that someone else will deal with the problem.

If we're going to succeed in addressing this crisis, we need to recognize that this is on *all* of us. We must see ourselves as stakeholders in taking on this crisis, at a one-to-one level with our families and the people we know, and in educating ourselves and those around us. We need to engage with each other and foster a culture that doesn't shame substance abuse.

We also need to be involved in our communities, in helping people in need find additional recovery resources, in supporting law enforcement to save lives, in becoming and staying connected. The solution to this crisis requires all of us to be engaged and moving in the same direction. I launched the #notanotherstat campaign (described in more detail at the end of this book) as a way to share resources around particular facets of the crisis, to encourage people to share their stories and become proactive parts of tackling the opioid crisis. I hope you will join me in the effort to grow the community of awareness and engagement to make a difference in communities across America.

Fixing Our Flawed Healthcare System

As a society, we need to closely examine our healthcare system and the many ways it is deficient in fostering "health." Our healthcare is costlier than almost any other nation, but with surprisingly poor outcomes. We have the most inefficient healthcare system in the advanced industrialized world. Why? Because we're spending a fortune to treat people with late-stage diseases, including opioid addictions, that could have been managed with early support and prevention efforts.

We need to redefine health as a bigger concept than having the appropriate blood pressure and cholesterol levels. That means moving away from waiting to treat people when they are really sick and instead finding new, cost-efficient ways to provide care and support to those who are most likely to need it. There are opportunities for us to help at an early stage by focusing on the social determinants of health: those variables that affect healthcare earlier in peoples' lives, when we can have a more significant, positive impact on their health outcomes.

We need more focus on data- and technology-driven health management strategies, especially for chronic issues that require ongoing care, such as addictions, and a bit less on late-stage treatment. We must reconsider the priorities of our system and strike a better balance for population health.

Before we can begin to reexamine our healthcare system and its failings, though, our healthcare providers must adopt a reasonable approach to helping those in our midst who are in pain. Our providers have gone from addressing pain—and overprescribing for it—to concentrating on stopping the resulting plague of opioids. Those in pain accordingly experienced a massive shift, from easy access to opioids to almost no access, regardless of pain severity. We need to find a middle ground for those who need help.

Strengthening Our Communities and Purpose

The "gift" of the opioid crisis and other underlying challenges of suicidality, pain, anxiety, depression, and hopelessness may be that they offer something to fight for—a reason to call upon each other, to gather and support our communities in a fight to vanquish this plague. In contrast to the issues that divide us as Americans, the opioid crisis holds a unique opportunity to bring Americans together across every divide. If we were ever in need of a shared purpose, look no further.

In many ways, the choice to invest in addressing the opioid crisis is a choice about the future of America. Do we have the resolve to take on this massive challenge? Or are we prepared to live with a shocking death toll? If we think about the opioid crisis as the "canary in the coal mine," it's warning us that we need to address a much bigger, toxic set of problems. What could be a better restoration of purpose than this crisis?

No issue presents the divergence between two possible futures quite so starkly. The pressure continues to ratchet up on our federal and state governments, healthcare organizations, schools, employers—and on all of us—to do more work on prevention of overdoses and addiction, intervention, improving access to and effectiveness of treatment, and addressing all aspects of this crisis.

As I mentioned in my introduction to this book, there is no single pattern to the lives disrupted by this crisis. The risks cut across socio-economics, age, race, ethnicity, and geography. Given how the opioid crisis has cut across all social lines, it will take a truly united approach. Maybe the opioid crisis will be the issue that brings people together.

I've tried to offer some personal strategies for how we can be effective in preventing and intervening with opioid and other drug abuse issues in the lives of everyone around us, whether it's our children or other relatives, our friends, our coworkers, or others in our wider circles.

The way forward in overcoming addiction is simultaneously about rebuilding social networks and also about intensive one-on-one work. People need support, ideally from peers, to mentor them and model a path towards greater strength and resilience—having higher self-esteem, a sense of their own efficacy, and better communication and coping skills.

There is enormous work ahead of us. I wrote this book not merely to recap my experiences working as an attorney on these issues, but to offer a roadmap of what I believe are opportunities for shared focus for healthcare providers, behavioral health organizations, and policymakers. I am devoting all proceeds of this book to Fighting for Opioid Relief through Collaborative Effort (FORCE), a project of the Behavioral Health Association of Providers (BHAP) working in partnership with other organizations, to support further initiatives to help build out specific models of items described above. This includes developing training programs and resources to empower more people to do the necessary work ahead within the contours of our laws and regulations. I am committed to using the #NotAnotherStat campaign and website as a way to share resources.

Together, we can stem the murderous opioid tide, save lives, and improve the care of people struggling with pain and people living with addiction. First though, we must more deeply understand the opioid crisis. That has been the overarching goal of my book as much as proposing ways for us as a society to move toward eradicating this insidious and devastating disease. Wherever you fall on the spectrum of people affected by opioids, as you read these concluding words, I hope you feel more connected and able to take action in dealing with opioid-based challenges. Important as our individual steps forward are, the powerful synergy we can produce facing the opioid crisis together is what will save us.

KEY TAKEAWAYS | CHAPTER 10

- The governmental and health policy responses to the opioid crisis itemized in Chapter 9 have been tactical rather than strategic. Moving from stopgap responses to the opioid crisis to meaningful solutions requires us to address (that is, prevent and intervene in) three distinct problems: people dropping dead of opioid overdoses, people living in pain, and people living with opioid use disorders or addictions. These three strands of the crisis require different resources, without which any proposed solution to the crisis will be incomplete.

- The most powerful way to overcome the opioid crisis is through all of us taking the time to learn and develop the skills of prevention and intervention. Rather than waiting for government solutions, the keys to addressing the crisis are reaching out proactively at home, in schools, in the workplace, and in our communities, opening up communication and expressing concern, without shame, blame, judgment, or criticism so that people can address the deeper issues. In addition to opening up communication, we need to develop the missing segments of our health system to meet the needs of the millions of Americans living in pain and with use disorders.

- On a broader societal level, if ever there was a project that should be a unifying call to arms across all social divides, it is the opioid crisis. Overcoming the opioid crisis calls upon all of us to come together with a renewed sense of purpose to do what we can to rebuild communal foundations that keep people healthy.

GLOSSARY:
ABBREVIATIONS AND TERMS

abstinence: the avoidance of alcohol or drugs (other than prescribed or medically necessary medications) and other problem activities with addictive potential.

Accreditation Council for Continuing Medical Education (ACCME): a national certifying organization that develops national training standards beginning in medical school and continuing through residency and private practice.

advanced electronic data (AED): data used by the US Customs and Border Protection (CBP) to identify potential drug shipments, including fentanyl and heroin entering the US illegally, using analysis of senders, recipients, and other data.

Affordable Care Act (ACA): the 2010 federal law (more formally known as the Patient Protection and Affordable Care Act and more commonly referred to as "ObamaCare") that mandated that insurance companies, employer-sponsored health plans, and Medicaid were required to include coverage in all health plans to treat substance use disorders (SUDs) as an "essential health benefit" (EHB).

Alcohol, Drug Abuse, and Mental Health Agency (ADAMHA): the federal agency formed in 1973 within the US Department of Health and Human Services to reduce the impact of substance abuse and mental illness in the US communities. ADAMHA was reorganized into the Substance Abuse and Mental Health Services Administration (SAMHSA) in 1992.

Alcoholics Anonymous (AA): an international fellowship of people dedicated to recovery from alcohol use, abuse, and addiction through the Twelve Steps. AA is nonprofessional, self-sustaining, and available globally through local meetings.

American Academy of Pain Medicine (AAPM): a medical society (originally named the American Academy of Algology) comprised of physicians focused on pain medicine, which was not recognized as a distinct physician specialty until 1983.

American Academy of Pediatrics (AAP): an organization devoted to children's health with over 67,000 physicians specializing in pediatrics and advocating for the optimal physical, mental, and social health and well-being for all infants, children, adolescents, and young adults.

American Board of Addiction Medicine (ABAM): a medical specialty board that grew out of the American Society of Addiction Medicine (ASAM) that offers board certification of addiction medicine physicians across a range of medical specialties. ABAM sets standards for physician education, assesses physicians' knowledge, and requires and tracks lifelong education.

American Foundation for Suicide Prevention (AFSP): a voluntary health organization, established in 1987, that gives those affected by suicide a nationwide community empowered by research, education, and advocacy to take action against this increasing cause of death for both men and women.

American Medical Association (AMA): an organization founded in 1847 that works to create a healthier future for patients, including advocating against racial and ethnic disparities in healthcare and for scientific advancement, standards for medical education. The AMA has played an important role in the development of US medicine, including developing a program of medical ethics and numerous initiatives focused on improving public health.

American Pain Society (APS): a multidisciplinary community founded in 1987 that brings together a diverse group of scientists, clinicians, and other professionals to increase the knowledge of pain and transform public policy and clinical practice to reduce pain-related suffering.

American Society of Addiction Medicine (ASAM): a professional medical society founded in 1954 and representing over 5,500 physicians, clinicians, and associated professionals in the field of addiction medicine and focused on increasing access and improving the quality of addiction treatment.

Americans with Disabilities Act (ADA): a 1990 federal civil rights law that prohibits discrimination against individuals with disabilities in all areas of public life, including jobs, schools, transportation, and all public and private places that are open to the general public.

Automation of Reports and Consolidated Orders System (ARCOS): an Electronic Data Interchange (EDI) Program created by the Controlled Substances Act of 1970, under which controlled substances pharmaceutical manufacturers and distributors are required to report their controlled substances transactions to the Drug Enforcement

Administration (DEA) through an automated reporting system tracking drugs from the point of manufacture through commercial distribution channels to point of sale or distribution at the dispensing/retail level.

ayahuasca: a hallucinogenic beverage prepared from the bark of a South American woody vine that is classified as a Schedule I controlled substance, but nonetheless has received attention as a potential treatment for opioid addiction.

Behavioral Health Association of Providers (BHAP): a national membership association (for the sake of full disclosure, chaired by the author of this book, Harry Nelson) that provides educational resources, develops standards, and advocates for the advancement of quality and access in addiction treatment and behavioral health.

benzodiazepine: a class of non-opioid, psychoactive drugs that include tranquilizers, sedatives, and anti-anxiety drugs, including alprazolam (Xanax), carisoprodol (Soma), clonazepam (Klonopin), diazepam (Valium), Iorazepam (Ativan), midazolam (Versed), ternazepam (Restoril), and triazolam (Halcion). The combination of benzodiazepines and opioids creates a heightened health risk, and are present in many fatal overdoses.

Big Pharma: a commonly used nickname referring to large drug companies as a politically influential industry. The advocacy group most commonly associated with Big Pharma is the Pharmaceutical Research and Manufacturers of America (PhRMA).

Big Tobacco: a commonly used nickname referring to large tobacco companies as a politically influential industry.

buprenorphine: an opioid partial agonist that is used as a form of medication assisted treatment (MAT) for opioid dependence under brands such as Subutex, Suboxone (in combination with naloxone), and Sublocade, an extend release injectable. Buprenorphine produces more subdued analgesic effects than more typical opioids, enabling a person addicted to opioids to transition without experiencing the extreme discomfort of withdrawal symptoms.

California Department of Public Health (CDPH): the California state licensing agency for healthcare facilities and protection of the public's health. Every state has a distinct agency that licenses health facilities, and in many cases, multiple agencies for different types of facilities.

cannabinoids: the various naturally occurring, biologically active, chemical compounds extracted from cannabis or hemp, such as tetrahydrocannabinol (THC), cannabidiol (CBD), cannabigerol (CBG), and cannabinol (CBN), each of which is being studied for potential therapeutic effects.

carfentanil: a synthetic opioid that is an analogue of (that is, has a similar chemical structure to) fentanyl but is up to 100 times more potent than fentanyl and marketed under the brand Wildnil for use in large mammals, such as elephants. Illegal carfentanil trafficking has been lethal due to its high potency.

Center for Behavioral Health and Statistics Quality (CBHSQ): the federal government's lead agency for behavioral health statistics, as designated by the Office of Management and Budget (OMB).

Center for Substance Abuse Treatment (CSAT): the unit within the Substance Abuse and Mental Health Services Administration (SAMHSA) in 1992 to increase the availability of treatment and recovery services, including medication assisted treatment (MAT). CSAT participates in SAMHSA's national outcomes reporting efforts.

Centers for Disease Control and Prevention (CDC): the federal agency under the oversight of the US Department of Health and Human Services (HHS) that provides data, resources, and expertise to promote and protect public health from threats and to prevent injury and disease.

Centers for Medicare & Medicaid Services (CMS): the federal agency within the US Department of Health and Human Services (HHS) that administers the Medicare program and works in partnership with state governments to administer Medicaid.

chronic obstructive pulmonary disease (COPD): a health condition involving two lung problems—chronic bronchitis (increased cough and mucus production caused by inflammation of the airways) and emphysema (associated with damage of the air sacs and/or collapse of the smallest breathing tubes in the lungs).

chronic traumatic encephalopathy (CTE): a degenerative brain disease found in athletes, military veterans, and others with a history of repetitive injuries to the brain. In CTE, a protein called Tau forms clumps that slowly spread throughout the brain, killing brain cells.

CIDP (chronic inflammatory demyelinating polyneuropathy): a neurological disorder in which there is inflammation of nerve roots and peripheral nerves and destruction of the fatty protective covering (myelin sheath) over the nerves, resulting in neuropathic pain, weakness, paralysis and/or impairment in motor function.

cognitive behavioral therapy (CBT): a technique used to help an individual talk through and manage an undesirable pattern of thought and action (including but not limited to addiction) by understanding the pattern, such as recognizing triggers for an undesirable action, and learning to redirect thoughts and reactions away from the undesirable action.

community health workers (CHWs): lay members of the community who work either for pay or as volunteers in association with the local healthcare system in both urban and rural environments.

Compassionate Use Act (CUA): a 1996 California referendum that voters passed to decriminalize medicinal cultivation and use of marijuana. The CUA was the first statewide law liberalizing the use of cannabis.

complex regional pain syndrome (CRS): a form of chronic pain that usually affects extremities (for example, an arm or leg), most commonly after an injury, surgery, stroke, or heart attack, with resulting pain that is out of proportion to the severity of the initial injury.

Comprehensive Addiction and Recovery Act (CARA): the 2016 federal law enacted with bipartisan support to provide funding for multiple initiatives intended to respond to the opioid crisis, including funding for addiction prevention, treatment, expanded use of medication assisted treatment (MAT), and expanded use of the overdose drug, naloxone.

Comprehensive Drug Abuse and Prevention and Control Act (CDAPCA): a federal law passed in 1970 to implement the Single Convention on Narcotic Drugs, a 1961 international treaty, that included the Controlled Substances Act (CSA).

continuing medical education (CME): educational programs required to be completed by physicians and other professionals to maintain and improve knowledge, skills, and professional performance, as well as to understand relationships with patients, the public, and the profession.

Controlled Substance Utilization Review and Evaluation System (CURES): California's prescription drug monitoring program (PDMP) and database, implemented in 1996 but underfunded and not fully mandatory for prescribing, ordering, administering or furnishing Schedule II through IV controlled substances until 2018.

Controlled Substances Act (CSA): the 1970 law that was part of the broader Comprehensive Drug Abuse and Prevention and Control Act (CDAPCA) implementing the Single Convention on Narcotic Drugs, a 1961 international treaty. The CSA combined four dozen different federal drug laws into one unified system establishing the schedules of controlled substances and focused simultaneously on managing prescription drugs and stopping the flow of illegal drugs.

Drug Abuse Warning Network (DAWN): a public health surveillance system created in 1972 to monitor drug-related deaths and hospital emergency department encounters, DAWN operated under SAMHSA auspices until it was discontinued in 2011 in favor of other data monitoring programs.

Drug Addiction Treatment Act (DATA) of 2000/DATA 2000: the federal law that permitted physicians who completed an eight-hour training course on its use to obtain DEA waivers to use buprenorphine in medical office settings, outside of Opioid Treatment Programs (such as methadone clinics).

Drug Enforcement Administration (DEA): the unit of the US Department of Justice that enforces the Controlled Substances Act of 1970 (CSA), overseeing prescription narcotic distribution and illegal drug interdiction.

durable medical equipment (DME): a category of medical supplies and equipment reimbursed by health insurance, often referred to by the broader category of DMEPOS, durable medical equipment, prosthetics, orthotics, and supplies.

electronic health records (EHRs): medical and other health records that are updated, maintained, and stored in digital format through health information technology (HIT).

emergency medical responders (EMRs): certified personnel who are "first responders," meaning the first medically trained personnel who come into contact with a patient after an emergency response. EMRs have less training than emergency medical technicians or paramedics, but provide transport and immediate lifesaving interventions while waiting for additional resources to arrive at the scene of an emergency.

emergency medical technicians (EMTs): licensed first responders who provide basic, noninvasive interventions to help save lives by stabilizing and safely transporting patients, as well as reducing harm at emergency sites, providing the majority of out-of-hospital care.

Emergency Medical Treatment and Labor Act (EMTALA): the 1986 federal law that requires hospitals with emergency departments to screen and stabilize people in need of emergency medical care without regard to their ability to pay.

employee assistance programs (EAPs): voluntary, work-based programs that offer employees free and confidential assessments, short-term counseling, referrals, and follow-up services for personal and/or work-related problems, including substance use-related issues.

Essential Health Benefit (EHB): the ten categories of services that the Affordable Care Act (ACA) required health insurance plans to cover, including physician services, inpatient and outpatient hospital care, prescription drug coverage, pregnancy and childbirth, mental health services, and substance use disorder (SUD) treatment.

Fair Housing Act (FHA): a federal law protecting people from certain types of discrimination, such as race, religion, sex, and national origin, when renting, buying, or securing financing for housing. In 1988, the FHA was amended to prohibit housing discrimination based on disability, extending protection to recovery residences providing sober housing for people in recovery from addiction.

False Claims Act: the federal law that enables whistleblowers to bring claims to the attention of the government for a share of the recovery to combat fraud against the government. The False Claims Act dates back to the Civil War, when it was enacted to combat fraud by suppliers of the Union Army.

Federal Bureau of Narcotics (FBN): the federal agency within the US Department of the Treasury formed in 1930 to enforce the Harrison Narcotics Tax Act. The FBN was a forerunner of the Drug Enforcement Administration.

fentanyl: a synthetic opioid narcotic analgesic that has approved variations of medications that are Schedule II controlled substances, such as the brands Duragesic and Sublimaze, as well as illegal forms that are Schedule I controlled substances distributed by drug traffickers. The low cost and proliferation of illegal fentanyl has become the primary driver of the rising overdose death toll since 2013, surpassing heroin as a killer.

Food and Drug Administration (FDA): the federal agency within the US Department of Health and Human Services (HHS) that oversees the manufacturing and distribution of drugs, medical devices, food, tobacco, and other consumer products. The FDA was established in

1906 through the enactment of the Food and Drugs Act, and authorized by the Food, Drug, and Cosmetic Act (FDCA) in 1938 with oversight of food, drug, device, and cosmetic safety.

Harrison Narcotics Tax Act: the 1914 law that utilized a tax to eliminate opium and heroin from widespread use.

health information technology (HIT): the digital infrastructure to support the computer systems and the secure exchange of health information between patients, health professionals and facilities, and payers.

Health Insurance Portability and Accountability (HIPAA): the 1996 federal law and regulations that establish privacy and data security standards for health information.

Health and Human Services, Department of (HHS): the federal agency that oversees US health policy through multiple divisions, including the Centers for Disease Control and Prevention (CDC), the Centers for Medicare & Medicaid Services (CMS), the Food and Drug Administration (FDA), the National Institutes of Health (NIH), and the Substance Abuse and Mental Health Services Administration (SAMHSA).

heroin: a highly addictive narcotic morphine derivative that was sold as a branded painkiller in the late 1890s until 1910 and is today a prohibited Schedule I controlled substance. Black tar heroin, a solid resin form that users typically melt down and inject or smoke, became an increasing cause of opioid deaths in 2010 as government pressure led to reduced physician prescribing of opioid medications and people turned to heroin as an alternative.

HillaryCare: the failed 1993 healthcare reform initiative proposed by President Clinton.

Hippocratic Oath: the oath embodying the code of medical ethics undertaken by the medical profession.

hydrocodone: an opioid derivative of codeine that is typically combined with other drugs as an analgesic or cough sedative, such as in the brands Vicodin and Norco, both hydrocodone-acetaminophen combinations.

IBD (inflammatory bowel disease): a term for two conditions (Crohn's disease and ulcerative colitis) characterized by chronic inflammation of the gastrointestinal (GI) tract.

ibogaine: a psychoactive substance from West African shrub iboga that produces psychedelic experiences that are believed to override the discomfort of withdrawal symptoms and cravings caused by opioid dependency. Ibogaine is a Schedule I controlled substance, illegal in the United States but legal as a form of addiction treatment in many other countries, including Canada, Mexico, Brazil, and several European countries.

IMD (Institutes for Mental Disease): the term for state-run psychiatric hospitals. At the time of Medicaid's enactment in 1965, the fear that states would shift costs for psychiatric hospitalization led to the IMD exclusion, a prohibition on Medicaid funding for residential facilities larger than sixteen beds.

International Opium Commission: the 1909 meeting at which the US and thirty-three other counties met to discuss international drug prohibition, leading to the 1912 International Opium Convention to limit the importation and production of opium and opium derivatives, such as heroin.

Insys Therapeutics: the drug manufacturer that marketed Subsys, a fentanyl spray. In 2017, Insys and several of its executives were charged criminally for alleged kickbacks to physicians. While numerous opioid manufacturers and distributors have faced civil lawsuits, Insys is the only opioid manufacturer (other than Purdue Pharma executives) to face criminal charges.

Jessie's Law: federal legislation (not yet enacted) to permit greater communication between doctors and with families relating to substance use treatment history. Jessie Grubb, a thirty-year-old woman living in Ann Arbor, Michigan, was in recovery from heroin addiction. Due to privacy restrictions, her surgeon did not know that he was prescribing OxyContin to a person in recovery. The prescription led to her relapse and overdose death, raising questions about whether privacy protections have gone too far given the need for doctors and families to communicate to avoid risks in prescribing to people in recovery from addiction.

Joint Commission on the Accreditation of Healthcare Organizations (Joint Commission): an independent, not-for-profit organization that accredits and certifies nearly 21,000 healthcare organizations and programs in the United States, providing a nationally recognized symbol of quality and adherence to certain performance standards.

laudanum: a tincture preparation popularized for centuries in which opium was mixed with alcohol.

MBC (Medical Board of California): the California state agency that licenses physicians and oversees medical practice, including prescribing practices, statewide through its disciplinary enforcement process for the purpose of consumer protection.

Medicaid: the federal program (financed in part by states and in part by the federal government and administered by each state) adopted in 1965 to provide healthcare services for people unable to otherwise afford care based on income level.

Medicare: the federal program (financed and administered by the federal government throughout the Center for Medicare and Medicaid Services (CMS) to provide healthcare for people over age 65, disabled within the meaning of the Social Security and Supplemental Security Income disability program, or with end-stage renal disease (ESRD).

medication-assisted treatment (MAT): the use of medications, such as methadone, buprenorphine, and naltrexone to treat people with opioid addictions. MAT is intended to relieve symptoms of opioid dependence and withdrawal, with counseling and support groups or services.

Mental Health Parity and Addiction Equity Act (MHPAEA): the 2008 federal law that declared an end to discrimination against mental health and substance use disorder (SUD) treatment relative to medical and surgical care, such as imposition of more restrictive financial requirements and treatment limitations mental health and SUD benefits.

methadone: a synthetic opioid full agonist that is used as a form of medication-assisted treatment (MAT) to treat heroin dependence. Methadone is an addictive narcotic, but it produces more subdued effects than heroin, enabling an addicted person to refrain from heroin use.

naloxone: a medication best known by the brand Narcan and commonly referred to as the "overdose drug" for its ability to reverse the effect of opioid overdoses when administered by injection or nasal spray. When administered while a person overdosing from opioids is still breathing, naloxone acts as an antagonist of narcotic drugs and causes the pain relief, euphoria, and respiratory suppression caused by opioids to end. Naloxone is also combined with buprenorphine in a brand of medication-assisted treatment (MAT) known as Suboxone.

naltrexone: a medication that acts as an opiate antagonist, cancelling out the euphoria associated with narcotics or alcohol, and used as a form of medication-assisted treatment (MAT). Naltrexone is well known by the brand Vivitrol, an extended-release injectable form that is effective for several weeks after each injection. In low doses, naltrexone has been shown to act as an anti-inflammatory on the nervous system and to reduce the severity of various pain syndromes, including fibromyalgia, multiple sclerosis, and complex regional pain syndrome (CPRS).

Narcotics Anonymous (NA): a community-based organization founded in 1953 and growing out of Alcoholics Anonymous that utilizes the Twelve Steps and social model recovery through local mutual support groups around the world.

National Alliance on Mental Illness (NAMI): the nation's largest grassroots mental health organization dedicated to building better lives for the millions of Americans affected by mental illness.

National Alliance for Recovery Residents (NARR): a recovery community organization (RCO) that works on improving access to quality recovery residences through developing standards, support services, placement, education, research, and advocacy.

National Bureau of Economic Research (NBER): a private, nonprofit, nonpartisan organization founded in 1920 that is dedicated to conducting economic research and to disseminating research findings among academics, public policy makers, and business professionals.

National Committee for Education on Alcoholism (NCEA): now known as the National Council on Alcoholism and Drug Dependence (NCADD), NCEA was founded in 1944 to advocate for the interests of people struggling with and in recovery from alcoholism and drug addiction and the consequences of alcohol and other drug use. Among other things, NCEA championed the idea of addiction as both an individual disease and a public health crisis, and advocated for detoxification in hospital settings and education and clinics to diagnose and treat alcoholism.

National Council on Alcoholism and Drug Dependence (NCADD): an advocacy organization formerly known as the National Committee on Education on Alcoholism (NCEA) that advocates for the interests of people struggling with or in recovery from alcoholism, drug addiction, and the consequences of alcohol and other drug use.

National Emergencies Act (NEA): a federal law that authorizes the President of the United States to declare a "national emergency" in response to extraordinary threats, triggering emergency authority and releasing funding to respond to the emergency. In 2017, President Trump directed the Department of Health and Human Services (HHS) to declare the opioid crisis a public health emergency, but he did not declare it a national emergency under the NEA. Federal funding to address the opioid crisis has been provided under two laws (CARA in 2016 and SUPPORT for Patients and Communities Act in 2018), but not under the NEA.

National Institute of Alcohol Abuse and Alcoholism (NIAAA): one of twenty-seven institutes and centers constituting the National Institutes of Health (NIH), originally created in 1970 under the auspices of NIMH and now its own unit, which is the largest research source in the world relating to the impact of alcohol use on health.

National Institute on Drug Abuse (NIDA): since 1992, one of twenty-seven institutes and centers constituting the National Institutes of Health (NIH), focused on advancing science on the causes and consequences of drug use and addiction, and applying to improve individual and public health through prevention and treatment of substance use disorders (SUDs) and enhance public awareness of addiction. NIDA traces its beginnings to a 1935 federal research project on addiction and formally came into being in 1974 under the Alcohol, Drug Abuse, and Mental Health Administration (a predecessor of SAMHSA), where NIDA was given oversight of the Drug Abuse Warning Network (DAWN) and National Household Survey on Drug Abuse (NHSDA).

National Institute of Mental Health (NIMH): one of twenty-seven institutes and centers constituting the National Institutes of Health (NIH), formed in 1946 to support research on mental disorders.

National Institutes of Health (NIH): the federal agency under the oversight of the Department of Health and Human Services (HHS) responsible for medical research.

nurse practitioners (NPs): licensed registered nurses who complete training and obtain a certification as advanced practice nursing professionals (APRNs), enabling them to provide certain medical services beyond traditional nursing, including examining, diagnosing, and treating patients. NPs work under physician supervision in many states, and they are permitted to practice independently in some states.

opiate: the natural derivatives of opium poppy, such as codeine, morphine, and heroin.

opioid: the broad class of drugs including prescription pain relievers, such as codeine, morphine, their semi-synthetic derivatives hydrocodone and hydromorphone, and pure synthetic forms, as well as illegal drugs, such as heroin and certain types of fentanyl. Opioids are valued for their ability to relax the body, relieve pain, and cause euphoria; they are dangerous due to their suppressing of the respiratory system and the high risk of physical dependency even when taken for short periods of time.

opium: opium refers to the dry latex extracted from the seed pod of the opium poppy (*Papaver somniferum*), which can be processed to extract morphine and codeine. These extracts can be further processed further to produce semi-synthetic derivatives, such as hydrocodone.

opioid-induced hyperalgesia (OIH): the phenomenon of patients experiencing new or worse pain while taking opioids that are prescribed for pain due to increased sensitivity caused by exposure to opioids.

opioid treatment program: a program engaged in medication-assisted treatment (MAT) opioid treatment of individuals with an opioid agonist medication.

opioid use disorder (OUD): a subset of substance use disorder involving opioids. OUDs can involve prescribed or illegal opioids.

Opium Wars: two armed conflicts in China in the mid-19th century between the forces of Western countries and of the Qing dynasty, which ruled China from 1644 to 1911–12. The first Opium War (1839–42) was fought between China and Britain, and the second Opium War (1856–60) was fought by Britain and France against China. In each case, the foreign powers were victorious and gained commercial privileges and legal and territorial concessions, including opium trade that made the problem of addiction pervasive in China.

over the counter (OTC): medications that are deemed to be sufficiently safe that a consumer can purchase the medication without a prescription and use it without physician supervision. Some OTC medications involve safety and potential abuse risks.

overdose prevention site: also known as supervised consumption sites or safe injection sites, overdose prevention sites are legally sanctioned, medically supervised facilities designed to provide a hygienic environment and reduce the nuisance of public drug use for individuals who consume illegal drugs intravenously, such as heroin. Typically, the overdose prevention site provides sterile needles and health professionals onsite to prevent overdose, along with counseling to encourage addiction treatment and recovery.

patient brokering: a crime, also referred to as body brokering, established by the SUPPORT for Patients and Communities Act making it illegal to give or receive money or anything of value in exchange for referring a patient to an addiction treatment program, recovery residence, or laboratory. Paying for patient referrals was already designated as a form of fraud and abuse by the federal Anti-Kickback Statute when occurring within federal health programs such as Medicare and Medicaid, but the new law covers kickbacks irrespective of whether payer is a federal health program.

patient financial responsibility: the portion of a healthcare claim reimbursed by insurance that is required to be paid by the patient, including any deductible, co-payment, or co-insurance (i.e., the percentage of charges required to be paid for by the patient).

paramedics: the highest level of first responders/licensed emergency responders, trained to do invasive and pharmacological interventions.

PDMP (Prescription Drug Monitoring Program): an electronic database that tracks controlled substance prescriptions and dispensations in each state for the purpose of identifying potential safety, risk, or abuse issues in access to medication.

physician assistants (PAs): health professionals who are trained and licensed to provide basic medical services, including examining, diagnosing, and treating patient under the supervision of a licensed physician practice medicine on teams with physicians, surgeons, and other healthcare workers.

primary care physicians (PCPs): physicians who provide the first contact for a person with an undiagnosed health issue and continuing care for many medical conditions, typically on an outpatient basis and in nonemergency circumstances.

PTSD (post-traumatic stress disorder): a health condition triggered by a terrifying event, in which a person may have uncontrollable thoughts, flashbacks, anxiety, nightmares or other reactions that cause the person to reexperience the original terror.

Purdue Pharma: the drug manufacturer that misled doctors and the FDA about the addictiveness of its best-selling prescription opioid, OxyContin, which played a central role in beginning the opioid crisis in the late 1990s.

Pure Food and Drug Act: the 1906 law that required medications containing morphine, heroin, or cocaine to be labeled with identification of their contents.

Racketeer Influenced and Corrupt Organizations (RICO) Act: a federal law designed to combat organized crime and misconduct through prosecution and civil liability for activities performed as part of an ongoing criminal enterprise.

recovery: a process of change, most commonly associated with overcoming a substance use disorder (SUD) or addiction, through which a person improves his or her health and wellness, lives a self-directed life, and strives to reach his or her potential.

recovery community organizations (RCOs): organizations that collaborate with various elements in helping people achieve and sustain recovery.

recovery residences: housing, commonly referred to as sober living homes or sober housing, intended to support substance-free communal living for people in recovery from SUDs or addiction.

recovery support services (RSS): resources that help people in the early stages of recovery through continuing care, peer-to-peer mutual help programs, education, jobs, and life-skills training for abstinence and living without substance use or abuse.

Risk Evaluation and Mitigation Strategy (REMS): a drug safety program that the Food and Drug Administration (FDA) requires for certain medications with serious safety concerns, including opioids, to help ensure the benefits of the medication outweigh its risks. REMS are intended to reinforce safe medication use beyond regular labelling requirements.

Rogue Rehabs: the title of a 2012 report by the California Senate Office of Oversight and Outcomes concerning unsafe practices by drug and alcohol treatment facilities resulting in patient deaths.

Ryan Haight Online Pharmacy Consumer Protection Act (Ryan Haight Act): a 2008 federal law enforced by the DEA regulating internet prescriptions of controlled substances in response to abusive distribution by internet pharmacies.

Schedule I controlled substance: drugs that are determined by the DEA to be unsafe, at high risk of abuse, and have no accepted medical treatment use that would permit them to be prescribed by physicians, including illegal fentanyl, heroin, and cannabis. Possession, use, and distribution of Schedule I substances are illegal under federal law.

Schedule II controlled substance: drugs that are determined by the DEA to have an accepted medical use in treatment but high potential for abuse, including the risk of severe physical or psychological dependence, and are subject to prescribing limitations to prevent abuse. Examples of Schedule II controlled substances are many prescription opioids, such as prescription fentanyl and the brands OxyContin, Vicodin, and Percocet.

Schedule III controlled substance: drugs that are determined by the DEA to have an accepted medical use in treatment but potential for abuse (less than Schedule I or II controlled substances), including the risk of moderate or low physical or psychological dependence, and are subject to prescribing limitations to prevent abuse. Buprenorphine, the active ingredient in Suboxone, is a Schedule III controlled substance.

Schedule IV controlled substance: drugs that are determined by the DEA to have an accepted medical use in treatment but low risk of abuse and dependence, and are subject to prescribing limitations to prevent abuse. Many benzodiazepines, such as the anti-anxiety drug alprazolam (Xanax) and diazepam (Valium) are Schedule IV controlled substances.

Screening, Brief Intervention and Referral to Treatment (SBIRT): an evidence-based interventional approach to identify, reduce, and prevent problematic use, abuse, and dependence on alcohol or illegal drugs.

SEGO: an acronym for "something else going on," useful to denote when the real reason for an action or communication is neither stated nor acknowledged by the person or organization acting or communicating.

SMART Recovery: a non-Twelve Step program of social model recovery that is asserted to have a scientific foundation (contrasting with Twelve Step's spiritual foundation) and emphasizes self-help through learning skills of coping with urges, sustaining motivation to abstain, and managing thoughts, behaviors, and feelings to maintain independence from alcohol, drugs, and other addictive behaviors.

social model recovery: an approach to recovery from substance use disorders (SUDs), addiction, and other disabilities based on participation in a community of interpersonal sharing of experiences, insights, and strategies, peer support and mutual help, and emphasizing recovery as a process and interaction between a person and his or her environment. Historically, social model recovery has been an abstinence-based model.

Substance Abuse and Mental Health Service Administration (SAMHSA): a federal agency formed in 1992 under the oversight of the Department of Health and Human Services (HHS) to reduce the impact of substance use disorders (SUDs) and mental illness in America by making information, services, and research available.

substance use disorder (SUD): a condition, also known as a drug use disorder, in which a person uses alcohol or drugs, including opioids, in a recurring manner that is mild, moderate, or severe as measured by clinically or functionally significant impairment, such as health problems, risky behavior, or failure to meet responsibilities at work, school, or home.

Substance Use-Disorder Prevention that Promotes Opioid Recovery and Treatment for Patients and Communities (SUPPORT for Patients and Communities Act): a 2018 federal law, also known as HR 6, enacted with bipartisan support in response to the opioid crisis, increasing access to opioid addiction prevention and treatment resources in Medicare, Medicaid, and other health programs. Noteworthy provisions of the law include increased access to medication-assisted treatment with buprenorphine, expanded use of telehealth, and a criminalization of patient brokering and kickbacks for referrals to addiction treatment programs, recovery residences, and laboratories.

Title 42, Code of Federal Regulations (CFR) Part 2: federal privacy regulations specific to substance abuse treatment that impose stricter limitations than HIPAA on sharing information about a person in treatment with family or other physicians.

Twelve Steps: guidelines developed by the founders of the Alcoholics Anonymous program, which provide principles to overcome addiction through an incremental process involving a spiritual component and the support of a community of shared values.

United Nations Single Convention on Narcotic Drugs: a 1961 international treaty creating worldwide prohibitions on the manufacturing, importation, possession, use, and distribution of opioids and other substances.

urine drug screen (UDS): the use of urine testing to monitor and detect recent drug use, through qualitative point-of-care (POC) testing in which immunoassay strips in the POC cup change color to indicate positive results and/or quantitative laboratory testing measuring the amount of drug quantities detected.

Veterans Health Administration (VHA): the largest integrated healthcare system in the US, providing care at 1,243 healthcare facilities, including 172 VA Medical Centers and 1,062 outpatient sites to more than nine million veterans enrolled in the VA healthcare program.

War on Drugs: the government-led initiative that began in the 1970s to stop domestic illegal drug use, importation, and trafficking by increasing and enforcing penalties for offenders (both users and traffickers).

GRAPHICS AND DATA

The Three Waves of the Opioid Crisis:
Overprescribing, Heroin, and Fentanyl

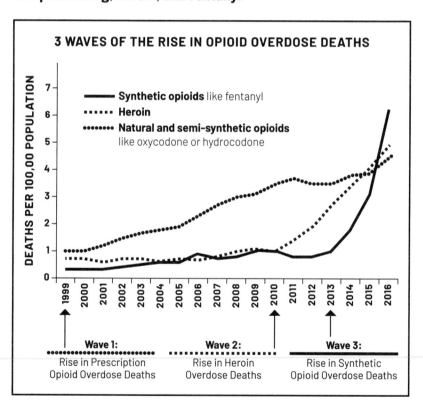

The opioid crisis is marked by three distinct waves of spiking death rates—from prescription opioids beginning in 1999, from heroin beginning in 2010, and from synthetic opioids, especially fentanyl, beginning in 2013.[1]

How many people have died in the opioid crisis to date?

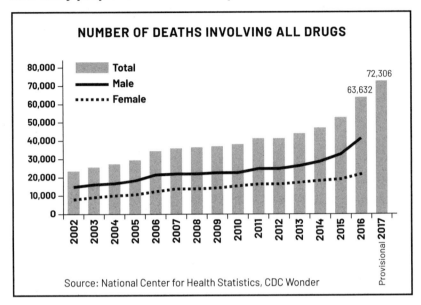

From 2002 to 2017, there was a threefold increase in the total number of US overdose deaths involving all drugs.[2]

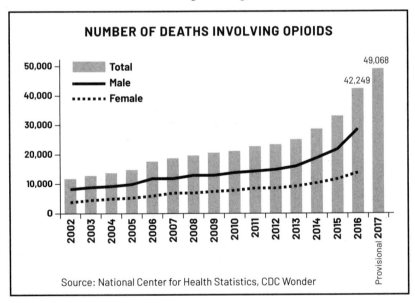

From 2002 to 2017, there was a fourfold increase in the total number of US overdose deaths involving opioids.[3]

How do opioids compare to other preventable causes of death?

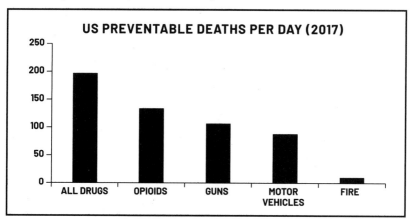

US PREVENTABLE DEATHS PER DAY (2017)

All Drugs[4]	Opioids[5]	Gun-Related[6]	Motor Vehicles[7]	Fire-Related[8]
197/day	134/day	107/day	88/day	9/day
72,000	49,000	39,000	32,000	3,400

There are more deaths per day from drug overdoses than there are from guns and cars combined.

How big is America's drug problem?

	Estimated #
US Total Population[9]	326 million
US Adult Population (18+)	253 million
US Adults prescribed opioids in 2015[10]	92 million
US Adults with a SUD[11]	20 million
US Adults reporting an OUD[12]	11.5 million
Americans diagnosed with an OUD[13]	1.5 million

Nearly four out of ten adults in the US were prescribed opiates in 2015. Of 253 million adults in the US, approximately 8 percent have a substance use disorder.

How many Americans are living in pain?

	Estimated #
US Total Population[14]	326 million
US Adult Population	253 million
Americans suffering from chronic pain most days or every day in the past 6 months[15]	50 million
Americans experiencing chronic pain that limits "life or work activities on most days or every day in the past 6 months"	20 million

One in five adults experiences chronic pain. For one in twelve adults, chronic pain limits life and work activities most or all of the time.

How do synthetic opioids compare to the potency of opiates?[16]

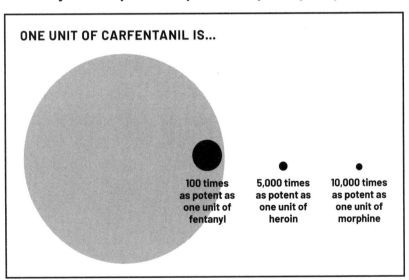

Synthetic opioids of extreme, highly deadly potency increasingly are showing up on the streets. Carfentanil, a synthetic opioid, is 10,000 times as potent as one unit of morphine, and 100 times as potent as one unit of fenatanyl.

How addictive are opioids?

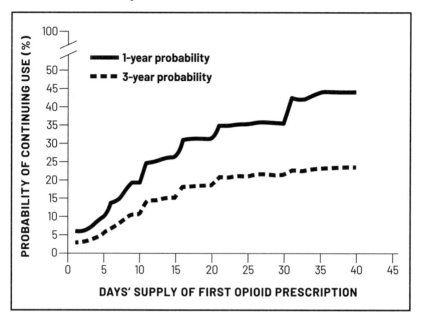

For patients in the hospital, the number of days of the initial pre-scription is predictive of the risk of continued, long-term opioid use for a year or more.[17] A five-day initial opioid supply translates into a 10 percent risk of use for a year or more; a ten-day supply translates into a 20 percent risk; and a thirty-day supply translates into a 45 percent risk.

RESOURCE GUIDE

FOR THOSE STRUGGLING WITH ADDICTION AND THEIR FAMILIES

Faces & Voices of Recovery

1.202.737.0690

Email: info@facesandvoicesofrecovery.org

https://facesandvoicesofrecovery.org/resources/overview.html

Educational, training, and advocacy resources to promote addiction recovery, including position papers, reports, toolkits, and information on other recovery resources.

MotherToBaby

Toll-free helpline 866.626.6847, text line 855.999.3525

http://www.mothertobaby.org/opioids

MotherToBaby provides evidence-based information about exposures, like opioids, during pregnancy and breastfeeding. It has fifteen affiliates across the country that provide this service to all fifty states as well as the US territories. The site features resources for healthcare providers, addiction specialists, and women struggling with addiction to prescription and illicit drugs, and offers live chat and email-an-expert services.

Narcotics Anonymous

General information: http://www.na.org/

To find an NA meeting: https://www.na.org/meetingsearch/

This website offers extensive information about NA local meetings, other resources, and support for people seeking support for recovery from addiction and maintaining a drug-free lifestyle.

#NotAnotherStat

http://www.notanotherstat.com

This project, launched by author Harry Nelson to provide more information and support community about topics addressed in this book, offers resources for people in recovery as well as those continuing to struggle with addiction and pain, as well as friends and loved ones. The goal of #NotAnotherStat is to increase awareness and recognition of substance use disorders (SUDs), end shame and stigmatization around addiction and pain, and empower people to take a meaningful part in tackling the opioid crisis.

Opioid Treatment Program Directory

http://dpt2.samhsa.gov/treatment/directory.aspx

SAMHSA provides a list of opioid treatment programs in each state.

Partnership for Drug-Free Kids Helpline

1.855.DRUGFREE (378.4373)

http://www.drugfree.org/get-help/helpline/

Trained bilingual parent support specialists are available Monday–Friday, 9 a.m. to 5 p.m. ET, to take calls from concerned parents and loved ones about SUD-related challenges involving children.

SAMHSA National Helpline

1.800.662.HELP (4357)

TTY 1.800.487.4889

Order free publications: store.samhsa.gov

Treatment facility finder: https://www.findtreatment.samhsa.gov/

The SAMHSA National Helpline is a confidential, free, 24-hour-a-day, 365-day-a-year, information service, in English and Spanish, for individuals and family members facing mental and/or substance use disorders. This service provides referrals to local treatment facilities, support groups, and community-based organizations.

SAMHSA Opioid Overdose Prevention Toolkit

https://store.samhsa.gov/system/files/safety-advice-for-patients-family-members.pdf

This downloadable publication and toolkit offers safety advice for patients and family members, as well as strategies for communities and local governments in developing practices and policies to help prevent opioid-related overdoses and deaths.

Suicide Prevention Lifeline

1.800.273.TALK (8255)

TTY: 1.800.799.4889

http://www.suicidepreventionlifeline.org

This 24-hour, toll-free, confidential suicide prevention hotline is available to anyone in suicidal crisis or emotional distress. Your call is routed to the nearest crisis center in the national network of more than 150 crisis centers.

Veterans Crisis Line

1.800.273.TALK (8255)

TTY: 1.800.799.4889

http://www.veteranscrisisline.net

This service connects veterans in crisis (and their families and friends) with qualified, caring Department of Veterans Affairs responders through a confidential, toll-free hotline, online chat, or text.

FOR EMPLOYERS

Drug-Free Workplace
1.800.WORKPLACE (967.5752)

http://www.samhsa.gov/workplace/resources/drug-free-helpline

This site assists employers and union representatives with policy development, drug testing, employee assistance, employee education, supervisor training, and program implementation.

Fighting for Opioid Relief through Collaborative Effort (FORCE), a project of the Behavioral Health Association of Providers (BHAP)
1.888.958.2282

Email: help@bhap.us

http://www.bhap.us/force

This project, spearheaded by the Behavioral Health Association of Providers (BHAP), provides resources and tools for employers to substance use disorders (SUDs) within the workplace through wellness programs and other means. (For more information about BHAP, see Resources for Healthcare Providers.)

FOR COMMUNITY LEADERS AND FAITH-BASED ORGANIZATIONS

#NotAnotherStat

1.888.958.2282

http://www.notanotherstat.com

Email: help@bhap.us

This campaign, launched by author Harry Nelson with the support of the Behavioral Health Association of Providers (BHAP), provides education, advocacy, and other tools for leaders and organizations to improve awareness and recognition of substance use disorders (SUDs) and other behavioral health issues within local communities.

Opioid Epidemic Practical Toolkit

https://www.hhs.gov/sites/default/files/hhs-partnership-ctr-opioid-practical-toolkit-unremediated.pdf

This toolkit provides resources to help faith-based and community leaders bring hope and healing to communities.

FOR FIRST RESPONDERS

SAMHSA Opioid Overdose Prevention Toolkit

https://store.samhsa.gov/system/files/five-essential-steps-for-first-responders.pdf

Five Essential Steps for First Responders

FOR HEALTHCARE PROVIDERS

Behavioral Health Association of Providers (BHAP)

1.888.958.2282

http://www.bhap.us

This is the organization chaired by author Harry Nelson to provide education and advocacy resources to improve the quality of behavioral healthcare services. BHAP provides extensive resources for healthcare organizations and professionals to address opioid-related issues.

Centers for Disease Control and Prevention (CDC)
Guideline for Prescribing Opioids for Chronic Pain

https://www.cdc.gov/drugoverdose/prescribing/guideline.html

These recommendations for prescribing opioid pain medication for chronic pain in primary care settings offer a valuable starting point for assessing best practices in opioid prescribing.

SAMHSA Opioid Overdose Prevention Toolkit

https://store.samhsa.gov/system/files/information-for-prescribers.pdf

This SAMHSA publication provides information for physicians and other prescribers in treating patients to reduce the risks of opioid use disorders (OUDs) and overdoses, as well as to bill claims for opioid related services appropriately.

FIGHTING FOR OPIOID RELIEF THROUGH COLLABORATIVE EFFORT

ALL PROCEEDS FROM THE SALE of *The United States of Opioids* are going to support Fighting for Opioid Relief through Collaborative Effort (FORCE), a project spearheaded by the Behavioral Health Association of Providers (BHAP), as well as other nonprofit partner organizations participating in this effort. FORCE seeks to accelerate cooperation and coordination among government, nonprofit, and private organizations focused on reducing opioid-related overdose deaths and expanding access to effective addiction treatment and pain management. FORCE also provides resources and tools to increase awareness, offer ways for individuals to participate in opioid crisis response, and drive innovation towards meaningful solutions to the opioid crisis.

We gratefully acknowledge all of the generous supporters who have made FORCE a reality. For more information on FORCE initiatives and how you or your organization can participate, please visit https://bhap.us/force or email help@bhap.us.

#NOTANOTHERSTAT

LOOKING FOR MORE DETAILS on particular facets of the opioid crisis? Interested in sharing your opioid story and helping move the conversation from paralysis to action, from shame to courage? Wondering how you can be a proactive part of the solution in spreading awareness, prevention, and intervention?

Join the conversation at http://www.notanotherstat.com.

Don't let anyone else become another stat in the opioid crisis.

ACKNOWLEDGMENTS

THE SEEDS FOR THIS BOOK were planted by my parents, Rabbi David and Alicia Nelson, who have set a lifelong model for me of what it means to work tirelessly for the sake of community, both at a one-on-one level for people in need and also in being a change agent wherever necessary. Mom and Dad, I am grateful for your love and instilling in me the value of forging inclusive communities and not being limited by anyone's expectations.

I am deeply grateful to my sister, Reva Nelson, editor extraordinaire, who provided invaluable feedback and editorial support in thinking through this project and suggesting how to write about policy in a way that would still tell a good story, and to Amy Spungen, for her editing and pushing to support and refine the ideas stated here. Thank you to Justin Batt, Lauren Delamater, and the Forbes team for pushing me to complete this book in the face of a thousand competing priorities, and to Charlie Fusco and the TGC team for guidance in thinking strategically about the resources needed that extend far beyond the book. I am grateful to Lisa Marie Presley for her willingness to share her story in support of the message of this book, and to everyone who has supported the efforts to spread the message.

Nick Merkin, CEO of Compliagent, offered valuable input about organization and took time to help me reorganize this book. I am grateful for the many friends whose feedback was invaluable, including my friend and guitar legend Richard Peikoff; my dear friend and mentor, Beth Berke; and the many healthcare providers who shared their insights: Mark Honzel, MD; Jon Hoenig, MD; Joe Englanoff, MD; psychologists Keith Valone, PhD, PsyD, MSCP, and Dan Kaplan, PhD; Loren Beck; Sheila Scott; Epstein Becker & Green partner Paul Gilbert; and writer and director Larry Trilling.

I am grateful to Montrece McNeill Ransom at the Centers for Disease Control and Prevention (CDC) and to the American Health Lawyers Association for feedback and for encouraging me, and bringing me into conversations with the leadership of key government agencies and organizations, clinicians, and others who provided invaluable feedback on my perspective.

The feedback of Andrew Martin, COO of the Behavioral Health Association of Providers, was invaluable in this book, as well as development of the Fighting for Opioid Relief through Collaborative Effort (FORCE) project to implement the resource development needed. I am grateful for many friends and teachers throughout the addiction treatment community, including Pete Nielsen, CEO of the California Consortium of Addiction Programs and Professionals; Dave Sheridan, President of the National Alliance of Recovery Residences; Anelia Shaheed and Julie Allison, and Dee McGraw of C4 Recovery Solutions.

Many others have also been a source of strength and support, including several people who were generous to provide insights anonymously. For the sake of attorney-client privilege, I am omitting the names of the many clients who have trusted me with so many sensitive and complex issues and taken the time to educate me on the issues around pain management and addiction treatment. As I think through that long list, I want to publicly acknowledge the important role of one friend and teacher who is no longer with us, Robert Pfeifer, of blessed memory.

I have been blessed with incredible partners and colleagues at Nelson Hardiman. I am grateful to my partners, Mark Hardiman, Hope Levy-Biehl, Stacie Neroni, Rob Fuller, and John Mills, who have supported me not only in this effort, but in driving our group to do things differently and have a broader impact on our health system. I am particularly grateful for the leadership of Kathryn Edgerton, Zach Rothenberg, Lee Arian, and John Mills in thinking through different pieces of the opioid puzzle and embracing this journey with me. I would be nowhere at all without Jill Frankel, who points me in the right direction and helps me navigate through all the working hours of the day. Jennifer Coren, Jessica Dunning, and Miguel Saldate all provided invaluable support on communications, graphics, IT support, and much more.

Finally, I could not have written this book without the support of my wife, Dorit, who is, hands down, the kindest, most loving and generous person I know. Dorit, I am grateful for the many things big and small you do every day to hold things together and realize our dreams together. Even at many points when it was not easy, you gave me the time, space, and support to make this book possible. I love you.

ABOUT THE AUTHOR

HARRY NELSON IS A FOUNDER of Nelson Hardiman, a healthcare and life sciences law firm that has been recognized nationally for its leadership and innovation. He is coauthor of the 2017 book *From ObamaCare to TrumpCare: Why You Should Care* about the past, present, and future of US health policy. Since 2016, Harry has chaired the board of the Behavioral Health Association of Providers (BHAP), a national education and advocacy organization with over thirty-one thousand subscribers developing evidence-based standards to improve the quality of addiction treatment and behavioral health. Harry spearheaded the Fighting for Opioid Relief through Collaborative Effort (FORCE) project, an effort to accelerate cooperation and coordination among government, nonprofit, and private organizations towards reducing opioid-related overdose deaths and expanding access to effective addiction treatment and pain management. Harry also works to provide resources to support education and community engagement through the #NotAnotherStat project. Harry has been called upon as a problem-solver by the healthcare industry and federal and state regulators to address challenges facing American healthcare, with a particular focus on behavioral and digital health.

ENDNOTES

CHAPTER I

1   Martha Bebinger, "Fentanyl-Laced Cocaine Could Be 'Next Wave' of Opioid Crisis, Some Warn," 90.9 WBUR-FM, CommonHealth (March 27, 2018), www.wbur.org/commonhealth/2018/03/27/fentanyl-cocaine-addiction-crisis

2   Centers for Disease Control and Prevention, "Understanding the Epidemic" (Aug. 30, 2017), https://www.cdc.gov/drugoverdose/epidemic/index.html (Note: this article uses the figure of 630,000 drug deaths. As noted in note 4 below, 2018 reports have estimated an undercounting of 70,000 based on death certificate errors, which is the basis for the 700,000 figure

3   *Ibid.*

4   Centers for Disease Control and Prevention, "Overview of the Drug Overdose Epidemic: Behind the Numbers" (July 18, 2017), https://www.cdc.gov/drugoverdose/data/index.html; F.B. Ahmad et al., "Provisional Drug Overdose Death Counts," National Center for Health Statistics (2018), https://www.cdc.gov/nchs/nvss/vsrr/drug-overdose-data.htm

5   Centers for Disease Control and Prevention, "U.S. Drug Overdose Deaths Continue to Rise; Increase Fueled by Synthetic Opioid" (March 29, 2018), https://www.cdc.gov/media/releases/2018/p0329-drug-overdose-deaths.html

6   Jeanine Buchanich et al., "The Effect of Incomplete Death Certificates on Estimates of Unintentional Opioid-Related Overdose Deaths in the United States, 1999–2015," *Public Health Reports* 133 (June 27, 2018): 423-31, https://doi.org/10.1177/0033354918774330

7   Martin Finucane, "70,000 Opioid Deaths May Have Gone Uncounted from 1999 through 2015, Researchers Say," *Boston Globe* (June 27, 2018), www.bostonglobe.com/metro/2018/06/27/researchers-opioid-deaths-may-have-gone-uncounted-from-through/dwpnTStVQOBwR9LQQx127K/story.html

8   Centers for Disease Control and Prevention, "Opioid Painkiller Prescribing: Where You Live Makes a Difference" (2018), https://www.cdc.gov/vitalsigns/opioid-prescribing/index.html

9   SAMHSA, "Associations of Nonmedical Pain Reliever Use and Initiation of Heroin Use in the United States," *CBHSQ Data Review* (Aug. 2013), https://www.samhsa.gov/data/sites/default/files/DR006/DR006/nonmedical-pain-reliever-use-2013.htm

10 National Institute of Drug Abuse (NIDA), Overdose Death Rates (1999–2017), https://www.drugabuse.gov/related-topics/trends-statistics/overdose-death-rates

11 PubChem Open Chemistry Database, "Carfentanil," https://pubchem.ncbi.nlm.nih.gov/compound/carfentanil

12 *Burlington Free Press*, Obituaries (Oct. 21, 2018), https://www.legacy.com/obituaries/burlingtonfreepress/obituary.aspx?n=madelyn-ellen-linsenmeir&pid=190469930

13 U.S. Food & Drug Administration, "Information by Drug Class, Timeline of Selected FDA Activities and Significant Events Addressing Opioid Misuse and Abuse" (July 11, 2018), www.fda.gov/Drugs/DrugSafety/InformationbyDrugClass/ucm338566.htm

14 Tim Craig and Nicole Lewis, "As Opioid Overdoses Exact a Higher Price, Communities Ponder Who Should Be Saved," *The Washington Post* (July 15, 2017), www.washingtonpost.com/world/as-opioid-overdoses-exact-a-higher-price-communities-ponder-who-should-be-saved/2017/07/15/1ea91890-67f3-11e7-8eb5-cbccc2e7bfbf_story.html?utm_term=.7ce61c9df66e

15 CA Health & Safety Code § 11165

16 Lewis v. Superior Court of California (S219811—Supreme Court of California, July 17, 2017), https://caselaw.findlaw.com/ca-supreme-court/1868096.html

17 50 U.S.C. § 1601-1651

CHAPTER 2

1   Aldous Huxley, "Adventures of the Mind 12: Drugs That Shape Men's Minds," *The Saturday Evening Post* 231 (Oct. 18, 1958)

2   Nora Volkow and Thomas McClellan, "Opioid Abuse in Chronic Pain—Misconceptions and Mitigation Strategies," *New England Journal of Medicine* 374, no. 13 (March 31, 2016): 1253–63, https://www.nejm.org/doi/full/10.1056/NEJMra1507771

CHAPTER 3

1   Erick Trickey, "Inside the Story of America's 19th-Century Opiate Addiction," Smithsonian.com (Jan. 4, 2018), https://www.smithsonianmag.com/history/inside-story-americas-19th-century-opiate-addiction-180967673

2   Nick Miroff, "From Teddy Roosevelt to Trump: How Drug Companies Triggered an Opioid Crisis a Century Ago," *The Washington Post* (Oct. 17, 2017), www.washingtonpost.com/news/retropolis/wp/2017/09/29/the-greatest-drug-fiends-in-the-world-an-american-opioid-crisis-in-1908

3   Edward Marshall, "Uncle Sam Is the Worst Drug Fiend in the World," *The New York Times* (March 12, 1911), www.druglibrary.org/schaffer/History/e1910/worstfiend.htm

4   United States v. Doremus, 249 U.S. 86 (1919)

5   Webb v. United States, 249 U.S. 96 (1919)

6   Jin Fuey Moy v. United States, 254 U.S. 189 (1920)

7   United States v. Behrman, 258 U.S. U.S. 280 (1922)

8   Ronald T. Libby, "The DEA's War on Doctors: A Surrogate for the War on Drugs," Congressional Briefing on the Politics of Pain (Sept. 17, 2004), www.aapsonline.org/painman/paindocs2/libbystatement.pdf

9   Linder v. United States, 268 U.S. 5 (1925)

CHAPTER 4

1   "Addiction Rare in Patients Treated with Narcotics," *New England Journal of Medicine* 302, no. 123 (Jan. 10, 1980), www.nejm.org/doi/10.1056/NEJM198001103020221

2   Patricia Sullivan, "Inventor of Valium, Once the Most Often Prescribed Drug, Dies," *The Washington Post* (Sept. 5, 2005), www.washingtonpost.com/wp-dyn/content/article/2005/09/30/AR2005093001963.html

3   Mike Mariani, "How the American Opiate Epidemic Was Started by One Pharmaceutical Company," *The Week* (March 4, 2015), from *Pacific Standard*: http://theweek.com/articles/541564/how-american-opiate-epidemic-started-by-pharmaceutical-company

4   "Purdue Pharma Used Deceptive Sales Tactic for OxyContin after Settlement, Ex-Sales Rep Says," Today's Rundown, *CBS This Morning* (June 21, 2018), www.cbsnews.com/news/oxycontin-purdue-pharma-former-sales-representative-deceptive-sales-psuedoaddiction

5   Patrick Radden Keefe, "The Family That Built the Empire of Pain," *The New Yorker* (Oct. 30, 2017), www.newyorker.com/magazine/2017/10/30/the-family-that-built-an-empire-of-pain

6   Barry Meier and Eric Lipton, "Under Attack, Drug Maker Turned to Giuliani for Help," *The New York Times* (Dec. 28, 2007), www.nytimes.com/2007/12/28/us/politics/28oxycontin.html

7   Barry Meier, "In Guilty Plea, OxyContin Maker to Pay $600 Million," *The New York Times* (May 10, 2007), https://www.nytimes.com/2007/05/10/business/11drug-web.html

8   Nate Raymond, "U.S. to Narrow Opioid Bribe Case Against Insys founder, Others," Reuters (July 24, 2018), https://www.reuters.com/article/us-insys-opioids/u-s-to-narrow-opioid-bribe-case-against-insys-founder-others-idUSKBN1KE2GD

9   Nate Raymond and Andy Thibault, "Update 3-Insys to Pay $150 Million to Settle U.S. Opioid Kickback Probe," Reuters (August 8, 2018), https://www.cnbc.com/2018/08/08/reuters-america-update-3-insys-to-pay-150-mln-to-settle-u-s-opioid-kickback-probe.html

10   Emily Sullivan, "Florida Sues Walgreens, CVS For Alleged Role in Opioid Crisis," NPR (Nov. 19, 2018), https://www.npr.org/2018/11/19/669146432/ florida-sues-walgreens-cvs-for-alleged-role-in-opioid-crisis

11   Marlene Satter, "Pharmacy Benefits Managers in Crosshairs of Latest Opioid Lawsuit," Benefits Pro (Feb. 26, 2018), https://www.benefitspro. com/2018/02/26/pharmacy-benefits-managers-in-crosshairs-of-latest/

CHAPTER 5

1   Brian Zimmerman, "3 Quotes from Dr. Atul Gawande on the Role of Physicians in the Opioid Epidemic," Becker's Hospital Review (Sept. 11, 2017), www.beckershospitalreview.com/opioids/3-quotes-from-dr-atul-gawande-on-the-role-of-physicians-in-the-opioid-epidemic.html

2   Jane Porter and Hershel Jick, "Addiction Rare in Patients Treated with Narcotics," New England Journal of Medicine 302, no. 2 (Jan. 1980): 123, https://www.nejm.org/doi/10.1056/NEJM198001103020221

3   R. K. Portenoy and K. M. Foley, "Chronic Use of Opioid Analgesics in Non-Malignant Pain: Report of 38 Cases," Pain 25, no. 2 (May 1986): 171–86, www.ncbi.nlm.nih.gov/pubmed/2873550

4   Zimmerman, "3 Quotes from Dr. Atul Gawande," www.beckershospitalreview. com/opioids/3-quotes-from-dr-atul-gawande-on-the-role-of-physicians-in-the-opioid-epidemic.html

5   Michael Fine, "Quantifying the Impact of NSAID-Associated Adverse Events," American Journal of Managed Care 19, no. 14 (Nov. 20, 2013), https://www.ajmc.com/journals/supplement/2013/a467_nov13_nsaid/ a467_nov13_fine_s267

6   Jared Younger, Luke Parkitny, and David McLain, "The Use of Low-Dose Naltrexone (LDN), as a Novel Anti-Inflammatory Treatment for Chronic Pain," Clinical Rheumatology 33, no. 4 (2014): 451–459, www.ncbi.nlm.nih. gov/pmc/articles/PMC3962576

7   Anuj Shah, Corey J. Hayes, and Bradley C. Martin, "Characteristics of Initial Prescription Episodes and Likelihood of Long-Term Opioid Use—United

States, 2006–2015," *CDC Weekly* 66, no. 10 (March 2017): 265–269. www.cdc.gov/mmwr/volumes/66/wr/mm6610a1.htm

8   Food and Drug Administration, "Statement from FDA Commissioner Scott Gottlieb, M.D., on the Agency's Scientific Evidence on the Presence of Opioid Compounds in Kratom, Underscoring Its Potential for Abuse" (Feb. 6, 2018), https://www.fda.gov/newsevents/newsroom/pressannouncements/ucm595622.htm

9   *Ibid.*

10   Edward Boyer, "Self-Treatment of Opioid Withdrawal Using Kratom (Mitragynia speciosa korth)," *Addiction* 103, no. 6 (June 2008): 1048-50, https://www.ncbi.nlm.nih.gov/pmc/articles/PMC3670991/

11   R. K. Portenoy and K. M. Foley, "Chronic Use of Opioid Analgesics in Non-Malignant Pain: Report of 38 Cases," *Pain* 25, no. 2 (May 1986): 171–86, www.ncbi.nlm.nih.gov/pubmed/2873550

12   M. B. Max, "Improving Outcomes of Analgesic Treatment: Is Education Enough?" *Annals of Internal Medicine* 113, no. 11 (1990): 885–889, https://doi.org/ 10.7326/0003-4819-113-11-885

13   J. N. Campbell, "APS 1995 Presidential Address," *Pain Forum* 5 (1996): 85–88

14   D. W. Baker, "History of the Joint Commission's Pain Standards: Lessons for Today's Prescription Opioid Epidemic," *JAMA* 317, no. 11 (March 2017): 1117–1118

15   William Sullivan and Logan Plaster, "Four West Virginia Cities Sue the Joint Commission," *Emergency Physicians Monthly*, epmonthly.com (Dec. 5, 2017), http://epmonthly.com/article/four-west-virginia-cities-sue-joint-commission

16   Owen Amos, "Why Opioids Are Such an American Problem," *BBC News* (Oct. 25, 2017), https://www.bbc.com/news/world-us-canada-41701718

17   Roger Chriss, "It's a Myth America Consumes 80% of World's Opioids," Pain News Network (March 8, 2018), https://www.painnewsnetwork.org/stories/2018/3/8/the-myth-that-americans-consume-80-of-the-worlds-opioids

18   Olga Khazan, "America Experiences More Pain Than Other Countries," *The Atlantic* (Dec. 20, 2017), www.theatlantic.com/health/archive/2017/12/america-experiences-more-pain-than-other-countries/548822

19   Zimmerman, "3 Quotes from Dr. Atul Gawande," www.beckershospitalre-view.com/opioids/3-quotes-from-dr-atul-gawande-on-the-role-of-physicians-in-the-opioid-epidemic.html

20   Centers for Disease Control and Prevention, "Vital Signs: Risk for Overdose from Methadone Used for Pain Relief – United States, 1999–2010," *Morbidity and Mortality Weekly Report (MMWR)* 61, no. 26 (July 6, 2012): 493–497

21   Art Van Zee, "The Promotion and Marketing of OxyContin: Commercial Triumph, Public Health Tragedy," *American Journal of Public Health* 99, no. 2 (Feb. 2009): 221–227

22   Vivek Murthy, "The Surgeon General's Call to End the Opioid Crisis," *Turn the Tide*, https://turnthetiderx.org

CHAPTER 6

1   Hawre Jalal, Jeanine M. Buchanich, Mark S. Roberts, Lauren C. Balmert, Kun Zhang, and Donald S. Burke, "Changing Dynamics of the Drug Overdose Epidemic in the United States from 1979 through 2016," *Science* 361, no. 6408 (Sept. 21, 2018)

2   Sabrina Tavernise, "U.S. Suicide Rate Surges to a 30-Year High," *The New York Times* (April 22, 2016), http://www.nytimes.com/by/sabrina-tavernise

3   Susan Scutti, "US Suicide Rates Increased More Than 25% Since 1999, CDC Says," CNN (June 22, 2018), www.cnn.com/2018/06/07/health/suicide-report-cdc/index.html

4   Jamieson Webster, "Why Are Suicides Among American Women Rising?" *The Guardian US Edition* (April 26, 2016), www.theguardian.com/commentisfree/2016/apr/26/suicide-rate-rising-american-women-cdc-report

5   American Foundation for Suicide Prevention, "Suicide Statistics" (accessed July 27, 2018), https://afsp.org/about-suicide/suicide-statistics/

6   Emiko Petrosky et al., "Chronic Pain Among Suicide Decedents, 2003 to 2014: Findings From the National Violent Death Reporting System," *Annals of Internal Medicine* (Oct. 2, 2018), annals.org/aim/fullarticle/2702061/chronic-pain-among-suicide-decedents-2003-2014-findings-from-national

7   Scott Stanley, "Young and Cueless: Thinking About the Big Rise in Anxiety," *Psychology Today* (Nov. 7, 2017), www.psychologytoday.com/us/blog/sliding-vs-deciding/201711/young-and-cueless-thinking-about-the-big-rise-in-anxiety

8   R. Mojtabai, M. Olfson, and B. Han, "National Trends in the Prevalence and Treatment of Depression in Adolescents and Young Adults," *Pediatrics* 138, no. 6 (December 2016), http://pediatrics.aappublications.org/content/138/6/e20161878

9   Jeffrey Bernstein, "The Rising Epidemic of Anxiety in Children's and Teens," *Psychology Today* (Jan. 23, 2016), www.psychologytoday.com/us/blog/liking-the-child-you-love/201601/the-rising-epidemic-anxiety-in-children-and-teens

10 National College Health Assessment, "Undergraduate Student Reference Group, Executive Summary," http://www.acha-ncha.org/docs/NCHA-II%20SPRING%202016%20UNDERGRADUATE%20REFERENCE%20GROUP%20EXECUTIVE%20SUMMARY.pdf (cited in Benoit Denizet-Lewis, "Why Are More American Teenagers Than Ever Suffering From Severe Anxiety?" *The New York Times* (Oct. 11, 2017), www.nytimes.com/2017/10/11/magazine/why-are-more-american-teenagers-than-ever-suffering-from-severe-anxiety.html

11 American Academy of Pediatrics News, "Children's Hospitals Admissions for Suicidal Thoughts, Actions Double During Past Decade (May 4, 2017), www.aappublications.org/news/2017/05/04/PASSuicide050417 (cited in Benoit Denizet-Lewis, "Why Are More American Teenagers Than Ever Suffering From Severe Anxiety?")

12 Seth Stephens-Davidowitz, "Don't Let Facebook Make You Miserable," *The New York Times* (May 6, 2017), www.nytimes.com/2017/05/06/opinion/sunday/dont-let-facebook-make-you-miserable.html

13 Olivia Goldhill, "Depression Diagnosis Is Up 33 in the US and That's a Good Thing," Quartz/Silver LInings (May 14, 2018), https://qz.com/1276314/depression-diagnosis-is-up-33-in-the-us-and-thats-a-good-thing

14 David G. Blanchflower and Andrew Oswald, "Unhappiness and Pain in Modern America," *National Bureau of Economic Research* (Nov. 2017), www.nber.org/papers/w24087

15 Steven E. Mock and Susan M. Arai, "Childhood Trauma and Chronic illness in Adulthood: Mental Health and Socioeconomic Status as Explanatory Factors and Buffers," *Frontiers in Psychology* 1 (2010): 246, https://doi.org/10.3389/fpsyg.2010.00246

16 John E. Sarno, *Healing Back Pain: The Mind-Body Connection* (New York: Warner Books, 1991); *The Mindbody Prescription: Healing the Body, Healing the Pain* (New York: Warner Books, 1998); *The Divided Mind: The Epidemic of Mindbody Disorders* (New York: Regan Books/Harper Collins, 2006)

17 D. Schechter et al., "Outcomes of a Mind-Body Treatment Program for Chronic Back Pain with No Distinct Structural Pathology—A Case Series of Patients Diagnosed and Treated as Tension Myositis Syndrome," *Alternative Therapies in Health and Medicine* 13, no. 5 (Sep.–Oct. 2007):26–35, https://www.ncbi.nlm.nih.gov/pubmed/17900039

18 Harry Nelson and Rob Fuller, *From ObamaCare to TrumpCare: Why You Should Care* (Los Angeles: RX4 Group, 2017)

19 Robert Putnam, "Bowling Alone: America's Declining Social Capital," *Journal of Democracy* 6, no. 1 (1995): 65–78, http://xroads.virginia.edu/~hyper/detoc/assoc/bowling.html

20 "America's Changing Religious Landscape," Pew Research Center (May 12, 2015), www.pewforum.org/2015/05/12/americas-changing-religious-landscape/

21 Sabrina Tavernise, "Married Couples Are No Longer the Majority, Census Shows," *The New York Times* (May 26, 2011), www.nytimes.com/2011/05/26/us/26marry.html

22 Martin Ford, *The Rise of Robots: Technology and the Threat of a Jobless Future* (New York: Basic Books, 2015)

23 Jay Shambaugh and Ryan Nunn, "Why Wages Aren't Growing in America," *Harvard Business Review* (Oct. 24, 2017), https://hbr.org/2017/10/why-wages-arent-growing-in-america

24 Federal Reserve Bank of New York, "The Labor Market for Recent College Graduates" (July 25, 2018), www.newyorkfed.org/research/college-labor-market/college-labor-market_underemployment_jobtypes.html

25 CBS News, "Workers with No College Degree Fall Further Behind Than Ever," *Money Watch* (Jan. 13, 2017), www.cbsnews.com/news/workers-with-no-college-degree-fall-further-behind-than-ever

26 Rick Warren, *The Purpose Driven Life* (Grand Rapids, MI: Zondervan, 2002)

27 Abraham Maslow, *A Theory of Human Motivation* (1943)

CHAPTER 7

1 Beth Warren, "Tired of Going to Funerals, This Doctor Treats Addiction with Drugs," *Louisville Courier Journal* (June 27, 2018), www.courier-journal.com/story/news/local/2018/06/21/louisville-doctor-treats-drug-addiction-suboxone-treatment/602640002/

2 Centers for Disease Control, "Wide-Ranging Online Data for Epidemiologic Research (WONDER)," National Center for Health Statistics, https://wonder.cdc.gov

3 US Department of Health and Human Services (HHS), Office of the Surgeon General, "Facing Addiction in America: The Surgeon General's Spotlight on Opioids," Washington, DC: HHS (Sept. 2018), https://addiction.surgeon-general.gov/sites/default/files/Spotlight-on-Opioids_09192018.pdf

4 "New York State Inebriate Asylum," National Park Service, https://www.nps.gov/places/new-york-state-inebriate-asylum.htm

5 William White Papers, "Significant Events in the History of Addiction Treatment and Recovery in America," *William White Papers*, www.williamwhitepapers.com/pr/AddictionTreatment&RecoveryInAmerica.pdf

6 Gabrielle Glazer, "The Irrationality of Alcoholics Anonymous," *The Atlantic* (April 2015), www.theatlantic.com/magazine/archive/2015/04/the-irrationality-of-alcoholics-anonymous/386255/

7 National Institutes of Health, "Methadone and Buprenorphine Reduce Risk of Death after Opioid Overdose," citing Larochelle et al., "Medication for Opioid Use Disorder after Nonfatal Opioid Overdose and Association with Mortality. A Cohort Study," *Annals of Internal Medicine* (June 19, 2018), www.nih.gov/news-events/news-releases/methadone-buprenorphine-reduce-risk-death-after-opioid-overdose)

8   Nancy Gibbs, "Betty Ford, 1918–2011," *Time* (July 8, 2011), https://en.wikipedia.org/wiki/Betty_Ford)

9   J. W. Finney, "Assessing Treatment and Treatment Processes," in John P. Allen and Veronica B. Wilson, eds., *Assessing Alcohol Problems: A Guide for Clinicians and Researchers,* US Department of Health and Human Services, Public Health Service National Institutes of Health, http://pubs.niaaa.nih.gov/publications/AssessingAlcohol/finney.pdf

10   J. Mann, "Forum on Public Policy, *Substance Abuse Control: How Do We Measure Success?*" (2009), citing M. Fendrich and P. Miller, "Pathways and Obstacles in Drug Use Measurement: Editor's Introduction," *Journal of Drug Issue* 30 (2000): 1–8

11   Anne M. Fletcher, *Inside Rehab: The Surprising Truth About Addiction Treatment—and How to Get Help That Works* (Viking, 2013)

12   Bankole Johnson, "Why Rehab Doesn't Work," *Dallas News* (Aug. 2010), https://www.dallasnews.com/opinion/commentary/2010/08/14/Bankole-Johnson-Why-rehab-doesn-2725; review of Project MATCH (Matching Alcoholism Treatments to Client Heterogeneity) 22, no. 6 (Sep. 1998):1300–11; study led by the National Institute on Alcohol Abuse and Alcoholism

13   Jane Brody, "Effective Addiction Treatment," *The New York Times* (Feb. 4, 2013), https://well.blogs.nytimes.com/2013/02/04/effective-addiction-treatment

14   "Evidenced-Based Treatment Practices for Substance Abuse Disorders," *National Quality Forum* (2005): workshop summary, www.apa.org/divisions/div50/doc

15   National Institute on Drug Abuse Advancing Addiction Science, *Principles of Drug Addiction Treatment: A Research-Based Guide* (Third Ed.; website last updated Jan. 2018), www.drugabuse.gov/publications/principles-drug-addiction-treatment-research-based-guide-third-edition/preface

16   John Hill, "Rogue Rehabs: State Failed to Police Drug and Alcohol Homes, with Deadly Results" (prepared Sept. 4, 2012), *sooo.senate.ca.gov*, https://sooo.senate.ca.gov/sites/sooo.senate.ca.gov/files/Rogue%20Rehab%209_4_12.pdf

CHAPTER 8

1   Peter Hecht, "Former Surgeon General Calls for Marijuana Acceptance," *Sacramento Bee* (Feb. 13, 2016), https://www.sacbee.com/news/state/california/california-weed/article60273726.html

2   Kate Sheridan, "Where Marijuana Is Legal, Opioid Prescriptions Fall," *Scientific American* (Apr. 2, 2018), https://www.scientificamerican.com/article/where-marijuana-is-legal-opioid-prescriptions-fall/

3   Christopher Ingraham, "How Many Americans Regularly Use Pot? The Number Is, errr, Higher Than You Think," *Sacramento Bee* (Apr. 20, 2017), https://www.sacbee.com/news/nation-world/national/article145681414.html

4   Conant v. Walters, 309 F.3d 629 (9th Cir. 2002)

5   Ethan B. Russo, "Cannabinoids in the Management of Difficult to Treat Pain," *Therapeutics and Clinical Risk Management* (Feb. 2008), https://www.ncbi.nlm.nih.gov/pmc/articles/PMC2503660/; Gabrielle Campbell et al., "Effect of Cannabis Use in People with Chronic Noncancer Pain: Findings from a 4-Year Prospective Cohort Study," *The Lancet* (July 2018), https://www.thelancet.com/journals/lanpub/article/PIIS2468-2667(18)30110-5/

6   Ethan Russo, "Cannabinoids in the Management of Difficult to Treat Pain," *Therapeutics and Clinical Risk Management* 4, no. 1 (Feb. 2008): 245–259. https://www.ncbi.nlm.nih.gov/pmc/articles/PMC2503660/

7   Martin De Vita, "Association of Cannabinoid Administration with Experimental Pain in Healthy Adults: A Systematic Review and Meta-Analysis," *JAMA Psychiatry* (Sept. 19, 2018), https://jamanetwork.com/journals/jamapsychiatry/article-abstract/2701671

8   *Ibid.*

9   Alison Mack and Janet Joy, *Marijuana as Medicine? The Science Beyond the Controversy* (Washington, DC: National Academies Press, 2000), Ch. 9, "Marijuana and Glaucoma," https://www.ncbi.nlm.nih.gov/books/NBK224386/

10 I. Tomida et al., "Cannabinoids and Glaucoma," *Journal of Ophthalmology* (May 2004), https://www.ncbi.nlm.nih.gov/pmc/articles/PMC1772142/

11 Martin Mulcahey, "The Case for Treating PTSD in Veterans With Medical Marijuana," *The Atlantic* (Jan. 17, 2012),

https://www.theatlantic.com/health/archive/2012/01/
the-case-for-treating-ptsd-in-veterans-with-medical-marijuana/251466/

12 Attilah Olah et al., "Cannabidiol Exerts Sebostatic and Antiinflammatory
Effects on Human Sebocytes," *The Journal of Clinical Investigation* (Sept.
2014), https://www.ncbi.nlm.nih.gov/pmc/articles/PMC4151231/

13 A. W. Zuardi et al., "Effects of Ipsapirone and Cannabidiol on Human
Experimental Anxiety," *Society Journal of Psychopharmacology* (January
1993), http://journals.sagepub.com/doi/10.1177/026988119300700112;
A. R. de Mello Schier et al., "Antidepressant-like and Anxiolytic-like Effects
of Cannabidiol: A Chemical Compound of *Cannabis sativa*," CNS Neurological Disorders Drug Targets (2014), https://www.ncbi.nlm.nih.gov/
pubmed/24923339

14 Yasmin Hurd et al., "Early Phase in the Development of Cannabidiol as a
Treatment for Addiction: Opioid Relapse Takes Initial Center Stage," *Neu-
rotherapeutics* (Aug. 2015), https://www.ncbi.nlm.nih.gov/pmc/articles/
PMC4604178/

15 Gustavo Gonzalez-Cuevas et al., "Unique Treatment Potential of Cannabidiol
for the Prevention of Relapse to Drug Use: Preclinical Proof of Principle," *Neu-
ropsychopharmacology* (March 22, 2018), https://www.nature.com/articles/
s41386-018-0050-8

16 K. A. Babson et al., "Cannabis, Cannabinoids, and Sleep: A Review of the
Literature," *Current Psychiatry Reports* (April 2017), https://www.ncbi.nlm.
nih.gov/pubmed/28349316

17 Adi Aran et al., "Cannabidiol-Based Medical Cannabis in Children with
Autism—A Retrospective Feasibility Study," *Neurology* (April 2018), http://n.
neurology.org/content/88/15_Supplement/P3.318

18 Peter Zygmunt et al., "Tetrahydrocannabinol and Cannabinol Activate Cap-
saicin-Sensitive Sensory Nerves via a CB1 and CB2 Cannabinoid Receptor-
Independent Mechanism," *Journal of Neuroscience* (June 2002), http://www.
jneurosci.org/content/22/11/4720.full

19 D. Brierley et al., "Cannabigerol Is a Novel, Well-Tolerated Appetite Stimulant
in Presatiated Rats," *Psychopharmacology* (2016), https://www.ncbi.nlm.nih.
gov/pubmed/27503475

20   A. G. Granja et al., "A Cannabigerol Quinone Alleviates Neuroinflammation in a Chronic Model of Multiple Sclerosis," *Journal of Neuroimmune Pharmacology* (Dec. 2012), https://www.ncbi.nlm.nih.gov/pubmed/22971837

21   R. G. dos Santos et al., "Phytocannabinoids and Epilepsy," *Journal of Clinical Pharmacy and Therapeutics* (2015), https://www.alchimiaweb.com/blogfr/wp-content/uploads/2015/11/Phytocannabinoids-and-epilepsy-Santos_et_al-2015-Journal_of_Clinical_Pharmacy_and_Therapeutics.pdf

22   F. Borrelli et al., "Beneficial Effect of the Nonpsychotropic Plant Cannabinoid Cannabigerol on Experimental Inflammatory Bowel Disease," *Journal of Biochemical Pharmacology* (May 2013), https://www.ncbi.nlm.nih.gov/pubmed/23415610

23   Simone Tambaro et al., "Cannabinoid-Related Agents in the Treatment of Anxiety Disorders: Current Knowledge and Future Perspectives," *Recent Patents on CNS Drug Discovery* (Apr. 2012), https://www.ncbi.nlm.nih.gov/pmc/articles/PMC3691841/

24   Joanna Jacobus, "Effects of Cannabis on the Adolescent Brain," *Current Pharmaceutical Design* (Dec. 2014), https://www.ncbi.nlm.nih.gov/pmc/articles/PMC3930618/

25   Claudia Wallis, "What Pot Really Does to the Teen Brain," *Scientific American* (Dec. 1, 2017), https://www.scientificamerican.com/article/what-pot-really-does-to-the-teen-brain/

26   Jennifer Matesa, "The Great Suboxone Debate," *The Fix* (Apr. 13, 2011), https://www.thefix.com/content/best-kept-secret-addiction-treatment

27   Deborah Sontag, "Addiction Treatment with a Dark Side," *The New York Times* (Nov. 16, 2013), https://www.nytimes.com/2013/11/17/health/in-demand-in-clinics-and-on-the-street-bupe-can-be-savior-or-menace.html

28   Alex Hannaford, "Dying to Get Clean: Is Ibogaine the Answer to Heroin Addiction?" *The Guardian* (Dec. 10, 2017), https://www.theguardian.com/society/2017/dec/10/ibogaine-heroin-addiction-treatment-gabon-withdrawal-danger-death

29   K. R. Alper et al., "Treatment of Acute Opioid Withdrawal with Ibogaine," *The American Journal on Addictions* 8, no. 3 (Summer 1999): 234-42

30   Tamar Tabo, "Who's To Blame For Ibogaine? A Debate Over Whether Big Government Or Big Pharma Is Keeping Heroin Addicts From Getting Well," *Above the Law* (Feb. 6, 2014), https://abovethelaw.com/2014/02/whos-to-blame-for-ibogaine-a-debate-over-whether-big-government or-big-pharma-is-keeping-heroin-addicts-from-getting-well/

31   Royce Amy Morales, "Brain Restoration: 'Too Good To Be True' for Addiction and Disease?" *The Fix* (March 20, 2014), https://www.thefix.com/content/brain-restoration-'too-good-be-true'-addiction

CHAPTER 9

1   Atul Gawande, *Better: A Surgeon's Notes on Performance* (Profile Books, London: 2008)

2   Kate O'Neill, interviewed by Scott Simon, "The Viral Obituary of an Opioid Addict: 'She's Just One Face' of the Epidemic," NPR Weekend Edition Saturday (Oct. 20, 2018), https://www.npr.org/templates/transcript/transcript.php?storyId=659122537

3   Lloyd D. Johnston et. al., "Monitoring the Future: National Survey Results on Drug Use, 1975–2017," The University of Michigan Institute for Social Research (July 2018), www.monitoringthefuture.org/pubs/monographs/mtf-overview2017.pdf

4   President's Commission on Combating Drug Addiction and the Opioid Crisis (Nov. 1, 2017), https://www.whitehouse.gov/sites/whitehouse.gov/files/images/Final_Report_Draft_11-1-2017.pdf

5   William Sullivan and Logan Plaster, "Four West Virginia Cities Sue the Joint Commission," *Emergency Physicians Monthly* (Dec. 5, 2017), http://epmonthly.com/article/four-west-virginia-cities-sue-joint-commission

6   David Baker, "Joint Commission Statement on Pain Management," *jointcommission.org* (April 18, 2016), https://www.jointcommission.org/joint_commission_statement_on_pain_management

7   Emily Mullin, "These New Devices Promise to Fight Pain without Opioids," *MIT Technology Review* (July 31, 2017), https://www.technologyreview.com/s/608256/these-new-devices-promise-to-fight-pain-without-opioids/

8   Cheri Harkleroad, "Naloxone: Everything You Need to Know," *Practical Recovery* (Oct. 30, 2018), https://www.practicalrecovery.com/prblog/naloxone-everything-you-need-to-know/

9   Charles Piller and Jia You, "Hidden Conflicts? Pharma Payments to FDA after Drug Approval Spark Ethical Concerns," *Science* (July 5, 2018), https://www.sciencemag.org/news/2018/07/hidden-conflicts-pharma-payments-fda-advisers-after-drug-approvals-spark-ethical

CHAPTER 10

1   *Burlington Free Press*, Obituaries (Oct. 21, 2018), https://www.legacy.com/obituaries/burlingtonfreepress/obituary.aspx?n=madelyn-ellen-linsenmeir&pid=190469930

2   The President's Commission on Combating Drug Addiction and the Opioid Crisis (Nov. 1, 2017): 44, https://www.whitehouse.gov/sites/whitehouse.gov/files/images/Final_Report_Draft_11-1-2017.pdf

3   Rebecca H. Bitsko, Joseph, R. Holbrook, Reem M. Ghandour, Stephen J.Blumberg, Susanna N. Visser, Ruth Perou, and John T. Walkup, "Epidemiology and Impact of Healthcare Provider–Diagnosed Anxiety and Depression Among US Children," *Journal of Developmental & Behavioral Pediatrics* 39, no. 5 (June 2018): 395–403, https://journals.lww.com/jrnldbp/Citation/2018/06000/Epidemiology_and_Impact_of_Health_Care.6.aspx

4   Dan Mangan, "Number of People with Health Insurance via Jobs Remains Steady with Obamacare," CNBC (July 13, 2016), https://www.cnbc.com/2016/07/13/number-of-people-with-health-insurance-via-jobs-remained-steady-with-obamacare.html

5   Sheryl Sandberg and Adam Grant, *Option B: Facing Adversity, Building Resilience, and Finding Joy* (Random House, 2017)

6   Tom Krisher, "Elon Musk Tells Newspaper He's Cracking under Stress of Tesla Job," *Chicago Tribune* (Aug. 17, 2018), https://www.chicagotribune.com/business/ct-biz-tela-elon-musk-overwork-20180817-story.html; Rupert Neale and Julia Carrie Wong, "Tesla Shares Crash after Elon Musk Smokes Joint on Live Web Show," *The Guardian* (Sept.

7, 2018), https://www.theguardian.com/technology/2018/sep/07/tesla-chief-elon-musk-smokes-marijuana-on-live-web-show

7   Kevin Love, "Everyone Is Going Through Something," *The Players Tribune* (March 6, 2018), https://www.theplayerstribune.com/en-us/articles/kevin-love-everyone-is-going-through-something

8   Putnam, *Bowling Alone*: 19

9   Michael J. Zoorob and Jason Lee Salemi, "Bowling Alone, Dying Together: The Role of Social Capital in Mitigating the Drug Overdose Epidemic in the United States," *Drug and Alcohol Dependence* 173 (Apr. 1, 2017): 1-9, https://www.ncbi.nlm.nih.gov/pubmed/28182980

10   Maia Szalavitz, "Why Social Capital Could Be the Key to Solving America's Overdose Epidemic," *The Guardian* (Aug. 6, 2017), https://www.theguardian.com/us-news/2017/aug/16/social-capital-us-opioid-epidemic-drugs-overdose

11   Olga Khazan, "A Shocking Decline in American Life Expectancy," *The Atlantic* (Dec. 21, 2017), https://www.theatlantic.com/health/archive/2017/12/life-expectancy/548981/

GRAPHICS AND DATA

1   L. Rossen, B. Bastian, Y. Chong, "Three Waves of the Rise in Opioid Overdose Deaths," Centers for Disease Control and Prevention, National Vital Statistics System Mortality File, https://www.cdc.gov/drugoverdose/epidemic/index.html

2   National Center for Health Statistics, CDC Wonder, "National Overdose Deaths: Number of Deaths Involving All Drugs" (rev. Aug. 2018), https://www.drugabuse.gov/related-topics/trends-statistics/overdose-death-rates

3   National Center for Health Statistics, CDC Wonder, "National Overdose Deaths: Number of Deaths Involving Opioids" (rev. Aug. 2018), https://www.drugabuse.gov/related-topics/trends-statistics/overdose-death-rates

4   Drug-Related Deaths/Day: 197 (2017 Year Avg: 70,000), https://www.drugabuse.gov/related-topics/trends-statistics/overdose-death-rates

5   Opioid-Related Deaths/Day: 134 (2017 Year Avg: 49,000), https://www.cdc.gov/drugoverdose/

6   Gun-Related Deaths/Day: 107 (2017 Year Avg: 39,000), https://www.cdc.gov/nchs/pressroom/sosmap/firearm_mortality/firearm.htm

7   Motor Vehicle-Related Deaths/Day: 88 (2017 Year Avg: 32,000), https://www.cdc.gov/vitalsigns/motor-vehicle-safety/index.html

8   Fire-Related Deaths/Day: 9 (2017 Year Avg: 3,400), https://www.usfa.fema.gov/data/statistics/

9   United States Census Bureau, "Quick Facts," 2017 Data, https://www.census.gov/quickfacts/fact/table/US/PST045217#PST045217

10   Dennis Thompson, "More Than 1 in 3 Americans Prescribed Opioids in 2015," *CBS News* (Aug. 1, 2017), https://www.cbsnews.com/news/more-than-one-third-americans-prescribed-opioids-in-2015/

11   Rachel N. Lipari and Struther L. Van Horn, "Trends in Substance Use Disorders Among Adults Aged 18 or Older," *The CBHSQ Report* (June 29, 2017), https://www.samhsa.gov/data/sites/default/files/report_2790/Short-Report-2790.html

12   Stoddard Davenport and Katie Matthews, "Opioid Use Disorder in the United States: Diagnosed Prevalence by Payer, Age, Sex, and State" (March 9, 2018), www.milliman.com/insight/2018/Opioid-use-disorder-in-the-United-States-Diagnosed-prevalence-by-payer--age--sex--and-state/

13   *Ibid.*

14   United States Census Bureau, "Quick Facts," 2017 Data, https://www.census.gov/quickfacts/fact/table/US/PST045217#PST045217

15   Alex Berezow, "Who Is Hurting? The Prevalence Of Chronic Pain In America," American Council on Science and Health (Sept. 14, 2018), https://www.acsh.org/news/2018/09/14/who-hurting-prevalence-chronic-pain-america-13407 (citing J. Dahlhamer, J. Lucas, and C. Zelaya et al., "Prevalence of Chronic Pain and High-Impact Chronic Pain Among Adults—United States, 2016" *Morbidity and Mortality Weekly Report* 67, no. 36 (Sept. 24, 2018): 1001-06. DOI: 10.15585/mmwr.mm6736a2)

16   Boston Globe staff, "Comparing the Lethality and Potency of Opioid Drugs," *The Boston Globe* (Nov. 15, 2017), https://www.bostonglobe.com/metro/2017/11/15/comparing-lethality-and-potency-opioid-drugs/6iEmKXzFDc2rjg9IIZeXWP/story.html; and https://www.cdc.gov/drugoverdose/opioids/fentanyl.html

17   Anuj Shah et al., "Characteristics of Initial Prescription Episodes and Likelihood of Long-Term Opioid Use—United States, 2006–2015," *Morbidity and Mortality Weekly Report* (March 17, 2017), https://www.cdc.gov/mmwr/volumes/66/wr/mm6610a1.htm2

INDEX

J

Jackson, Michael, 1, 11, 33
Janssen Pharmaceuticals, 76
Japan, 52
Jefferson, Thomas, 50
Jessie's Law, 29, 271
Jick, Hershel, 81, 313
Jin Fuey Moy v. United States, 54, 311
Joint Commission on the Accreditation of Healthcare Organizations, 95, 271
Joint Commission, the, 95-96, 108, 141, 199, 271, 314, 323, 337

K

Kadian, 76
Kapoor, John, 75
Keefe, Patrick Radden, 66, 69
Keeley, Leslie, 133
    Keeley Cure, The, 133, 337
Kefauver, Estes, 68
Kennedy, Patrick, 33
ketamine, 33, 87-88
ketorolac, 85
Khazan, Olga, 99, 314, 325
kickbacks, 73, 153, 157, 163, 189, 271, 277, 282
King, Stephen, 109
Klonopin, 60, 262
Kozinski, Alex, 168
kratom, 91-92, 314

L

Laos, 38
Laudanum, 50, 85, 271
Ledger, Heath, 11
levorphanol, 42
Lewis, Alvin, 28
Librium, 67
licensing of addiction treatment, 27, 30, 35, 137-138, 149, 160, 163-164, 263
Lidocaine, 87-88
Lincoln, Mary Todd, 50
Linder v. United States, 49, 56

Institutes of Health (NIH), 135, 147, 175, 269, 274-275

Outcomes Measures, 149

Neanderthal, 39

needle exchange, 204

Nelson, Harry (as author). *See From ObamaCare to TrumpCare*

nerve block, 87

neural pathways, 47, 116-117

Neurontin, 88

neurotoxicity, 178

New Jersey, 33, 199

Newport Beach, California, 152

nicotinamide adenine dinucleotide (NAD) infusion, 183

Nixon, Richard, 57

nonaddictive therapeutics, 201

nonmedical programs, 161

nonpharmacologic options for treating and managing pain, 90

nonsteroidal anti-inflammatory drug (NSAID), 85-86

Noplis, Charles, 129

Norco, 59, 76, 270

norepinephrine, 43, 176

Notanotherstat.com, 238, 292, 296, 301

Nucynta ER, 76

nurse practitioners, 189, 195, 217, 219, 275

O

Odyssey, The (Homer), 40

O'Neill, Kate, 16, 194, 233, 323

Opana ER, 76

opiates, 16, 38, 41, 50, 89, 133, 287-288

opioids

opioid antagonist, 142, 144

opioid-induced hyperalgesia (OIH), 45, 276

"opiophobia," 70-71, 78

"opioid properties," 92

opioid receptors, 144

O-P-I-O-I-D-S, 190-222

opioid treatment program, 276

opioid use disorder (OUD), 48, 130, 188, 214, 228-229, 276

prescribing, 6, 13, 63, 92, 130, 196, 211, 297

A Special Offer
from
ForbesBooks

Other publications bring you business news. Subscribing to *Forbes* magazine brings you business knowledge and inspiration you can use to make your mark.

- Insights into important business, financial and social trends
- Profiles of companies and people transforming the business world
- Analysis of game-changing sectors like energy, technology and health care
- Strategies of high-performing entrepreneurs

Your future is in our pages.

To see your discount and subscribe go to Forbesmagazine.com/bookoffer.

Forbes